Dashiell Hammett
and the Movies

Dashiell Hammett and the Movies

WILLIAM H. MOONEY

RUTGERS UNIVERSITY PRESS

NEW BRUNSWICK, NEW JERSEY, AND LONDON

Library of Congress Cataloging-in-Publication Data
Mooney, William H., 1948–
Dashiell Hammett and the movies / William H. Mooney.
pages cm
Includes bibliographical references and index.
ISBN 978–0–8135–6253–7 (hardcover : alk. paper) — ISBN 978–0–8135–6252–0 (pbk.:
alk. paper) — ISBN 978–0–8135–6254–4 (e-book)
1. Hammett, Dashiell, 1894–1961—Film adaptations. 2. Film adaptations—History
and criticism. I. Title.
PS3515.A4347Z78 2015
813′.52—dc23
2014000067

Visit our website: http://rutgerspress.rutgers.edu

Manufactured in the United States of America

CONTENTS

ACKNOWLEDGMENTS

I would like to thank President Joyce F. Brown and the Board of Directors of the Fashion Institute of Technology, State University of New York, for their continuing support, especially for a sabbatical leave that allowed me to develop the proposal for this book. Thanks also to FIT's Teaching Institute for research and conference travel grants, and to the Interlibrary Loan department of the Gladys Marcus Library, in particular Paul Lajoie, for fast and reliable help with research materials.

The collections of the Margaret Herrick Library of the Academy of Motion Picture Arts and Sciences were extremely useful—thank you, Jenny Romero, for making the use of the library such a convenient and enjoyable experience. I am grateful to the Harry Ransom Center, the University of Texas at Austin, for access to Dashiell Hammett's treatment for *City Streets*, and to *Literature/Film Quarterly* for permission to include here material from my 2011 article on film versions of *The Maltese Falcon*. A more personal thanks is due long-time friends and colleagues at the Literature/Film Association, particularly Peter Lev and Thomas Leitch for helpful advice on more than one occasion. Thank you, Gary Collins, for good copies of several films.

I am grateful to Leslie Mitchner, my editor at Rutgers University Press, for her initial enthusiasm and for the wisdom of experience she brought to the project. (Thanks also to Art Simon for suggesting Rutgers as a good place to submit the proposal.) Thank you, Jeffrey Riman and Brian Emery, for help with the photos. A special word of appreciation goes to my good friend Scott Stoddart, dean of the School of Liberal Arts at FIT, for his careful reading and editorial suggestions, and even more importantly for his encouragement and moral support at every stage. Finally, I owe my wife, Margaret Mercer, and son, William Mercer Mooney, a debt of gratitude for so many things, among them tolerating my preoccupation with this project.

Dashiell Hammett
and the Movies

Introduction

Inferior Hammett or
Exemplary Hollywood?

Dashiell Hammett is remembered, first and foremost, for his part in creating the hard-boiled detective story. With Carroll John Daly at the pulp-fiction magazine *Black Mask*, he was the writer whose groundbreaking work and reputation made him the emblematic figure of the new genre. First as the Continental Op, who appeared in numerous stories and two novels—most importantly *Red Harvest*—then as Sam Spade in *The Maltese Falcon*, Hammett's detective was the model of an investigator who, in the Op's words, "stirs things up" and by tough persistence as much as intelligence follows the evidence wherever it leads, with results that include disillusion and loss.[1] Hammett's reputation always had a biographical element, the recognition that he had worked as a Pinkerton operative before, and briefly after, World War I. He was fortunate in being admired and imitated by Raymond Chandler, whose Philip Marlowe developed and to some extent altered the type on which Hammett's enduring reputation depends. Our first surprise, then, in a book about the movies based on Hammett's writing is that almost none of the films—really only one among the nineteen considered here—focus on the hard-boiled detective.

Humphrey Bogart as Sam Spade is so enduring an image that he remains the iconic representative of Hammett's fiction on film. In fact, Bogart in *The Maltese Falcon* (1941), followed by his role as Philip Marlowe in Howard Hawks's *The Big Sleep* (1946), further consolidated the literary image of the hard-boiled detective, such that going forward any detective slouching along a dark rainy street would evoke some composite character we might think of as Spade-Marlowe-Bogart, associated in the minds of the uninstructed with that two-headed author, Hammett-Chandler. This detective was the figure that would remain a pop-culture icon throughout the latter part of the twentieth century, accreting aspects of the Hammett biography—from his elegant and aloof public persona to his reputation for drink and womanizing, his relationship with Lillian Hellman, and his politics, which included a willingness to go to prison rather than cooperate during the Cold War witch hunts.

Because of his association with the hard-boiled detective, Hammett's name is frequently forgotten in connection with his even more frequently revived movie, *The Thin Man* (1934), in which Myrna Loy and William Powell made Nick and Nora Charles an iconic couple with a cultural reach as extensive as Bogart's Spade. If Loy and Powell embody these characters in the public mind as Bogart is our image of Spade, their images are less associated with Dashiell Hammett—in fact, many who fondly remember that film forget or recall with surprise that Hammett is the author, a mistake no one makes concerning *The Maltese Falcon* (1941). The reason is obvious— the buoyant couple falls outside what is remembered as Hammett's greatest achievement, the hard-boiled detective story. *The Thin Man* (1934) is in a different register from the prototypical film noir, just as the novel on which it was based is different from those in the hard-boiled mode, a reason many critics found it inferior.

All of the Spade/Bogart/Hammett mythology must be put aside, then, as we consider the other films that Hollywood made from Hammett's work. A few, like the two earlier versions of *The Maltese Falcon*, remain within the conventions of Hollywood detective comedies of the 1930s, but others participate in genres from the newspaper film to the gangster film to screwball comedy to postmodern pastiche. These films remain significant in themselves: nearly all were A-list projects of major studios with important stars and directors, and taken together they offer a profile of the interaction of Hammett's work with the film industry, a case study of one author's dissemination and diffusion through the cultural machinery of the cinema.

In some instances, the process of their adaptation—particularly where there are several film versions—casts new light on Hammett's novels, highlighting the permutation of ideas of the couple in *The Thin Man*, for example, the dual plot structure of *The Maltese Falcon*, or the ethnic allegory performed by *The Glass Key*. *Dashiell Hammett and the Movies* furthermore draws attention to unknown and little-known films—particularly the early films *Roadhouse Nights* (1930), *City Streets* (1931), *The Maltese Falcon* (1931), *Woman in the Dark* (1934), and *Mister Dynamite* (1935), though my fondness for these may have become exaggerated from spending so much time with them. In any case, *Dashiell Hammett and the Movies* fills a void in the literature by examining the films from Hammett's writing and by bringing together in one volume information otherwise available only in widely scattered sources. While the book pretends neither to exhaustive research on any one film nor definitive coverage of the many intersecting areas of film study—from period history to genre to the nature of sequels to auteurist portrait or star reputation and reception—it undertakes to explain within wider cultural and industry contexts what shaped the films, emphasizing the events, choices, and relationships that governed the particular direction taken by each. In this respect, it contributes further detail to a growing understanding of the interrelationship of books, films, Hollywood, and their cultural context.

As a title, *Dashiell Hammett and the Movies* frames one of the book's primary challenges, which is to place the body of writing by a single author in its proper but extremely varied relationship with nineteen films, given that the role of Hammett's fictions ranges from determinant to merely one ingredient among many. Thus, in some degree, the book is about adaptation, though to announce this fact is to raise a host of theoretical and practical questions. Are we using "adaptation" as a noun or in its verb form, referring to a *product* to be viewed in a certain light or to a *process* of transmutation? Should we discuss *Satan Met a Lady* (1936) as an adaptation of Hammett's *The Maltese Falcon*, of the 1931 film of that name, or of both? Should we consider Hammett's screenplay for *Watch on the Rhine* (1943) as an adaptation of Lillian Hellman's stage play, an extension of the source text adapted in making the film, or as an intermediate text sharing qualities of the source while itself being subject to adaptation into the film? To what extent is *Mister Dynamite* an adaptation of Hammett when his contribution was a brief story outline at the beginning of an extended development process? If such issues of multiple sources, ambiguity about the status of precursor texts, and the serial authorship of film narratives

are fundamental to adaptation study, the movies made from Hammett's
writing are an excellent laboratory.

Even while we bear Hammett's work in mind in examining these films,
we must of course distance ourselves—along with the majority of adaptation
scholars in recent years—from any notion of fidelity as a primary goal or
measure of value. In his oft-cited 1984 essay, Dudley Andrew could already
complain that the "most tiresome discussion of adaptation" concerned
"fidelity and transformation," tiresome because of the repeated, unfounded
assumption "that the task of adaptation is the reproduction of something
essential about an original text."[2] Forty years earlier, André Bazin had suggested that filmmakers typically set goals that have more to do with the
needs of their audiences than with fidelity to the source.[3] As Thomas Leitch
has written recently, "It should be clear by now that fidelity, even as a goal,
is the exception to the norm."[4] Or in Linda Hutcheon's words, "There are
many and varied motives behind adaptation and few involve faithfulness."[5]
"Motives," as well as the contingences of changing historical contexts, are
indeed the crucial issue. Robert Stam has usefully described their combina-
tion in terms of "filters," of "studio style, ideological fashion, political and
economic constraints, *auteurist* predilection, charismatic stars, cultural values, and so forth," making an adaptation "an *interested* reading of a novel
and the *circumstantially shaped* 'writing' of a film."[6]

With respect to the adaptation of Hammett, a question that repeatedly
arises is the degree of knowledge an audience has of the source text. For
most scholars the viewer's role is paramount in constructing the interrelationship between source(s) and film. Hutcheon, for example, writes of a
"constant oscillation between [the adapted work] and the new adaptation
we are experiencing."[7] Stam prefers the more broadly applicable idea of
"intertextuality," referring to an "effective co-presence of two texts."[8] In
any case, a work is understood as "intertextual" or as an adaptation only
in the degree that we are aware of a precursor text. If we do not know the
adapted work, as Hutcheon writes, "we will not experience the work *as an
adaptation*."[9] "It is only as inherently double, or multilaminated works," she
argues, "that they can be theorized as adaptations."[10]

This necessary recognition of the precursor text is the main reason
that adaptation scholars have focused on films from the best-known
sources—canonical and popular literary works, as well as inherited stories

of less certain origin—and where the debt is openly proclaimed. Thus Andrew narrowed his attention to *"the explicit, foregrounded relation* of a cinematic text to a well-constructed original text,"[11] echoed in Hutcheon's definition of adaptations as "deliberate, announced, extended revisitations of prior works."[12] But how many of the nineteen films from Hammett's writing fulfill these requirements? A third of them, at best. Screen credit acknowledging the legal debt of a film to a novel or its author is no guarantee that viewers will oscillate between texts, as Hutcheon suggested. Audiences would certainly not have done so as they watched *Roadhouse Nights*, loosely based on *Red Harvest*, when Hammett was little known. This would have been even more the case with *City Streets*, which was developed from a story Hammett wrote for hire at Paramount and to which audiences had no direct access. Warner Bros. used the title *Satan Met a Lady* to lead viewers away from the source novel and the earlier film of *The Maltese Falcon*. The five sequels to *The Thin Man* adapted mainly characters and a relationship, referencing primarily the 1934 movie and basing their narratives respectively on an original story by Hammett, an earlier *Black Mask* story that he incorporated into a new story outline, and three narratives by other writers. *Woman in the Dark* was based on a Hammett novella that was, and remains, significantly less known than his novels. In these cases and others, "motives" and circumstances of the moment were at work from the beginning in the selection of Hammett material and throughout the process of defining the films. Only John Huston's *The Maltese Falcon* and W. S. Van Dyke's *The Thin Man* can be imagined as having been conceived with any notion of fidelity to their source. Close consideration of the factors more obviously shaping the films leads us, in many cases, away from the Hammett source material.

Yet the book must maintain something of a double focus. By design, we deliberately oscillate between films and sources. We look for the signs of Hammett's contribution even where we realize that viewers would have ignored them, their minds occupied instead with memories of familiar stars, other recent films, and generic expectations, as well as with the circumstances of their lives outside the cinema. Only this double perspective of critic and ordinary viewer allows us to understand the process of dissemination and diffusion of Hammett's work through the films that absorbed or transmitted it.

What should be obvious, but which probably needs to be stated none-theless, is that Hollywood's values and images of the world were not those of Dashiell Hammett. Lovers of Hammett's fiction recognize the intellectual rigor in his artistry, a thoroughgoing understanding of the weight of words in their relationship to characters, events in the narratives, and the con-ceptual formulation of his novels. Yet Hammett's writings were embraced by Hollywood for more timely, superficial characteristics and themes—the gangsters, the corruption of urban life, political intrigue, mystery, adven-ture, and the celebration of Prohibition-era freedoms. The Hammett who was deeply and philosophically in sync with his era makes his way into the cinema surreptitiously, through Trojan horses of narrative, character, dia-logue, and imagery. Hollywood generally ignores the "something essential" in Andrew's definition of adaptation in favor of elements useful for its own economic projects and in its differently circumscribed cultural domain. Recognizing this difference between Hollywood and Hammett, we must ultimately insist on valuing the films as exemplary Hollywood rather than as inferior Hammett.

So the double focus on Hammett and on the films leaves us with two interrelated stories to tell. One emphasizes Hammett's contribution; the other finds its expression mainly in response to the question of what shaped any particular film. Was it an attempt to recapture something in Hammett's writing? Was it a desire to produce an exemplar of a popular genre? Was the goal to capitalize on the prior success of a star or story, or to sidestep Production Code censorship in delivering a predictably successful commodity? In most cases, the competing interests in a film's production are mediated through the rigorous craftsmanship and industrial machin-ery of the classical Hollywood studios.

Hammett's development as a writer occurred at a different pace and with a different logic from Hollywood studios and their audiences. This book generally follows his movie involvement, while it also brings together films related to the same source material. Chapter 1 examines three early films, *Roadhouse Nights*, *City Streets*, and *Mister Dynamite*. The first two were developed by Paramount, the third by Warner Bros. *Road-house Nights* was to be based on the gangster elements in *Red Harvest*, and shortly thereafter David O. Selznick advocated hiring Hammett to write a gangster film for Gary Cooper, which became *City Streets*. Before that film was released, Darryl Zanuck had signed Hammett to a contract to write a story for another picture. Hammett's outline—entitled "On the Make" and featuring a crooked private eye—was eventually rejected by Warner Bros., only to be revived by Universal after the success of *The Thin Man* and released as *Mister Dynamite*.

Chapter 2 is devoted to *The Thin Man*, Hammett's last novel yet the beginning of his important contribution to film. The extraordinary success of *The Thin Man*, in perfect harmony with the zeitgeist of 1933 and 1934 when the novel and the film appeared, transformed Hammett in the view of the film industry from an ordinary scribbler into a proven asset whose talent they hoped to exploit and whose name could be used in marketing a film. Chapter 3 takes up the five *Thin Man* films that followed, released over a period of eleven years from 1936 to 1947. These are best understood as extending and repeating a successful formula, initially as a sequel and then in a series, while accommodating the aging of the films' stars.

The Thin Man reflected Hammett's broader social experience after the literary success of *The Maltese Falcon*, including his relationship with Lillian Hellman. Chapter 4 proceeds to the other works reflecting this relationship: *Woman in the Dark* from the novella of the same name, with Luise Fischer as its strong protagonist, and *Watch on the Rhine* (1943), based on Hammett's screenplay from Hellman's Broadway hit.

Chapter 5 takes up the three Warner Bros. versions of *The Maltese Falcon*. Because of the dates of these successive productions, a comparative view reveals with unusual clarity how the development of industry self-censorship conditioned their adaptation. The first, which was released in 1931 and might otherwise be grouped with the early films, was developed with a pre-Code emphasis on Bebe Daniels's erotic appeal. The second, entitled *Satan Met a Lady*, was a screwball battle of the sexes reshaped by casting Bette Davis as the female lead opposite Warren William. The third, John Huston's *The Maltese Falcon*, the best-known Hammett film after *The Thin Man*, shifts the focus to Humphrey Bogart as the archetypal private detective and anticipates film noir.

Chapter 6 similarly focuses on the two Paramount versions of *The Glass Key* (1935 and 1942), crime films in which the gangsters and a mystery plot are transposed into the political arena of a Tammany Hall–style political machine and boss. *The Glass Key* was Hammett's most ambitious attempt to go beyond genre fiction, but the government corruption and the ethnic tribalism he portrayed, fundamental to the Tammany Hall system, were also areas of concern for the Production Code Administration. Thus, the first of the two films, while re-forming the novel's narrative within Hollywood conventions, shows the strain of repressing criticism of government and the immigrant/ethnic basis of the system; the second film strives above all to capitalize on the screen chemistry between Alan Ladd and Veronica Lake following the production of *This Gun for Hire* (1942). Chapter 7 follows Hammett's reputation in the 1970s and after, with particular attention to the Coen brothers' *Miller's Crossing* (1990), an homage to Hammett and a postmodern confection in complex dialogue with all versions of *The Glass Key*. Hammett, like all authors, focuses and transmits elements of the cultural environment that produced him. The fate of an author's books, like that of a body in the ground, is to return what has become of their ingredients to the soil, a sort of cultural composting. *Dashiell Hammett and the Movies* observes that process with particular emphasis on the role of cinema.

1

Three Early Films

Roadhouse Nights (1930), *City Streets* (1931),
and *Mister Dynamite* (1935)

Dashiell Hammett's introduction to Hollywood came during his most
productive period as a writer. He submitted *Poisonville* to Alfred A. Knopf
in February 1928,[1] and it was published as *Red Harvest* a year later. In the
meantime, between August and November 1928, Hammett was exchanging
ideas about revisions of *The Dain Curse* with Knopf editor Harry C. Block.[2] By
then *The Maltese Falcon* had already been submitted in June, so that Block
left it to Hammett to decide which book would be published first.[3] *The Dain
Curse* came out in June 1929 and *The Maltese Falcon* in February 1930, the
same month that Hammett completed his next novel, *The Glass Key*.[4]

As his literary reputation blossomed, Hammett quickly came to understand the potential for movie earnings. He was still an unknown when *Red
Harvest* was picked up by Paramount for a modest amount in September
1929,[5] but by the following June, Warner Bros. agreed with Knopf to pay
$8,500 for rights to *The Maltese Falcon*, Hammett getting 80 percent.[6] By July
1930, David O. Selznick was advocating that Paramount hire him for $300
a week, with a $5,000 bonus for the story that became *City Streets* (1931).[7]
In January of 1931, Darryl Zanuck at Warner Bros. offered him $5,000 to
sign another contract, which specified $5,000 more for a treatment, and
an additional $5,000 if the story was accepted for production.[8] Hammett
received the first $10,000, but "On the Make" was rejected by Warner Bros.
in April 1931; only later, after the success of *The Thin Man*, was this story
resold to Universal and made as *Mister Dynamite*. In April 1932, when *The*

Glass Key was published in the United States, the movie rights were sold to Paramount for $25,000.

It was the violence of *Red Harvest* that attracted Hollywood, its gangsters rather than the mystery story or detection, for gangsters were everywhere at the time. As Will Hays, president of the Motion Picture Producers and Distributors Association (MPPDA), would write, "The gangster cult had been a main theme of journalism for a decade."[9] Along with the acquisition of *Red Harvest*, Paramount studio head B. P. Schulberg, with Gary Cooper under contract, wanted Hammett to write "a gangster film for Coop."[10] But Hammett's literary reputation soon altered Hollywood's perception of him. By January 1931, after the publishing success of *The Maltese Falcon*, executives at Warner Bros. wanted Hammett to create, in Richard Layman's words, "an original Sam Spade story for a movie starring William Powell."[11]

Roadhouse Nights, City Streets, and *Mister Dynamite*—along with the 1931 version of *The Maltese Falcon* and *Woman in the Dark* (1934)—represent Hammett's transition from an unknown author to a successful novelist employed by the studios. Yet until the success of *The Thin Man*, he was still treated as a hack, a supplier of raw material for an industry turning out some four hundred movies each year. Thus *Roadhouse Nights* would be shaped primarily by another writer, Ben Hecht. *City Streets* would be organized around its star, the film's specific form dictated by an imposing director, Rouben Mamoulian. *Mister Dynamite*, following *The Thin Man*'s success for Metro-Goldwyn-Mayer, became a comedy for Edmund Lowe and Jean Dixon at a much weaker studio, Universal. In all three of these cases, Hammett's work was little more than a point of departure.

Roadhouse Nights (1930)

Red Harvest was a first novel by a little-known author—its initial printing of three thousand copies took a full year to sell. So the studio had no compunction in giving Ben Hecht, who had written the extremely successful film *Underworld* (Josef von Sternberg, 1927), freedom to reinvent Hammett's novel. He did so almost completely—Hecht's background in journalism and the box office record of *Underworld* largely explain the transformation of *Red Harvest* into *Roadhouse Nights*. In Hecht's detailed treatment for

Roadhouse Nights, William Nolan has written, "nothing of Hammett's novel remained."[12] This is only a slight exaggeration.

The film was Walter Wanger's second credited production, and it relied on much of the same crew as his first, *The Lady Lies* (1929): both films were directed by Hobart Henley, with William O. Steiner as cinematographer and Helene Turner as editor, and both featured Charles Ruggles. But Hecht made the story his own. He had begun as a newspaper reporter and active participant in Chicago's literary scene prior to World War I. After some success as a playwright in New York, he was famously summoned to Hollywood by a telegram from his friend Herman J. Mankiewicz, who had left the drama desk at the *New York Times* to write scripts: "There are millions to be grabbed out here," Mankiewicz wrote, "and your only competition is idiots."[13] With Charles MacArthur, Hecht had written the 1928 Broadway hit *The Front Page*, which became a film under the same title in 1931 and would also be the basis of *His Girl Friday* (Howard Hawks, 1940). And *Underworld*, his first credited screen story, won Hecht the Oscar for Best Original Story at the inaugural Academy Awards ceremony on May 16, 1929. Both *The Front Page* and *Underworld* derived from his experience as a reporter during the period of rising gangland crime in Prohibition-era Chicago. *Underworld*'s box office success is frequently credited with spurring the cycle of gangster films that concluded with Hecht's *Scarface* (Hawks, 1932). *The Front Page* (Lewis Milestone, 1931) holds a similar place with respect to newspaper films. If the success of *Underworld* made Hecht an obvious choice to adapt the Prohibition gangster novel *Red Harvest*, Hecht must equally have found it obvious to replace Hammett's private detective with a newspaperman: his experience in that profession was even more extensive than Hammett's as a Pinkerton operative.

Remaining from Hammett's novel are bootleggers attempting to take over a town, a murdered newspaperman, an investigator making trouble for the gangsters, and the character of Lola Fagan, who retains something of Hammett's Dinah Brand in *Red Harvest*, with her corruption and instinctive goodness as two sides of the coin of human nature. Yet the film's locale has nothing to do with the Montana mining town in *Red Harvest*, nor with the strikebreaking history of the Pinkerton agency that Hammett knew firsthand. The single gang of bootleggers in the film represents only one of many factions in the novel, that of Pete the Finn. Left out are those led by Reno Starkey, Lew Yard, "Whisper" Thaler, and Elihu Willsson, not to mention Dinah Brand's additional conquests—a bank clerk named Albury and the IWW union organizer Quint. In *Roadhouse Nights*, the murdered newspaperman is a reporter rather than a publisher, and his investigating colleague is a clever, cynical drunk rather than a professional detective.

Unlike the film, the novel is full of action scenes, including gangland shootouts, chases, a knife thrown into the neck of a boxer in the ring who had failed to take a dive, and one-on-one encounters between the Op and various attackers. But the most important aspect of the book passed over by Hecht is the Op's struggle to avoid going "blood simple": becoming so involved in killing as a solution to Poisonville's problems that he will lose his professionalism and commitment to the values of the Continental Detective Agency as embodied by the Old Man, the head of the agency and a paragon of objectivity. In the novel, the Op's struggle is that of every individual against the corruption of life in industrial society, a corruption exemplified by the bootlegging of the Prohibition era.

Rather than following the plot of *Red Harvest*, Hecht's story reworks that of *Underworld*, once again creating a love triangle between a gangster, his girl, and a passive, somewhat intellectual drunk. In both films, the ineffectual male is goaded into action out of love for a woman and a sense of loyalty. A difference between the two stories is that in *Underworld*, a gangster named Buck Mulligan (Fred Kohler), entirely violent and self-interested, is set up as the foil of a heroic gangster, Bull Weed (George Bancroft). But further continuity with *Underworld* is evident in the casting of Fred Kohler as Sam Horner, a figure who, like Mulligan, is without redeeming qualities. In *Roadhouse Nights*, Willie Bindbugel (Charles Ruggles) is a reporter sent to find his missing colleague who was murdered by Horner. On the scene he encounters Horner's moll, a singer named Lola Fagan (Helen Morgan), whom he recognizes as Lola Davies from his hometown, the "first girl I ever kissed." Their love reignited, Bindbugel and Davies attempt to escape, but they are surprised by Horner en route to the train station. Ultimately, with the help of an entertainer named Daffy (Jimmy Durante), they turn the tables on the gang—Lola rescues Bindbugel by shooting Horner, and the other gangsters are arrested.

The film also attempts to exploit the star image of Helen Morgan, capitalizing on her reputation as a torch singer and on audience memories of her success in *Applause* (Rouben Mamoulian, 1929) as Kitty Darling, a burlesque queen who does all she can to keep her daughter from discovering how low she has fallen. *Applause*—from an early script by Garrett Fort, who also wrote the "continuity" from Hecht's story for *Roadhouse Nights*—followed Morgan's 1927 Broadway success as the mixed-race Julie in *Show Boat*, and her reprise of Julie's "Can't Help Lovin' Dat Man" that was used as a prologue in the film version of the same (1929). Julie is an entertainer who suffers a fate not unlike that of Kitty in *Applause*, though Julie is rejected because of race, while Kitty is cast aside when age undermines her appeal as a burlesque performer. As Lola in *Roadhouse Nights*, Morgan is once more playing an entertainer whose life is on the brink of a fatal turn, as a dominating crime boss threatens to overwhelm the essential goodness of her character. Her doomed love in *Show Boat* and her sacrifice for her daughter in *Applause* prefigure the backstory of *Roadhouse Nights*, in which Horner had degraded Lola for ten years before she recovers her true identity through a rekindled girlhood infatuation for Bindbugel. In other words, the audience for *Roadhouse Nights* got to witness the rescue of Helen Morgan not only from Horner, but also from the fate she suffers in *Show Boat* and *Applause*.

Casting Ruggles as Bindbugel shaded *Roadhouse Nights* toward comedy. Already one can see, at this early stage in his career, the ingredients that would mark Ruggles's later screen persona, for example as Adolph in Ernst Lubitsch's *One Hour with You* (1932), a man unable to comprehend the woman he pursues even as he collects evidence on the wife he plans to divorce. Or as Major Horace Applegate in *Bringing Up Baby* (1938), a big game hunter who, in true screwball form, can't tell a loon's call from the roar of a leopard. Bindbugel is presented as an articulate half-wit who has given himself over to gambling and drink, and who only develops a sense of purpose when he finds the body of his former colleague washed up on a beach. Like most of Ruggles's characters, Bindbugel must work hard to understand the world that others inhabit naturally and from which he finds himself at a distance. In his stylized movements and in his voice that he modulates with everything he says, Ruggles portrays Bindbugel as a man for whom life is a game of adopting postures, of well-intentioned attempts to fit in. The performance bridges Kohler's gangster seriousness in the role of Horner and the roadhouse entertainers' world of song and make-believe.

The performers at the roadhouse also introduce the familiar trope of backstage musicals in which entertainers rescue life from banality; the show people are endowed with a talent for creating illusions that foster hope and aspiration. Morgan's singing laments life's difficulties, while Jimmy Durante brings a magical power into the world of the film. Durante, with Lou Clayton and Eddie Jackson, had been a vaudeville star since the mid-1920s. In the film he acts as Lola's agent, a Puckish figure in the employ of this Titania in contrast to the tyrannical Oberon of Horner. Through his timely interventions, the film becomes a fairytale of love triumphing over corruption, allowing the jaded torch singer and the cynical journalist to slough off the years and reenter a presexual childhood paradise.

Roadhouse Nights is routinely disparaged as badly representing an important first novel, but comparing the film to *Red Harvest* provides the wrong measure of value. Indeed, the film lacks the power of *Red Harvest.* Yet in spite of the technical limitations of its production in 1929, it has its own integrity, a product in some degree of what André Bazin famously called "the genius of the system."

City Streets (1931)

City Streets was based on a mere seven-page, handwritten outline by Hammett, but in this case the story was used as the basis of the film rather than ignored. After *The Maltese Falcon* was published in February 1930 and embraced by reviewers, Hammett became a sought-after prospect. By the following July, David O. Selznick would write to B. P. Schulberg, "We have the opportunity to secure Dashiell Hammett to do one story for us. . . . Hammett has recently created quite a stir in literary circles by his creation of two books for Knopf, *The Maltese Falcon* and *Red Harvest.* I believe that he is another Van Dine—indeed that he possesses more originality than Van Dine, and might very well prove to be the creator of something new and startlingly original for us."[14] S. S. Van Dine was the pseudonym of Richard Huntington Wright, the author of detective novels featuring the effete Philo Vance, which in turn became a series of popular films, three of them starring William Powell. Hammett detested Van Dine's work. But when Hammett was put under contract, Paramount focused on his originality; in writing a gangster film for Gary Cooper, he was asked for "something

with class. Something different."[15] One after another, Hammett sketched
out six stories in the hope of quickly being awarded the $5,000 bonus for
getting one produced. Finally, "After School" was accepted, to be developed
as *City Streets*.[16]

Much more directly than *Roadhouse Nights, City Streets* participated
in the gangster cycle of the early 1930s. It arrived on screens just three
months after *Little Caesar* (1931), one week before *The Public Enemy* (1931),
to be followed in less than a year by the delayed release of *Scarface* (1932).
"In retrospect," Carlos Clarens writes, "1931 looms as the peak year of
the gangster film," and though he qualifies his statement by pointing
out that only forty of the four hundred pictures released in the United
States that year were gangster films, 10 percent is a significant portion.[17]
Yet in surveys of the gangster film, *City Streets* is rarely mentioned, and
the reason is clear. At least for the pre-*Godfather* era, most critics have
relied in some degree on the definition outlined in Robert Warshow's
seminal 1948 essay "The Gangster as Tragic Hero." For Warshow, "the
typical gangster film presents a steady upward progress followed by a pre-
cipitous fall." The gangster "hurts people," his activity becoming "a kind
of pure criminality." "We gain the double satisfaction of participating
vicariously in the gangster's sadism and then seeing it turned against
the gangster himself."[18] While *City Streets* is set in the gangster milieu,
featuring bootlegging, competition for control of the liquor industry,
and the introduction of The Kid (Gary Cooper) into the gang, his story—
particularly his escape from the world of crime at the end—does not fit
the pattern that came to be recognized by audiences and critics as typical
of the genre. Thus Tom Milne can write that "*City Streets* is not, strictly
speaking, a gangster film. For one thing, there is not a single killing shown
on screen. . . . Instead, *City Streets* is first and foremost a love story looking
back to *Underworld* in its relationships and its stylized view of gangster-
dom."[19] He might have added that neither The Kid as a character, nor Cooper as a rising star, was coded as ethnic in a way that was typically part of
the gangster's profile, Irish in *The Public Enemy*, for example, or Italian in
Little Caesar and *Scarface*. Just the opposite—The Kid is presented as typical
of the nativist heartland, marked by an innocence associated with rural
life in contrast to the city. Most importantly, the love story of *City Streets*
has a happy ending rather than a "tragic" one.

In attempting to write for Cooper's screen persona, Hammett stayed close to his recent fiction. Few of Hammett's characters are either open or expressive of their feelings, but Hammett seems to have looked specifically to Wilmer in *The Maltese Falcon*, who, like the Roscoe Kid of "After School," is good with a gun and unable to look people in the eye. Here is the first description of Wilmer: "The boy . . . looked with small hazel eyes under somewhat long curling lashes at Spade's chest. He said, in a voice as colorless and composed and cold as his young face: 'What?'" After Spade has answered, "the hazel eyes' gaze went up Spade's chest to the knot of his maroon tie and rested there."[20] In "After School" Hammett wrote, "The boy doesn't look into anybody's face. The closest he comes to it is to look at their chests. He moves very deliberately, holding himself rather rigid, and has a cool, unsmiling, poker face."[21] Like Wilmer, the Roscoe Kid seems damaged and dangerous.[22]

Oliver Garrett's screenplay for *City Streets* softens The Kid's manner to naïve innocence and simplicity, his social awkwardness becoming shyness rather than a sociopath's isolation. Additional changes have to do with Nan, the gangster's stepdaughter who falls for The Kid. In both stories she gets in trouble as an accessory to a murder committed by her stepfather, but in the film she emerges from prison wiser and dedicated only to saving The Kid. In Hammett's outline, she was a high school student sent to reform school rather than prison, emerging five years later "hardened," a quality that makes her unattractive to the Roscoe Kid. In the film, Nan tries to avoid the gang leader's attentions, whereas in Hammett's version she is angered by the Roscoe Kid's withdrawal into himself and throws herself at the boss, even revealing to him the Roscoe Kid's plan to leave the gang. In Hammett's story, the Roscoe Kid's continuing self-discipline inspires Nan, whereas in the film his innocence and honesty make Nan try to win him back after he has begun to stray.

If creating the story for Cooper gave it a protagonist very different from the gangster stereotype, the actor's special reticence worked well in the gangster milieu, which is marked by an avoidance of verbal explanation. Cooper had worked on a cattle ranch, found stunt work in Hollywood, and a year after his success in *The Virginian* (1929) was paired with Marlene Dietrich in Josef von Sternberg's *Morocco* (1930). *Morocco*, which would be followed immediately by *City Streets*, takes full advantage of the deep-seated reserve that marked Cooper's personality, on- and off-screen.[23] As Legionnaire Tom Brown, he flees an emotional commitment to the almost equally independent Amy Jolly (Dietrich). In fact, he is an *homme fatal* in *Morocco*, a reversal for Dietrich and von Sternberg after *The Blue Angel,* where the allure of Dietrich's character leads to the destruction of a self-important gymnasium professor. As Jeffrey Meyers remarked on von Sternberg's presentation of Cooper in *Morocco*, "Languid and romantic, Cooper was lit and photographed as if he were a beautiful woman."[24] Ultimately, Jolly sacrifices a comfortable life with a rich lover, played by Adolphe Menjou, preferring to walk barefoot into the desert as Legionnaire Brown's camp follower. *City Streets* builds on and takes advantage of this star image of Cooper as an object of desire.

The reserve that Cooper brings to The Kid eases his character's acceptance in the underworld, which is defined by the unspoken. The single word "Beer" stands for the entire bootlegging racket, for example, while one cryptic phrase, "No hard feelings"—first used when the boss eliminates a rival in the opening moments—replaces verbal elaboration of any reasons for betrayals and executions. In a scene showing Nan (Sylvia Sidney) and The Kid at a beach, where troubled waves provide a metaphor for the turmoil they face, she expresses her feelings and waits for him to respond; his mouth forms words as if rehearsing them, only to come out with the minimal "It sure is." Everyone in the underworld understands the unspoken, but Nan ultimately proves to be the best at reading the signs, and especially at understanding The Kid's unique quality, his authenticity. The Kid, unlike the boss, Maskal (Paul Lukas), and all the lesser gangsters, is exactly what he seems to be. Nan understands this and desires him for it. When he visits her in prison—dressed in an outlandish fur-collared coat she doesn't even notice at first, she expresses her longing and adoration directly: "Boy, you're good to see," she says. "I wish . . . I wish I could just touch you." This is followed by a close-up showing her fingers pushing through the coarse screen to reach him. The Kid as embodied by Cooper becomes that which is valued above all else, desired, admired, to be protected and to be sacrificed for, a variation on von Sternberg's use of Cooper in *Morocco.*

Rouben Mamoulian further builds on the idea of the unspoken and Cooper's reticence by imposing a cinematic style based on a similar

"A gangster film for Coop" (*City Streets*, 1931)

restraint or indirection. Milne associates this with the director's having "thoroughly absorbed the techniques of silent film at its best." Of the cryptic dialogue in one scene, Milne writes that "the words are almost like stress marks, indicating the accents in a verse where the poetry is carried by the images, the rhymes by the editing and camera movement."[25] But Mamoulian's differences from standard Hollywood practice go well beyond the visual storytelling of the silent era—they include his sense of theatrical mise-en-scène, and more significantly an approach to editing and narrative most likely learned from Soviet cinema. Born in Tilisi (now Tbilisi), Georgia, Mamoulian moved to Paris, then attended the gymnasium and studied law in Moscow, where he also took classes at the Moscow Art Theatre (he met Stanislavsky but did not study with him).[26] Eventually, after working with student productions at an opera company George Eastman organized in Rochester, Mamoulian convinced the Theatre Guild to allow him to direct Dorothy and DuBose Heyward's *Porgy* on Broadway, the October 1927 success of which made possible Mamoulian's subsequent career in theater and film (he would also direct the better-known operatic adaptation *Porgy and Bess* in 1935, with music and lyrics by George and Ira

Gershwin). *The Jazz Singer* premiered just four days after the opening of *Porgy*; with theatrical expertise in demand for sound film, Mamoulian was lured to Paramount's Astoria studio to make *Applause*, then brought to Hollywood for *City Streets*.

The point to be emphasized is how Mamoulian's style, both visually and in his handling of the narration, builds on the reticence of Cooper's persona, the quality that Dashiell Hammett had initially attempted to address in "After School." A montage of the industrial production of beer is juxtaposed with the factory-like prison where the women appear as laborers among the heavy machinery: we see Nan through a web of threads as she and others fix bobbins on industrial sewing machines, Mamoulian emphasizing the impact of industrial labor on people's lives. And his visual technique is complemented by an indirection in the narration: the progress of the story is intentionally and persistently interrupted, as for example at a party thrown by Maskal in order to seduce Nan, in which the director frequently cuts to parallel and tangential developments rather than following the main characters' attention through eyeline matches that carry the story forward. Even the most significant plot development of the film—an apparently inevitable confrontation between The Kid and Maskal—never occurs. The logic of the production is profoundly coherent: The Kid's inherent reluctance, tied to a pre-urban simplicity and individualism, ignites Nan's desire and motivates her to interrupt the grinding gears of the urban gangster machine.

City Streets has one singular claim to fame. Prevailing over arguments that audiences would not understand his technique, Mamoulian introduced what has repeatedly been labeled the first use in cinema of voiceover to reveal a character's thoughts. As Nan is lying awake in an upper bunk in her prison cell, the camera moves slowly in until her face is framed in a tight close-up, and we see a tear below the corner of her eye. Then her voice begins, followed by The Kid's voice, fragments from their conversation gradually distorted and becoming obsessively repetitive.

Hammett was not impressed with the film. When *City Streets* was released in April 1931, he wrote to Lillian Hellman of the film's good reviews and modest box office receipts, "a fair $50,000 or $60,000 in New York."[27] But when he saw it a few days later he "found it pretty lousy, though Sylvia

"Beer" (*City Streets*, 1931)

Prison as a factory (*City Streets*, 1931)

Sidney makes the whole thing seem fairly good in spots. She's good, that ugly little baby, and currently my favorite screen actress."[28]

Mister Dynamite (1935)

Like *City Streets*, *Mister Dynamite* was based on a brief outline by Hammett, sold to Universal by Warner Bros. In 1935 Universal was the "eternal has-been of a lot," in one critic's words, with a "nickelodeon mindset," having refused to bank on stars in a star-oriented age.[29] Thus, *Mister Dynamite* is a sixty-seven-minute B-picture without a major star, directed by Alan Crosland at the end of a career remembered mainly for introducing sound with *The Jazz Singer* (1927). Darryl Zanuck's initial assignment to create an "original Sam Spade story" for William Powell was badly timed in terms of Hammett's development as a novelist. While Powell was fresh off his success playing Philo Vance in *The Benson Murder Case* (Frank Tuttle, 1930), Hammett was striving to move away from the detective genre entirely toward the realism evident in *The Glass Key*.

Hammett had been concerned with the issue he pursues in "On the Make" for some time. In all his novels, the protagonist walks a line between independence and transgression of the law and other social constraints. In *Red Harvest* and *The Dain Curse* these are represented by the ethical code of the Continental Agency, which he stretches to the limit. In *The Maltese Falcon*, even after Spade says, "Don't be too sure I'm as crooked as I'm supposed to be. That kind of reputation might be good business,"[30] the reader is kept guessing just how dedicated he is to helping his client as opposed to pursuing personal gain. Ned Beaumont in *The Glass Key* similarly keeps us guessing as to where the line is between loyalty and integrity as he defines them. In contrast to all of Hammett's other protagonists, Gene Richmond, the private detective in "On the Make" has no code beyond the profit motive, which cannot even be held in check by love. The dénouement of the story grows out of this flaw, which defines and condemns him.

Richmond is established as a small-time chiseler, who lies to his clients and pads his expense accounts. He is hired by a man named Pomeroy, who is fearful of being ensnared in an investigation of a murder involving his bootlegger. Immediately Richmond demands an outsized fee of $25,000, but in the course of the investigation he falls in love with his

client's daughter, Ann. He conceals evidence that will solve the case so that
he has more time to win her over, but things go wrong: Ann is kidnapped,
and when the police rescue her, everyone learns of Richmond's dishonesty.
Ann turns her back on him as he confesses, "I'm in the game for money.
Sure, I'm always on the make."[31] Richmond is torn between the woman and
his greed, but "On the Make" turns the relationship with the femme fatale
on its head: Ann draws Richmond toward a worthwhile relationship from
which he is excluded because of his persistent dishonesty.

Hammett's downbeat outline, however, was transformed into a classic
detective comedy full of witty banter between its male and female protagonists. Acquiring "On the Make" in September 1934, Universal hoped to
emulate the success of *The Thin Man*. Thus, in the screenplay by Doris Mal-
low and Harry Clork, the protagonist has been rehabilitated—now called
T. N. Thompson, or Dynamite (Edmund Lowe), he proves he can ultimately
be trusted to do the right thing. And a spirit of anarchic comedy dominates
the film to the point that issues of integrity, and ultimately the coherence
of ideas in the narrative, are no longer of central importance.

If Richmond's dishonesty is mitigated in *Mister Dynamite*, a second
important change is the substitution of a Svengali pianist/composer for the
bootlegger of "On the Make"; he is now called Jarl Dvorjak (Victor Varconi)
and is contrasted with an honest and down-to-earth casino owner named
Clark Lewis (Minor Watson), as if to evoke the exploration of the American
Northwest. The contrast of concert hall versus casino allows the film to
dwell on the Hollywood commonplace that the popular and ordinary are
superior to high culture that is frequently a sham.[32] And the allegory of
high and low culture is worked throughout the film visually as well as in the
narrative. The unspoiled Mona Lewis (Verna Hillie) is contrasted implicitly
with Dvorjak's rotten offspring Boris (Frank Lyman), and the staging of the
moment where Dynamite falls for Mona in a rose garden on Lewis's patio is
designed to drive home the juxtaposition between pretense and unspoiled
natural beauty. Dynamite moves through the doors to the patio garden on
a lower level and looks down, where an eyeline match to his gaze shows
Mona crying. To join her he passes in front of a large semicircular window,
a bright fan of light that creates a silhouette of a statue with great simi-
larity to the Venus de Milo, so that Dynamite's conversation with Mona
transpires under the auspices of Venus. While it is appropriate to have the

Dynamite under the eyes of Venus (*Mister Dynamite*, 1935)

goddess of love overseeing the moment where Dynamite develops his feelings for Mona, equally clear is the distinction between the ossified knock-
off statue and the freshness of Dynamite and Mona as an embodiment of
modern American romance. This point is driven home when Dynamite
compares Mona not to the statue, but to a rose in the garden, telling Lewis,
"You have a particularly fine one out there."

Ultimately the allegory breaks down in ways that betray the studio's
limited investment, or at least the low priority given this aspect of the
script. Ideas are ignored in favor of funny lines—Lowe and Jean Dixon, who
plays Lynn Marlo, Dynamite's long-suffering sidekick, were clearly cast
based on their ability to swap wisecracks. Dixon's screen career lasted but
fifteen films, of which *Mister Dynamite* was her fifth; she was frequently
used as the friend and comic foil of the heroine. Lowe had worked steadily
since 1915 in a range of roles that at first took advantage of his physical
energy, then later of a liveliness of personality and wit. The two actors
converge at a moment in Hollywood history that saw both tightening censorship and a great deal of effervescent comedy. When the dated gangster
element of Hammett's "On the Make" was eliminated, models of comic

performance beyond *The Thin Man* included *It Happened One Night* (1934) and other screwball comedies. These flourished especially after censors' attacks on Mae West's ribald sexuality in *Belle of the Nineties* (Leo McCarey, 1932), *She Done Him Wrong* (Lowell Sherman, 1933), and *I'm No Angel* (Wesley Ruggles, 1933). These years were the high point of W. C. Fields's career—he made twelve films between 1931 and 1935—and there was the banter of Fred Astaire and Ginger Rogers in their RKO musicals. Particularly relevant to *Mister Dynamite* were Groucho Marx's antics and wordplay in *The Cocoanuts* (Robert Florey and Joseph Santley, 1929), *Animal Crackers* (Victor Heerman, 1930), *Monkey Business* (Norman Z. McLeod, 1931), *Horse Feathers* (Norman Z. McLeod, 1932), and *Duck Soup* (Leo McCarey, 1933).

Some of the clowning in *Mister Dynamite* has a screwball element, such as Lynn leaving town on the train not with luggage but with a goldfish in a tank, or when she tries to talk with a clothespin in her mouth and Dynamite says, "Finest secretary in the world—she has three championships for hog calling." Yet many of the asides have the timing and irrelevance to plot that recall the Marx Brothers, as when Lynn first hears Jarl Dvorjak's name and comments, "That sounds like a mouthwash." Or when she cracks wise as Dynamite plays a note on the musician's prized organ: "Pretty," she says; "sounds like a cow with cramps." Dialogue regularly upstages the action: when Lynn enters the casino wearing a fur coat she knows Dynamite has acquired fraudulently, an attendant says, "I'll take your wrap," and she responds, "No thanks, honey, I'll take the rap for this myself." To an older man's invitation to leave the casino with him, she says, "Hold on to your arthritis, honey—everything in due time." Dynamite follows Lynn's lead. When she asks, "All right, Sherlock, who did it?" he answers, "Your curiosity's going to get the upper hand some day." At one point, Dynamite says to a butler, "You may show me out in the manner to which I am accustomed." At another he remarks to the police chief: "I'll do my best, which when you look at it from all sides is pretty darn good." As he searches the corpse of Dvorjak's business manager, Dynamite even addresses the dead body: "If I found anything, you'd wake up and claim 20 percent." Lowe's vaudeville delivery, with a twinkle in his eye that amounts to a wink at the audience, deliberately undercuts all other kinds of emotional engagement with events.

As with *Roadhouse Nights* and *City Streets*, in *Mister Dynamite* the particular goals of the production largely displace the trajectory and ideas of Hammett's story outline. Once his reputation was fully established, this would occur to a lesser extent. In a *New York Times* review of *Mister Dynamite* on May 25, 1935, Hammett's name is invoked: "Mr. [*sic*] Dynamite . . . is the creation of Dashiell Hammett, who wrote *The Thin Man*. Mr. Hammett's distinction among mystery tale spinners is that he never takes his corpse as seriously as his detective; and he never lets his detective take himself seriously at all." The claim might be true of Nick Charles, but certainly not of Hammett's other protagonists; inadvertently the reviewer is underscoring the extent to which Hammett, by this date, was associated primarily with *The Thin Man*.

2

Celebrity

The Thin Man (1934)

No film is as important to Dashiell Hammett's movie career as *The Thin Man*, not only because it remains—along with *The Maltese Falcon* (1941)—his best known, but because the rest of Hammett's movie success grew out of the celebrity he acquired as the creator of Nick and Nora Charles. As rarely occurs in Hollywood, the filmmakers at Metro-Goldwyn-Mayer set out to make their movie as much as possible like the book. Several circumstances aligned their project with Hammett's novel. For one thing, after praise for *The Maltese Falcon*—some reviewers had called it the best American detective novel ever written—many in the audience would know Hammett's later work. More importantly, much of the book's appeal for Hollywood was its celebration of a definitive turn in the century-long political struggle over alcohol signaled by popular rejection of Prohibition. The novel and film were created within a year of each other between May 1933 and May 1934. Hammett wrote *The Thin Man* during a six-month period ending just as states began voting to ratify the repeal of the Eighteenth Amendment. *Redbook* published a condensed version in its December 1933 issue, the same month that the Twenty-first Amendment was ratified. A few weeks later, on January 8, 1934, Alfred Knopf published the novel just as the bars and nightclubs were reopening legally, only four months before MGM released the film. Social life in the film, as in the novel, would be organized around drinking. And beyond the legalization of alcohol, Nick and Nora's behavior reflected the more profound social changes that had come about by the end of the 1920s.

The novel was Hammett's last, drawing on his personal experience of New York and on the relationship he had developed with Lillian Hellman, and in the trajectory of his work as well as that of his life, it represents a culmination. Nick Charles, middle-aged and retired, a reflective and somewhat passive man, concludes the evolution of the private detective through Hammett's stories and novels, from the Op through Sam Spade and the political operative Ned Beaumont. But in three other respects, *The Thin Man* also represents a final stage of Hammett's evolution: in the development of his female characters, in his defining characters through their use of alcohol, and in the pairing of his protagonists with partners who are also their adversaries.

As Hammett's detectives had roots in his Pinkerton experience before and briefly after World War I, Nora in *The Thin Man* reflects his wider exposure to society—and specifically to New York—that came with success. Before becoming a writer, Hammett had married a nurse he met in the hospital where he had been sent for tuberculosis during World War I; they had two children, then separated in the early 1920s. He had since become involved with the novelist Nell Martin, among others, whom Diane Johnson describes as also having been a "newspaperwoman . . . , a musical comedy soubrette, vaudeville actress, cabaret entertainer, Proofreader, and erstwhile operator of a laundry mangle."[1] They went to New York in the fall of 1929 as *The Maltese Falcon* was in preparation for publication. By then, as Richard Layman writes, Hammett "was a minor literary celebrity, and he learned quickly that such a distinction was more meaningful in New York than in San Francisco."[2] In the fall of 1930 he began his long relationship with Hellman. Martin, Hellman, and Dorothy Parker were among many accomplished women Hammett knew, and the development of his women characters paralleled this broadening of his social experience. In his early fiction, the women were for the most part stereotypical femmes fatales. With Dinah Brand in *Red Harvest*, continuing with Brigid O'Shaughnessy in *The Maltese Falcon* and Janet Henry in *The Glass Key*, the women become more active and more complex. In *The Thin Man*, Nora Charles is an equal partner with Nick. Hellman has recounted how Hammett told her that she was the model for Nora Charles, as well as for the less attractive female characters in the novel.[3]

Drinking was more than fashionable during Prohibition, and temperance rhetoric was commonplace. Yet from the beginning Hammett had gone well beyond truisms of the century-long debate over alcohol in signaling strength of character by his protagonists' ability to resist the effects of drink. In "Nightmare Town" (1924), for example, where Steve Threefall makes a bet that he can drive all day across a boiling desert drinking only "bitter white liquor," the feat is performed as a test of the strength of character he will need to tame the town.[4] "The Golden Horseshoe" (1924) offers a more complex instance. The tale is set in Tijuana, a liminal zone between U.S. law and lawless Mexico, and the town's main thoroughfare is defined by its bars, "six or seven hundred feet of dusty and dingy street running between two almost solid rows of saloons."[5] The Op ventures into this limbo looking for clarity about a man whose actions and identity are a mystery. When he finds the man, he spends three days in what turns out to be "a drinking contest pure and simple. He was trying to drink me into a pulp—a pulp that would easily give up all its secrets—and I was trying the same game on him. Neither of us made much progress."[6] This standoff offers a paradigm of Hammett's deployment of alcohol in many of the stories and in all his novels—drinking calibrates character and is the medium of a contest between characters.

The third element central to the plots of the novels is a relationship between the protagonist and someone who is his partner as well as his adversary. In *Red Harvest*, the relationship is with Dinah Brand, in *The Dain Curse* with Owen Fitzstephan. Sam Spade partners and competes with both Brigid O'Shaughnessy and Casper Gutman in *The Maltese Falcon*, as in *The Glass Key* Ned Beaumont competes and is allied with both Janet Henry and Paul Madvig. In *The Thin Man* Nora is Nick's affectionate wife while competing with him in drinking and in trying to solve the mystery of Clyde Wynant's disappearance, while Herbert MacCaulay is also a partner/adversary, a seemingly helpful acquaintance who turns out to be the murderer.

Part of the novel's appeal to Hollywood was that while it seemed fresh, it also fit within familiar industry genres. Detective films had received particular impetus with the arrival of sound because, as William Everson wrote in 1972, "there was a great emphasis on the kind of movie in which the story had to be told by prolonged dialogue exchanges." The B-detective film "quickly became as standardized as the 'B' western," with comedy an important part of the formula[7]—one has only to think of the popular Charlie Chan series. In spite of MGM's higher-than-average budget and production values, *The Thin Man* was conceived as just such a film. Hammett's novel already included the ingredients of a classic detective story, the step-by-step unfolding from murder to investigation, to assembling the suspects to the detective's revelation of the guilty party and explanation of the crime.

With respect to the Hays Office, *The Thin Man* was also suitable, even as the Production Code was entering a period of newly robust enforcement under the leadership of Joseph Breen. Magazine editors had considered the novel immoral, so much so, in fact, that Hammett's agent, Ben Wassen, had difficulty placing it for serial publication. The *Redbook* version was bowdlerized, and one line in particular caused a stir when the novel appeared in book form. After Nick has subdued Mimi when she has a fit, Nora says to Nick: "Tell me the truth: when you were wrestling with Mimi, didn't you get an erection?" Nick's answer: "A little." In advertising the book, Knopf referred to the line—citing the page number—while boasting that "twenty thousand people don't buy a book within three weeks to read a five-word question."[8] The phrase was inflammatory enough that British and later U.S. editions substituted "excited" for "an erection."[9] But such dialogue was easily deleted, and the narrative had the more fundamental advantages of being a sexy love story without explicit sex and a crime novel without violence.

Furthermore, the script would be shaped under the especially conservative management at MGM. Louis B. Mayer, the studio's all-powerful head, had been heard to mutter, "I don't care what DeMille does, with his naked slave girls. No Mayer picture will have a bedroom scene, even where the couples are married."[10] MGM's producers, directors, and writers all functioned with an understanding of this policy—even a romance between man and wife, set in the sinful heart of metropolitan Manhattan, would have no bedroom scenes, and the Charles's luxury hotel would provide them with modest single beds. Moreover, an attempt would be made to frame the independent couple within a more conventional narrative of separated lovers brought together in marriage in the film's final moments. By the time Joseph Breen reviewed the script of *The Thin Man* for the Production Code Administration, the only negative comment addressed what he considered excessive drinking. Intrinsic to the social fabric presented in the film, the drinking remained: there is no correspondence in the PCA files that suggests negotiation over the issue, only a final laudatory note from Breen communicating how much he enjoyed the picture.[11]

Within the constraints at MGM, the film was ultimately shaped by director W. S. Van Dyke, who, because of his stature and the trust of Mayer and producer Hunt Stromberg, had extensive preproduction involvement as well as complete control of filming on the set. Van Dyke's career stretched back to running errands for D. W. Griffith on *Intolerance* (1916), and his silent-film experience marked his visual style, particularly in his use of mise-en-scène and occasionally jarring close-ups. He first established his reputation by rescuing a disastrous production of *White Shadows in the South Seas* (1928) in Tahiti, relieving Robert Flaherty, famous for *Nanook of the North* (1922). Following *White Shadows*, Van Dyke directed adventure movies such as *Trader Horn* (1931), some of the Tarzan movies, and eventually films like *Penthouse* (1933) with Myrna Loy and *Manhattan Melodrama* (1934) with both Loy and William Powell. When Stromberg acquired *The Thin Man* for $21,000 and showed it to Van Dyke, he was immediately excited.[12] "While it was a good enough mystery story," he later said, "there was something else about the book that struck me. Here was something new and fresh and charming, a romance between a man and his wife. It's the story of a couple of kids that understand each other, and have a blessed confidence in each other. Beneath all the casualness and all the wise cracking, there's a lovely wholesome relationship, something really deep and spiritual and inspiring."[13] This understanding of the novel drove the casting and the development of the screenplay. Van Dyke requested Powell and Loy for the roles of Nick and Nora, while molding the work of screenwriting team Frances Goodrich and Albert Hackett to highlight Nick and Nora's relationship. His method of shooting fostered the actors' spontaneity, set the film's pace, and defined its visual style.

Myrna Loy and William Powell

Stromberg and Van Dyke immediately identified Loy as right for Nora, and concluded, as William Nolan writes, that "the only actor who could play Nick Charles with total conviction was William Powell."[14] Mayer challenged both choices. In his view Powell, at forty-one and with his popularity waning, was too old, while Loy lacked the sophistication for Nora.

From her debut in *What Price Beauty* (1925), Loy had played a succession of exotic vamps, most recently at MGM as Fu Manchu's daughter in *The Mask of Fu Manchu* (Brabin, 1932)—this was the Loy that Mayer had difficulty imagining as Nora Charles.[15] But Van Dyke was more familiar with her, especially from *Penthouse* (1933). Stromberg had produced and Van Dyke directed the film, from a script by Goodrich and Hackett. In it Loy plays Gertie Waxted, who begins the film as a young beauty with a bad reputation. She is introduced to the protagonist Jack Durant (Warner Baxter) as "the kind you can take home to dinner and no hard feelings if you don't ask her to stay to breakfast," to which Durant replies, "And no hard feelings if you do!" Gertie seems almost disappointed that Durant doesn't immediately jump into bed with her, but by the end of the story she demonstrates herself to be honest, loyal, and witty, worthy of marrying Durant. The film features New York nightclubs as well as the theme of class difference, though in *Penthouse*—the reverse of the situation in *The Thin Man*—the lower-class woman marries the upper-class man. Gertie is as independent as Nora Charles, but a pronounced stiffness between Loy and Baxter makes this film far less satisfying than *The Thin Man*. Van Dyke developed *The Prizefighter and the Lady* specifically for Loy, though that film was written by John Lee Mahin and John Meehan, and Van Dyke shared direction with Howard Hawks. Stromberg and Van Dyke had also seen Loy, on loan from MGM to Paramount, in Rouben Mamoulian's *Love Me Tonight* (1932), a film that showed her ability to make people laugh:[16] she played Valentine, in Loy's words "a pent-up aristocrat hungry for life and men," a description that might fit Nora Charles.[17] Certain that Loy would be able deliver the sophistication and the comic timing of Nora Charles, Stromberg and Van Dyke were able to overcome Mayer's doubts.

Powell's history was much longer than Loy's; by the time of *The Thin Man* he had been a major star for several years. As Loy had been pigeon-holed as an exotic vamp, Powell was at first known for playing villains. Eventually, however, he had an opportunity to play comic parts—several across from Bebe Daniels, who would play Ruth Wonderly in *The Maltese Falcon* (1931)—and he made the shift from villain to hero in three films released in 1930: *Street of Chance* (John Cromwell), where he is a gambler who sacrifices his life to save his brother from a similar life; *Shadow of the Law* (Louis J. Gasnier), in which he risks his life to protect a female companion with a shady past; and *For the Defense* (Cromwell), where as an attorney he saves his wife who has allowed him to defend her as innocent when she is guilty of bribing a juror. By 1930, Powell was among the industry's biggest male box-office attractions; along with John Barrymore, Ronald Colman, and several others, he received a 100 percent rating as a "Top *Photoplay* Male Performer."

What made Powell especially plausible for the role of Nick Charles, however, was the public's identification of him with Philo Vance. In fact, Powell developed much of his manner for Nick Charles in his four films as Vance. The first was *The Canary Murder Case* (1929), initially shot as a silent by Malcolm St. Clair, then reshot by Frank Tuttle with dialogue. In it Powell seems physically constrained, yet the film, which co-starred Louise Brooks as the seductive "Canary" of the title, was a success. After *The Greene Murder Case* (1929) and the faster-paced *Benson Murder Case* (1930), both directed by Tuttle, Ben Washer could write in the *New York Telegram* that "William Powell is most often thought of by the moviegoer as Philo Vance, that super detective."[18]

By the *Kennel Murder Case* (1933), an MGM film directed by Michael Curtiz, the Powell familiar to us from *The Thin Man* fully inhabits the character of Vance. His tone, as when he arrives at the crime scene and addresses a police sergeant played by Eugene Pallette, is one of dry sarcasm: "Doesn't it strike you as rather odd that a man would commit suicide while changing from his street clothes to his pajamas?" Nothing, however, shows better how short a step it was to *The Thin Man* from *The Kennel Murder Case* than a moment in the opening scene. The film begins at a dog show at the Long Island Kennel Club. A series of establishing shots shows the genteel participants taking dogs to and from the judging

"Miss Loy, I presume?" (*Manhattan Melodrama*, 1934)

posts while spectators mill around on a pleasant summer afternoon. Gradually the focus of the scene narrows, a public address system presenting the contestants, including, "in ring number two, Captain Mac-Tavish, shown by its owner, well-known fancier Philo Vance." Vance's Scottish terrier wins third prize, and a medium shot of Powell carrying Captain MacTavish shows him, leisurely and smiling, addressing the dog just as Nick Charles would address Asta: "Don't be down-hearted, Captain; you're still champion with me." Except for the color of the dog, a clip from the scene could pass for an outtake from *The Thin Man*. This was the "heyday of the debonair private detective," in Everson's words, and "no player essayed his role as well (or with so many variations) as William Powell."[19]

The assumption has frequently been made that Van Dyke recommended Loy and Powell for *The Thin Man* based on their easy collaboration on the set of *Manhattan Melodrama* (1934), which he directed;[20] in fact they had been offered the roles in *The Thin Man* long before—only a delay in starting *The Thin Man* allowed *Manhattan Melodrama* to be shot first. That film, however, did help to establish their rapport, and it previewed qualities of Loy that would help make her a star in *The Thin Man*.[21]

The Screenplay

Following the assembly-line model of 1930s Hollywood, *The Thin Man*'s narrative was established in advance of the shooting, but in this case the development of the screenplay was directly supervised by Van Dyke, so that both his view of the novel and his plans for shooting the film were already represented in the narrative shaped by screenwriters Goodrich and Hackett. According to Powell's biographer Charles Francisco, Van Dyke demanded "eight romantic sequences" between Nick and Nora.[22] Goodrich remembers a more categorical directive: "I don't care anything about the story; just give me five scenes between those people."[23] Because of Van Dyke's method of concentrating on a few key moments in the narrative, Goodrich's "five scenes" would dominate the film. To achieve the focus Van Dyke wanted, the screenwriters dismantled Hammett's novel, then artfully reassembled it using as much of the original material as they could.

Their most obvious rearrangements include creating a prologue so as to avoid exposition in the dialogue about events that precede Nick and Nora's arrival in New York. And the screenwriters consolidated the later chapters of the novel, concentrating the revelation of the criminal and explanation of the crime into a single scene, now set in the Charles's hotel suite, Nora's domain, which thus also keeps Nora in the story when Hammett had left her offstage. A story of young lovers temporarily separated would also be added, yet the mystery of Wynant's disappearance remains the same, and the movie is still very much about New York at the end of Prohibition. For the rest, the richness of a longer novel is merely reduced to achieve the clarity and relative simplicity of a ninety-minute film—several couples and characters are eliminated, and Goodrich and Hackett soften the harder edge of Hammett's tone.

The screenplay maintains the pretext Hammett created for Nick and Nora's excess and *carpe diem* philosophy: they are on holiday. They have traveled from the West to the East Coast to escape seasonal responsibilities to Nora's family. In fact everyone is on holiday, celebrating during the period between Christmas and New Year's Eve during which the story unfolds. Furthermore, within this atmosphere of Saturnalia, Nick is retired—he is always on holiday, and his reluctance to get involved seems further justified, at least retrospectively, by the thinness of the case. The missing Clyde Wynant, long dead, is as insubstantial as the man described as "so thin he had to stand in the same place twice to throw a shadow"[24]—concern for his wellbeing is ultimately much ado about nothing. Finally, along with all these other reasons for Nick and Nora to turn their backs on life's drudgery, they find themselves in the capital of loose living, Prohibition New York.

In carrying out Van Dyke's orders, Goodrich and Hackett followed Hammett in defining Nick and Nora against a spectrum of other couples. These include Clyde Wynant and Mimi, Wynant and Julia Wolf, Mimi and Chris Jorgenson—who remains married to his first wife—Julia and the gangster Shep Morelli, the stool-pigeon Nunheim and Marion (Miriam in the novel), as well as one invented by the screenwriters, Dorothy Wynant and her fiancé, Tommy. Except for Dorothy and Tommy, all the relationships are dysfunctional in ways that highlight aspects of the success of Nick and Nora. The mismatch of Wynant's brains with Mimi's shallow opportunism, for example, repeated in Wynant's relationship with Wolf, is a grotesque version of the quid pro quo represented in the pairing of Nick's experience with Nora's beauty, wit, and wealth. Similarly, the handsome Jorgenson lives off Mimi's money as Nick depends on Nora's; yet Jorgenson has never worked while Nick has been a highly successful detective. Nunheim and Marion offer a crude, lower-class version of dysfunctional complementarity. Excluded from the film are the Edges, a pedantic intellectual and his silly wife, and, more importantly, the Quinns. As in the novel, the factor common to most of the broken relationships is jealousy, motivated by duplicity and infidelity. By contrast, Nora is merely amused by Nick's reputation as a womanizer; with less detail in the screenplay than in the novel, her remaining unfazed at finding Dorothy Wynant being consoled in Nick's arms bears more weight in showing her security in the relationship.

Similarly, commentary on the idea of family in the film is less explicit than in the novel. The Wynants are still the primary example, in contrast with Nick and Nora, who are happy without children. Yet in Hammett's version, Gilbert and Dorothy are as monstrous as their parents, an affliction on the parents brought about by their own flawed nature and incompetence. Dorothy has no direction in life and shares her mother's profound dishonesty, while Gilbert has inherited both his father's lack of judgment as well as his mother's amorality. "This family's a family," Nick tells Nora, his way of saying that the apples haven't fallen far from the tree, but which also suggests that the Wynants perfectly represent the concept of family.[25] Mimi underscores her motherhood status as a point of superiority over Nora, asking, "You don't have children, do you?" Nick's response is to comment ironically to Nora that she is obviously "missing a lot," adding about Gilbert: "I hoped he had stopped being the whining little nuisance he was as a kid."[26] With the Wynants as the only model of family, it is obvious why the mature Nick and Nora prefer keeping a dog to having a child. Dorothy's transformation for the film, as we will see, comes about because of the added love story, which is an attempt to shift Hammett's emphasis.

For although most critics dismiss Hammett's last novel as veering from his earlier hard-boiled style,[27] it is important to recognize the ways in which it remains connected to his earlier hard-boiled writing and the realism evident in *The Glass Key*. These connections include both his framing of ideas and his style. For one thing, Hammett emphasizes the fact that the couple's freedom of action depends on Nora's wealth. Without the windfall of her inheritance, Nick would still be a working detective like Sam Spade. Other hard realities, underscored through Nora's response to them, include Morelli's drug habit, Dorothy's claim that she cannot go home because her stepfather will force her to have sex with him, as well as Gilbert's internal bleeding after a beating by a tough cop—not to mention his suspect obsession with learning about pain, heroin addiction, incest, and cannibalism. Part of the insistent reality of the novel is that both Dorothy and Gilbert are damaged human beings because of the neglect of their egocentric parents.

In fact, Mimi in the novel is vicious in the hard-boiled mode of Hammett's earlier work—the metaphor of a dangerous cat beneath the feminine exterior shows her kinship to the femmes fatales of his *Black Mask* stories. When she is confronted by Nick about one of her lies, "she made a claw of her right hand and struck at my face with her pointed nails. Her teeth were together, her lips drawn back over them."[28] Her most remarkable transformation occurs during her fit: "Mimi's face was becoming purple. Her eyes protruded, glassy, senseless, enormous. Saliva bubbled and hissed between clenched teeth with her breathing, and her red throat—her whole body—was a squirming mass of veins and muscles swollen until it seemed they must burst."[29] This brutality, more appropriate to literary naturalism than to the detective genre, is the core underlying Mimi's civilized veneer. In describing her, Hammett's prose, animated with the excess of Mimi's monstrosity, overflows the bounds of Nick's cool observation. In the film she is merely foolish and ridiculous.

Hammett's realism is most evident in the conversation Nick has with Alice Quinn when he brings home her drunken husband, and it goes beyond motives and narrative plausibility to prose style. The passage gets to the heart of the question of why the Quinns were eliminated from the screenplay:

Alice opened the door when I rang. She had on green pajamas and held a hairbrush in one hand. She looked wearily at Quinn and spoke wearily: "Bring it in." . . .

"I'll tuck him in," I said and loosened his tie.

"If you want to. I've given up doing it." I took off his coat, vest, and shirt.

"Where'd he pass out this time?" she asked with not much interest. She was still standing at the foot of the bed, brushing her hair now.

"The Edges." I unbuttoned his pants.

"With that little Wynant bitch?" The question was casual.

"There were a lot of people there."

"Yes," she said. "He wouldn't pick a secluded spot." She brushed her hair a couple of times. "So you don't think it's clubby to tell me anything."

Her husband stirred a little and mumbled: "Dorry." I took off his shoes.

Alice sighed. "I can remember when he had muscles." She stared at her husband until I took off the last of his clothes and rolled him under the covers. Then she sighed again and said, "I'll get you a drink."

"You'll have to make it short: Nora's waiting in the cab."

She opened her mouth to speak, shut it, opened it again to say: "Righto." I went into the kitchen with her.

A moment later she asks Nick:

"What do people think about my staying with Harrison with him chasing everything that's hot and hollow?"

"I don't know, Alice."

"What do you think?"

"I think you probably know what you're doing and whatever you do is your own business."

She looked at me with dissatisfaction. "You'll never talk yourself into any trouble, will you?" She smiled bitterly. "You know I'm only staying with him for his money, don't you? It may not be a lot to you, but it is to me—the way I was raised."

"There's always divorce and alimony. You ought to have—"

"Drink your drink and get the hell out of here," she said wearily.[30]

In contrast to Nick, Quinn is the image of a man for whom excess drinking marks his failure of character, while Nick's willingness to undress Quinn and put him to bed shows Nick's nonjudgmental empathy, with which he also takes in Alice's bitterness. He will not, however, be drawn into lingering over a drink with her, nor yield to her self-pity or her excuses about money and "the way [she] was raised." Alice's language is hard and cynical; her intelligence, in contrast to Nora's, is directed by bitterness. This passage highlights the way that in the novel the Quinns' broken relationship presents the opposite pole of a world that includes Nick's and Nora's mutual affection. Quinn in the film is just a name attached to one of the drunks at the Charles's Christmas Eve party; he then turns up as the drab middle-aged man in the final scene with whom Dorothy was about "to take [her] first false step."

The Quinns of the novel have no place in an MGM detective comedy, and one has the impression that, as magazine editors had, the studio felt uncomfortable with the freedom Nick and Nora exhibit within their marriage, and their indifference to family. What else can explain the introduction into the screenplay of the second couple, a now innocent and idealistic Dorothy paired with a stereotypically decent upper-middle-class college boy from Connecticut who wants nothing more than to marry her. The couple and their marriage plans are presented in the prologue, which is filmed with expressionistic shadows thrown high on the wall, Wynant's demonic concentration creating the mood of a science fiction or horror film. But that genre framing disappears immediately, when Wynant's assistant (William Augustin) announces Dorothy (Maureen O'Sullivan) and Tommy (Henry Wadsworth), who have come to announce their engagement. Clearly the goal of adding this second couple is to counterbalance the unusual relationship of Nick and Nora, framing it within the more conventional comic context of renewal—marriage and the promise of family.

This marriage subplot brings with it ideas not found in the novel. The murder mystery in the film derails Tommy and Dorothy's marriage plan because it raises questions—in Dorothy's mind as well as in the eyes of society—about the character of Dorothy's father. The assumption seems to be that criminality is a result of genetic inheritance, so Dorothy is no longer worthy of her fiancé. When Wynant's reputation is cleared, therefore, Dorothy can allow herself to return to Tommy, and the film can end with their departure on a wedding trip. In the novel, by contrast, the future of Dorothy, whom Nick distrusts and keeps at a distance throughout, is left unresolved. Hammett sees her character, and that of her brother, as deriving from the parents, but without the reductive genetic explanation of their flaws. Without the marriage subplot, the novel offers no encompassing pattern of salvation or renewal, only resignation in an imperfect world; Nora and Nick accept the limits of their ability to solve other people's problems. Thus on the last page when Nora asks, "What do you think will happen to Mimi, Gilbert, and Dorothy now?" Nick answers, "Nothing new. They'll go on being Mimi and Dorothy and Gilbert just as you and I will go on being us and the Quinns will go on being the Quinns." Nora finds this conclusion "pretty unsatisfactory," but such is life.

Making Nick and Nora the older couple in contrast to Dorothy and Tommy, the screenplay takes Powell's age into account. But the new pairing also further emphasizes the holiday aspect of the main story and rescues the idea of family as a trans-generational institution; escaping the shadow of Wynant and Mimi, the young couple's marriage is also a restoration of the normal order in contrast to the Charleses' unconventional behavior. In the dinner party scene, Tommy, young and respectable, helps dramatize the film's social and moral triage when he knocks the shoddy, middle-aged Quinn unconscious. The moment also shows the subtlety and thoroughness with which Goodrich and Hackett worked with the novel's text. When Nick requests that the policemen "remove that," treating Quinn's body as a worthless inanimate object, he is echoing Alice Quinn's words in the book when Nick brings home her drunken husband—she tells him to bring "it" in.

If the second love story represents MGM's idea of an appropriate message more than it does Hammett's skeptical worldview, it has little impact—Nick and Nora dominate the film as they do the novel. More memorable than this subplot, for example, and somewhat surprising in a film released by Mayer, is the direct reference to sex in the final scene, perhaps a vestige of the openness of Hollywood to the subject as late as 1933. The newlyweds are anxious to consummate their marriage, possibly beginning a new family. But Nick and Nora are also about to make love. Nora is the one alert to the young couple's desire, pulling Nick out of his too-rational clarification of the time change as they move west. When he continues his explanation back in their compartment, Nora pretends she will punish him by sleeping alone. Nick, however, tosses Asta to the top bunk in order to climb into the lower one with Nora; the camera then focuses on Asta, the dog covering his eyes, a surrogate for industry and cultural modesty concerning sex. The final image of the film is a long shot of the train, its whistle blowing as it moves through the night. That the couple are convincing as lovers is reflected in a comment by George Cukor about the impact of *The Thin Man:* "There had been romantic couples before, but Loy and Powell were something new and original. They actually made marital comedy palatable."[31]

Van Dyke's Direction: Method as Style

Van Dyke's method enhanced the chemistry between Loy and Powell, while giving the film a mise-en-scène that firmly places the couple's relationship in its end-of-Prohibition context. Nicknamed "One-Take Woody," Van Dyke was known for working fast. In fact, he had convinced Mayer to approve Loy and Powell in the first place by promising to shoot the film in twelve days. In the event, it took sixteen, with two additional days for retakes, still only about half the time required for most pictures of its kind.[32] In Van Dyke's view, shooting a film quickly, while it saved money for the studio, also helped him elicit natural performances from the actors. As he told Howard Sharpe in a 1936 interview:

> I have a few rules that I follow. The main one is speed—keeping ahead of the audience. The reckless pace . . . the heightened tension and lack of dreary rehearsals necessarily has its effect not only on the staff but on the players as well. . . . The stars naturally snap into everything they do with an alertness you don't find on other stages. It gives a crisp, vital quality to the final production, and since they haven't worn themselves out going over and over a scene until they're stilted in it, the performance has spontaneity—which, anyway, is the most important thing in acting. After spending all those years directing, I've finally learned that the first rehearsal—always the first take—is the best.[33]

"Tempo," Sharpe concluded from this, was "the secret of his pictures' invariable success. Perfection of detail, word-for-word regard for the script sacrificed to speed and spontaneity—equals good pictures."[34] Van Dyke's average shot duration, longer than that of many directors in the 1930s,[35] can be best understood in terms of making the most of the spontaneity of his actors in the scenes he felt were most important. It translates in *The Thin Man* into what Martha Nochimson describes as a "raw, documentary energy in the images produced by Powell and Loy that embeds the characteristic, uncanny sense of vitality into the *Thin Man* series."[36] This is evident where the characters are teasing each other—the characters become indistinguishable from the performers. But the "uncanny sense of vitality" goes well beyond their physical playfulness to include glances exchanged and postures that respond to the movements of their partner. For Nochimson, this "documentary energy" is the essence of the film, and "collaborations on such idiosyncratic and unpremeditated inventions are far more significant to enduring *Thin Man* pleasures than the script."[37] I would argue rather that they complement or extend the pleasures of the dialogue and narrative, for it is precisely the vitality of Nick and Nora's relationship in contrast to all others that guarantees the work of the narrative and dialogue. As Nochimson recognizes, their movements allow the connectedness of the couple to trump the disconnectedness and betrayal among other characters in the movie.

Van Dyke's ability to make pictures quickly came in part from his efficient commitment of time and resources to what he considered key scenes. As he told Sharpe: "Three-fourths of any picture is utterly unimportant anyway. . . . Out of the entire thing only a few scenes are so necessary to the effect of plot or characterization that you have to worry about them. The shots that I consider as merely builder-uppers can be finished as hurriedly as possible."[38] Hal Rosson, cameraman on *Penthouse* and other Van Dyke films, explained the implications of Van Dyke's attitude: "His thinking, as I recall it, was to emphasize certain things in a picture. In other words, the girl in his picture was supposed to be beautiful. So Van would permit you as a cameraman as much time as needed, within reason, to get a good result of the girl. If I was going to make a photograph of a piece of newspaper that had to be lying on that table, he wanted me to photograph that newspaper in one second, or only half a second if possible."[39] Van Dyke's comment that "three-fourths of any picture is utterly unimportant" echoes his words to Goodrich that for *The Thin Man* he didn't "care anything about the story." When it came time to shoot the film, the scenes "so necessary to the . . . characterization" were the five scenes "between those people" that he had requested of Goodrich and Hackett.

The scenes include the one in which Dorothy first approaches Nick at the bar in the elegant cafe where they are joined by Nora; the extended party at the Normandie; the scene the same evening when Morelli and then the police intrude on them and Nick is shot; the following morning when they exchange Christmas presents; and the final dinner-party scene at which MacCaulay is arrested and the crime explained. The scene of Nick

Glassware. (*The Thin Man*, 1934)

and Asta discovering Wynant's body buried in his shop also receives considerable attention, but like others, such as Mimi's discovery of Julia Wolf's body, it mainly serves the purpose of turning expository talk from the book into action for the film. For the scenes between Nick and Nora, Van Dyke creates a special iconography, using the sets and framing of shots, in Rosson's words, to "emphasize certain things" in the picture, mainly the end-of-Prohibition celebration of drinking.

Hammett's novel emphasizes alcohol to the point that it can be read as a work of anti-temperance literature. Temperance novels and plays—including the most famous, T. S. Arthur's *Ten Nights in a Bar-Room, and What I Saw There*, typically present alcohol as dangerous because it endangers the family, the cornerstone of society. Before women achieved the right to own property, a drunken husband led inevitably to the destitution of wife and children. Hammett's novel turns this model of society inside out: drink and the speakeasy abet freedom rather than threatening the social order; its breaking down of confining restrictions with respect to gender and class is liberating. Thus *The Thin Man* focuses on the value of

Nora serves the boxer (*The Thin Man*, 1934)

a relationship between consenting adults in the present, rather than on a broader imperative to reproduce and nurture children for the future. Van Dyke re-creates Hammett's repeated mention of drink through a mise-en-scène focusing on glassware.

The scene in which Dorothy first approaches Nick, for example—a variation on Hammett's opening scene from the novel—is staged against a wall of glassware. Her introduction is presented as an interruption of Nick's cocktail hour, and she only recognizes him because he is in his most characteristic posture, draining a drink. When she approaches, he reflexively asks the bartender for another glass, and when Tommy approaches, Nick repeats the request, an unvarying ritual of sociability. After Nora's arrival—among the most familiar moments in American cinema—she and Nick are similarly seated in front of the wall of glasses, Nora requesting six martinis to match her husband. Drink is thus a mark of their equality, and in conjunction with her shopping and attire, it marks Nora as the rich girl striving to stay in sync with this man of the people who is also a man of the world. The mise-en-scène—the couple framed against the wall of crystal martini glasses—perfectly expresses Nick's focused appreciation of alcohol

Drinks with dinner (*The Thin Man*, 1934)

in this film, in sync with the historical moment of New York nightlife at the repeal of Prohibition.

The ten-minute party scene at the Normandie continues the visual development of the theme. Following nine of what Van Dyke calls "builder-upper" scenes, it consolidates chapters 4–7 of the novel, bringing together characters from several locations over two days into a single evening at the hotel suite. One setting it replaces is Studsy Burke's Pigiron Club, the prime example of the Prohibition institution of the speakeasy, in reality and in Hammett's novel an institution that allowed transgression of social boundaries of all kinds, from sexual taboos to barriers of class.[40] The party scene emphasizes this same social diversity facilitated by drink. It opens with Nora adding a drink to a tray Nick is about to deliver to the guests. The camera then follows the glasses as Nick moves around the room, revealing the heterogeneous crowd, cutting at one point to a smaller tray that Nora is carrying. "Highballs and cocktails," Nick says, seeming to refer to the mix of tall and squat glasses, "the long and the short of it." Among the many quips about drink in the scene is Nick's when Nora tells him to get to work breaking ice: "What big glasses you have, my dear," he says, making Nora the wolf in women's clothing. The circulating trays tie these individuals together into a social group that includes elegant men and women, a boxer, and toothless ex-cons. Highballs and martinis are the key to harmonizing the diverse crowd that will end the evening in a drunken chorus of "O Tannenbaum." Nick articulates his philosophy here more directly than in the novel, when he sings, "For tomorrow may bring sorrow, so tonight let us be gay"—the sentiment is repeated at the final dinner party as "eat, drink and be merry, for tomorrow we die." Nick, of course, is not permitted to enjoy this party. The crimes—instigated by the lawyer MacCaulay's greed—intrude on his drinking and socializing. As in the film as a whole, the murder story seems an intrusion into this celebration. A line not found in Hammett's novel underscores Nick's effort to avoid the investigation. Asked if Nick is working on a case, Nora answers, "Yes, a case of Scotch—pitch in and help him."

If the glassware and drinking represent Nick's world, Nora's is represented by her gowns, and one of Nora's most striking costumes is the diaphanous candy-cane dress at this Christmas Eve party. Nora's movement around the room is a kind of dance in conjunction with the tray of glasses, representing how her grace, like the drinks, facilitates the social interaction. All Nora's costumes are striking, as are Dorothy's and Mimi's. But Mimi is a grotesque mirror image of Nora, avaricious and brutal, and her expensive, aggressively fashionable garments only underscore her self-indulgence. In order to set up the final dinner-party scene, Nick will ask Nora, "Have you got a nice evening gown?" To which she responds, "Yes, I've got a lulu." The costuming and drinking iconography come perfectly together the morning after Nora's six martinis when she wakes up with a hangover—she enters the room to greet MacCaulay wearing an ice bag on her head as if it were an elegant hat.

The final dinner-party scene once again begins with a display of glassware. Material from the final two chapters of the novel has been consolidated at the Normandie, where Nick, almost as a demonstration to please Nora, solves and explains the mystery. The opening shots present the table as a forest of empty glasses, an extension of the abundant flower arrangement, as if the stemware has exploded into bloom, part of the garden of

High-fashion hangover (*The Thin Man*, 1934)

earthly delights over which Nick and Nora preside. In this post-Prohibition moment, rather than preventing the guests from drinking, the police force them to drink, specifically Morelli, Nunheim's girlfriend Marion (Gertrude Short), and Tanner (Cyril Thornton). Nick's resolution of the troublesome case allows him and Nora to return to the pursuit of pleasure in their "wet" heaven, New York, before taking a train west. This scene offers an example of the detective film at its most formulaic, with the detective telling the tale of the crime, holding the focus one by one on the various suspects as each proclaims his or her innocence, then finally revealing the guilty party. A survey of the people at the table shows an interesting accumulation of independent women, from Nora to Mimi to the wife who never divorced Jorgenson (Cesar Romero) to the skillet-throwing Marion. Even Dorothy is not without spirit, though she has been framed as a damsel in distress, rescued to become a bride and prospective mother, which creates a small rip in the film's ideological fabric, the result of shoehorning Hammett's novel into a Hollywood and MGM master narrative.

Consequences of the Film's Success

If the success of the film was assured by its timeliness, the anti-temperance window of opportunity that it took advantage of was extremely brief. An article in *Variety* from February 27, 1934, announced that what had been "smart" during Prohibition was changing with repeal: "Going on the wagon and staying there is threatening to reach epidemic proportions," the article claims; "though it was smart to drink, now it's smarter to refuse a drink." The parties in *The Thin Man*, conceived by Hackett and Goodrich just weeks before the article in *Variety* appeared, reflect a highpoint and a culmination. The century-long battle over alcohol was finished, to be replaced by other issues, among them the social impact of economic collapse, the New Deal, war in Europe, and the fear of communism. For twenty-first-century viewers, with the urgency of the struggle over alcohol now largely forgotten, *The Thin Man* is mainly remembered simply for the couple, their grace and wit, and their embrace of life as they find it.

For Dashiell Hammett—as for William Powell and Myrna Loy—the success of *The Thin Man* was life-changing. Hammett was not consulted during production of *The Thin Man*. Though his name was used to promote the film, he was ignored as most authors would have been, the purchased material handed over to the powerful studio's producer, literary department, and director. During the months of the film's production and release, Hammett went off to Homestead, Florida, to relax on the money he had made from the novel's sale.[41] Yet the magnitude of the film's success soon changed his relationship with the film industry. *The Thin Man* grossed over $2 million, nearly ten times its budget of $231,000. Furthermore, it received prestigious Academy Award nominations for Best Picture, Best Director, Best Actor in a Leading Role, and Best Writing, Adaptation. The most immediate result was the hiring of Hammett to write an original story for a sequel, but the impact was more general and long-lasting. In a letter to Hellman, Hammett expressed his surprise at his sudden elevation to a new level of importance in Hollywood: "People bring the Joan Crawfords and the Gables over to meet me instead of vice versa! Hot-cha!"[42] Hammett's work was now sought after, not only for additional *Thin Man* films and radio series, but for two versions of *The Glass Key* (1935 and 1942), for two additional versions of *The Maltese Falcon* (*Satan Met a*

Lady, 1936, and *The Maltese Falcon*, 1941), and for *Woman in the Dark* (1934). *Mister Dynamite* (1935) was acquired and produced by Universal. Perhaps, this time, as Richard Layman claimed of the more modest success that followed publication of *The Maltese Falcon*, Hammett's sudden affluence and fame ruined him as a writer—from this point on he produced little for publication or for the screen. Nonetheless, the release of *The Thin Man* marks the true beginning of Hammett's prominence in movies.

3

After *The Thin Man*

From Sequel to Series

The success of *The Thin Man* was such that Metro-Goldwyn-Mayer immediately planned to exploit it by creating a sequel and by developing additional vehicles for Myrna Loy and William Powell. When *After the Thin Man* (1936) generated even more revenue than the original film, the sequel became the second film in a series that included four additional pictures. Reducing risk through an emphasis on "pretested" or "presold" products was a fundamental strategy of the industry in the classical Hollywood era, manifest in imitating all aspects of successful movies, a practice that spawned cycles of films, fostered the genre system, and emphasized continuity in a star's roles from one picture to the next. Sequels and series films are an extension of these strategies, and MGM executives might from the beginning have considered the possibility of a series based on *The Thin Man*. After all, it had initially been conceived as a B-detective picture whose fading star was identified with the Philo Vance films. But too many uncertainties stood in the way of predicting five more successful *Thin Man* films over a period of thirteen years. No preexisting series of novels existed to provide recognizable titles and ready-made plots, and, more importantly, Powell's age meant that Nick and Nora would probably have to be played by different actors over time. Without looking too much into the future, then, MGM reassembled the team from *The Thin Man*—actors, producer, director, and writers—and worked to achieve a similar result for a single film. Dashiell Hammett was hired to create a story that picked up where *The Thin Man* left off, and the A-list production unit under Hunt Stromberg, with director W. S. Van Dyke and screenwriters Frances Goodrich and Albert Hackett, again made a "quality" film for first-run theaters. It was the overwhelming success of *After the Thin Man* that made clear the value of additional pictures featuring Loy and Powell. MGM paired them in a total of eleven films after *The Thin Man*, five of them part of the *Thin Man* series, and six unrelated films that were, on the whole, less successful.

Over time, the creative team on the *Thin Man* series would evolve. Hammett struggled to produce the stories for *After the Thin Man* and *Another Thin Man* (1939). In a sense, he had written serials for years, creating numerous detective stories and novels with the same protagonist—the unnamed "Operative" of the Continental Detective Agency. But he also preferred never to repeat himself. Each of his novels was deliberately set in a different milieu and was framed around a different set of relationships and issues. And while Hammett had worked at Paramount and Warner Bros. in 1930 and 1931, at that time he had only sketched out brief story ideas to be developed by others on the studio payroll. The longer grind of a detailed treatment to meet studio requirements frustrated him. He drank excessively and missed deadlines while writing the story for *After the Thin Man*, and his struggle to produce one for *Another Thin Man* led not only to arguments with Stromberg, but to a breakdown that put him in the hospital and made him realize, for one final time, that work for hire at the studios was not something he could make himself do. As a result, Hammett had no involvement with the last three films, *Shadow of the Thin Man* (1941), *The Thin Man Goes Home* (1945), or *Song of the Thin Man* (1947).

When *The Thin Man* was released, Powell was nearly forty-two years old, Loy almost twenty-nine, but by the time the studio understood that more *Thin Man* films should be made, executives also realized that the actors were too popular to replace without diminishing the value of the franchise. The only solution was to incorporate their drift into middle age into the films' stories, with appropriate changes in the characters' lives and relationship. Thus the freewheeling partnership based entirely on mutual affection and consent in *The Thin Man* was altered in *After the Thin Man* with Nora's announcement of her pregnancy. *Another Thin Man* made use of the couple's vulnerability as parents responsible for an infant. *Shadow of the Thin Man* emphasized the subjugation of the couple to the imperatives of child rearing, as well as to the family's progressively conventional, upper-middle-class position in society. As they became more conventional, their relationship began to reflect a more traditional patriarchy, Nora as mother and wife becoming less adventurous, Nick more paternalistic. *The Thin Man Goes Home* (1945) took Nick's transformation even further: in the World War II context, the film retrospectively recast him as a product of small-town America and enlisted him in defending the homeland from an enemy within. The last film, *Song of the Thin Man* (1947), with Powell fifty-five and Loy forty-two, presented Nick and Nora as having aged to the point that they were no longer evolving along with changes in society—they had become entirely out of sync with a new jazz generation.

Frances Goodrich and Albert Hackett left the production team when Hammett did, following *Another Thin Man*. Hunt Stromberg produced and W. S. Van Dyke directed three of the five films following the original. But Van Dyke died in 1943, committing suicide amid a long bout with heart disease and cancer. Everett Riskin produced *The Thin Man Goes Home*, which was written by his brother Robert and directed by Richard Thorpe. Nat Perrin produced the final film in the series, *Song of the Thin Man*, and also received a screenplay credit; it was directed by Edward Buzzell. With changes in the production personnel, inevitably, came additional changes in substance and style.

It is tempting to interpret the politically conservative perspective of the later films as a direct result of Hammett's departure. According to such a narrative, Hammett, a man of the left, leaves the series and the conservative values of Louis B. Mayer increasingly impose themselves; after a film that in some degree embraced social change, the series moves toward representing change as a loss of reason, an attack on civilization. This reading is not so much wrong as simplistic. Hammett was a political activist in the 1930s, but his novels offer a critique of flawed human nature that seems more Calvinist than Marxist; corruption takes new forms as society evolves, but his protagonists' posture is based on a personal code of behavior. Rather than breaking new ground as a critique of society, the first *Thin Man* film embraced ideas that were widely popular, celebrating a new era that had already arrived. The movement of the series in a conservative direction reflects the aging protagonists' development. Furthermore, the audience for these films aged along with Loy and Powell, while the political climate in the country also evolved, in the most sweeping sense from popular acceptance of the New Deal to an embrace of the anticommunism of the Cold War.

In changing times, *The Thin Man*'s interrelationship with its cultural moment was difficult to duplicate, and although they were released in very different contexts, the later films still celebrate the looser manners of the jazz age and Nick's fondness for drink. Instead of reflecting an evolving society, they answer mainly to memories of the earlier films, part of the raison d'être of both sequels and series, to capitalize on the successful elements of the original. Carolyn Jess-Cooke describes this as a common "investment in circularity and continuation."[1]

Yet there are differences between sequels and series films as well: sequels generally continue a narrative from the previous film, while series films attempt to repeat a formula again and again.[2] In Jess-Cooke's words, "Seriality and series defy change; the sequel champions difference, progress and excess."[3] And the two forms have typically targeted different audiences. In the 1930s and 1940s, sequels occurred as one-off continuations of successful A-list movies aimed at first-run theaters and relatively sophisticated audiences. Series, by contrast, were formulaic B-movies with lower budgets, relegated to secondary theaters and less discriminating audiences. According to Jennifer Forrest, "the 'true' sequel caresses a certain spectator's class sensibilities by appealing to his or her preference for works of quality, [promoting] itself as having distinctly more high-brow ambitions."[4] In this respect, as Forrest recognizes,[5] the *Thin Man* series is an exception that proves the rule—it was unique for its time in that, after an initial well-financed and heavily promoted sequel, the films that followed, even though falling into series practices of relying on repetition, continued to have large budgets, full-length running times, and release in first-run theaters. While the original *Thin Man* was made for a modest $231,000, *The Thin Man Goes Home* (1945), to choose one example, had a budget of a $1 million.[6] Certainly the later films in the series became less important relative to considerably more expensive MGM products, but the *Thin Man* budgets nonetheless remained far above those of typical, shorter detective programmers cranked out by poverty row studios.

After the Thin Man (1936)

Throughout the summer of 1934, audiences packed movie theaters to see *The Thin Man*, so that when Hammett returned to New York that fall, he was, in Richard Layman's words, "one of the most sought-after literary celebrities in America."[7] MGM was looking to hire him to write a sequel, and in spite of Louis B. Mayer's warning to the New York office about Hammett's "irregular habits," the studio signed him to a contract for ten weeks at $2,000 a week.[8] Hammett left New York for the West Coast toward the end of October.

If the public was hungry for a new film featuring the couple played by Powell and Loy, however, they would have to wait. Once he began, it took Hammett a year to write a new story, and in any case Loy had become engaged in a battle with MGM and Mayer over her contract. After *Evelyn Prentice* (1934)—made quickly with Powell and Loy to take advantage of *The Thin Man's* success—Loy demanded that her seven-year contract, originally signed in 1931, be renegotiated. She had been receiving $1,500 a week while Powell was paid twice that. Now his co-star, Loy demanded equal pay, as well as more control over the roles she would play. Mayer refused to negotiate. When MGM cast Loy inappropriately in a film called *Escapade*, eventually released with Luise Rainer and Powell in 1935, Loy rebelled. She went to New York, then on to Europe. The standoff lasted for most of 1935, until eventually, according to Loy, her lawyer Bill Sacks pitted Nicholas Schenck, president of Loew's Incorporated, the parent company of MGM, against Mayer. Mayer met Loy's contract demands and gave her a $25,000 bonus as well.[9] Back in the MGM fold, Loy quickly made *Whipsaw* (Sam Wood, 1935), which was rushed into release, then in 1936 several outstanding films including *Wife vs. Secretary* (Clarence Brown), *The Great Ziegfeld* (Robert Z. Leonard), *Libeled Lady* (Jack Conway), and finally *After the Thin Man*.

Powell was also extremely active while a script for *After the Thin Man* was being prepared. A divorce from Carole Lombard in August 1933 had left him dispirited, but shortly after making *The Thin Man* he began a relationship with Jean Harlow, his co-star in *Reckless* (Victor Fleming, 1935) and *Libeled Lady*—they were considering marriage at the time of her untimely death on June 7, 1937, but that was still in the future. The year 1936 turned out to be the high point of Powell's movie career: building on the success of *The Thin Man*, he starred in no fewer than ten films between it and the sequel, including *My Man Godfrey* (Gregory La Cava, 1936) and *The Great Ziegfeld* and *Libeled Lady* with Loy. The range of characters played by Powell and Loy during this period brought a further richness to audiences' experience of Nick and Nora in subsequent films.

By January 8, 1935, Hammett was able to give Stromberg thirty-four typewritten pages that contained the kernel of the story for the sequel. It still needed considerable work, however, and by March 9, 1935, Hammett's contract had expired. On June 19, as Layman writes,

> [Hammett] signed an extraordinary agreement, which stayed in effect, except for short periods when he was fired for drunkenness or unreliability, for the next three years. He was to serve as an assistant to Hunt Stromberg, 'as general editorial aide and/or assistant and/ or advising, not only in connection with preparation of stories and/or continuities, but as well in connection with actual production and photoplays. He agrees to attend conferences and assist in preparation and/or developing of ideas submitted by him or others and generally to render services as motion picture executive.'[10]

Hammett was to be paid $1,000 a week for working on scenes and dialogue, $1,750 a week when he was working on "complete continuity including dialogue of such screenplay."[11] The terms of this contract indicate a strong relationship between Hammett and Stromberg, who knew better than Mayer the "irregular habits" the studio head had referred to. A note to Alfred Knopf in June 1935 emphasizes Hammett's "executive" role of looking for new material, as well as his appreciation of Stromberg: "If you've anything coming out that looks like picture stuff, you might shoot it to me, as we are hunting for material. (I'm working with Stromberg, the chap who produced *The Thin Man*, and he listens to reason.)"[12]

The studio's desire to have the author of the original novel create the story for the new film is evidence of their intention to produce what Forrest calls a "quality" sequel, as is the manner in which *After the Thin Man* follows from the final scene of the first film. An early outline—before the January 8 draft—attempted to revive several characters, including Mimi and Gilbert. "We are going to make a picture with all the surviving members of the first cast," Hammett wrote in a letter to Lillian Hellman, "which won't be silly if I can devise a murder that grows with some logic out of the set-up I left everybody in at the end of the T.M."[13] According to William Nolan, Hammett "had the original killer, MacCaulay, escape from New York (disguised as a woman) and follow Nick to San Francisco."[14] Stromberg, however, rejected the carryover. The January 8 draft follows Nick and Nora Charles to San Francisco but otherwise begins with a fresh set of characters. The story takes its inspiration from a line in chapter 11 of Hammett's novel, where Nora explains to Inspector Guild that she and Nick "have to go away over the Christmas holidays every year because what's left of my family make a fuss over them and if we're home they come to visit us or we have to visit them, and Nick doesn't like it."[15] The new film would be about Nora's family. On September 17, 1935, Hammett submitted a polished 115-page draft to Stromberg that contained the plot, motivation of characters, and relationships essentially as they would be in the film.[16]

A sequel typically reopens the closure of the original film's ending, and in so doing prepares the way for a reassessment of issues that were presented as settled—it recapitulates features of the original but it also adds something new.[17] As a sequel to *The Thin Man*, *After the Thin Man* reframes Nick and Nora's relationship in terms of its value to her family, the ways her staid family will benefit from her liaison with the freewheeling Nick. Nick was the driving force of the first film, Nora's mentor and guide. In the sequel, Nora takes the upper hand; Nick's energies from the first film, leading to an escape from the confining family, are now harnessed to serve the interests of Nora and her family.

This film begins with a party that seems almost a continuation of the Christmas Eve gathering at the Normandie in the first film, yet here the couple is arriving exhausted from their trip—Nick and Nora have not instigated the event, and they see it as interfering with their sleep. In any case, they are immediately summoned to the house of Nora's Aunt Katherine (Jessie Ralph), where they learn that Robert (Alan Marshal), the husband of Nora's cousin Selma (Elissa Landi), has disappeared. Aunt Katherine, matriarch of the family, wants Nick to find him.

Like *The Thin Man*, this film—even more schematic as a classic detective tale moving from a murder to clues establishing the suspects to resolution and an explanation by the detective—is also shaped by Van Dyke's method of concentrating the story into a few key scenes. Besides the denouement where Nick identifies the killer, two major sequences develop the film's ideas: Nick and Nora's encounter with the family at Aunt Katherine's, and an extended sequence set in the Li-chee Club. The opening sequence at Aunt Katherine's establishes the world of Nora's conservative family, and the Li-chee sequence presents the principal challenge to their way of life, the open world of the nightclub. This film unfolds out of a logic based on the difference between Nora and Nick: Nora is part of a "respectable" family with a specific social position; Nick is an independent male, a freewheeling son of immigrants, identified with no particular social position. The question of the film is how such different types can be joined in a family or, phrased differently, how Nora's conservative clan, represented by Aunt Katherine's Victorian mansion, can absorb and benefit from the revitalizing energy of a changed society, represented by the nightclub.

The polarization between the family and the nightclub is an opposition between old and new, the past and the future. In this respect it encompasses not only the aging of Nora's relatives, but also of Nick and Nora—played by aging actors. Thus the problem faced by Nora's family, to be addressed in the story, is that even as the elder generation will soon be dying off, Selma, their hope for the future, has failed to successfully mate and reproduce—she chose the wrong partner in Robert, and in doing so turned the right partner, David (James Stewart), into a madman and killer. Receiving his assignment to find Robert from Aunt Katherine, Nick immediately points up Selma's confusion: "Do you want him back, or don't you?" In either case, Robert cannot play the role of taking the family into the next generation. If nothing is done, the family line will end. The ironic resolution of the problem is that Nick, who is appalled by Nora's stuffy family, will become part of it through Nora; her announcement at the close of the film that she is pregnant seals their success at producing an heir. By capturing a husband who represents the very best of the new age—with his Greek immigrant genes and competence at navigating the new realities of 1930s America—Nora has revitalized her moribund clan.

The class difference between Nora and Nick, given a positive value in *The Thin Man*, is reestablished in the opening moments of the sequel. Nick is at home among pickpockets, liquor truck drivers, and boxing fans. In pointed contrast, when Nick and Nora find themselves next to a wealthy couple in an elegant touring car, the well-dressed woman and a man in a top hat greet Nora while ignoring Nick, inspiring Nora to say to him, "Oh, you wouldn't know them—they're *respectable*." Thus, a difference that was secondary to what united the couple in *The Thin Man* is foregrounded as a problem in *After the Thin Man*, typical of the way a sequel can, and often does, revise its precursor.

Nora's Aunt Katherine Forrest, the matriarch of the family, is sturdy and tyrannical, with a hint of an Irish brogue that connects her to a San Francisco circle of nineteenth-century barons who made their fortunes in mining in the years following the Gold Rush. Her house is like a museum dedicated to the nineteenth century; the study, for example, is framed in heavy wood, with dark glass-front bookcases, mahogany tables, heavy drapery, an overstuffed chair and sofa. A globe, a sword hanging on one wall, chalices, a small sculpture of a man on horseback, and a golden eagle all suggest dreams of empire. In such an environment, man-of-the-people Nick becomes "Nicholas." That the clan is led by a woman speaks to the main thrust of the film, Nora's power to convert Nick from an independent man into a father.

Early in the film we feel the subterranean link between Nora's new firmness and Katherine's unvarnished command, especially when the

Aunt Katherine (*After the Thin Man*, 1936)

women and men are segregated into different rooms. The women are holding council over coffee and listening to Selma play a classical piece on
the piano, while the old men have fallen asleep at the dining table after
port and cigars. Their absence of thought is underscored as Nick mock-
ingly treats their snoring as an expression of their ideas: "No, really?" he
responds to one, and to another, "Would you explain that point a bit further?" When summoned by Nora, Nick lays flowers from the table on the
chest of one old gentleman as if he were dead. Although this scene is illus-
trative of an old pattern in which women manage domestic affairs while
men tackle obligations external to the household, these men offer the family no future.

The nightclub scenes are announced as an immediate contrast to
the "waxworks" of Aunt Katherine's house; Nick tells the chauffeur,
"We want to go someplace and get the taste of respectability out of our
mouths." Unrestrained by any archaic etiquette, the Li-chee Club is loud
and lively, and a place where all kinds of people mingle. The clothing
styles, accents, and manners that emphasize the underlying social diversity at the club stand in contrast to the static complexity of Victorian
ornamentation of Aunt Katherine's. Orientalist motifs of the popular
Charlie Chan movies are echoed in the Li-chee Club scenes and particularly in the subplot involving Lum Kee (William Law), whose brother
Nick had sent to prison. Lum Kee is presented as friendly, but stereotypically inscrutable. His early statement that he is Nick Charles's "friend"
only becomes intelligible at the end of the film; after he has helped Nick
disarm David, he explains that he did not like his brother, he liked his
"brother's girl." Lum Kee's practical motives, and those of his brother—
using a "tong war" as cover for robbing banks—undercut any stereotype
of oriental mystery. The operator of the Li-chee Club seems Italian rather
than Chinese; Dancer is played by the Maltese actor Joseph Calleia, veteran of a full range of foreign and ethnic roles. He would later be cast,
for example, as the Italian gangster in *The Glass Key* (Stuart Heisler, 1942).
And from the first moment of the Li-chee sequence, we realize that typical elements of Chinese-restaurant décor are lost in jazz and dancing that
could be found in any nightclub. The easy mixing of people of different
ethnicity in this setting stands in contrast to Aunt Katherine's insisting
on pronouncing Abrams' name as "Abraham" and "Abrahamson" as if to

evoke Old Testament (Jewish) origins. In the Li-chee Club, according to Nick, a "coming out" party is for ex-cons rather than debutantes. Like the world of the speakeasy in *The Thin Man*, the nightclub in this film frames the primary example of ethnic and class mixing, Nora's marriage to Nick.

As the setting for celebrating the New Year—meeting place of the alpha and omega, the beginning and the end—the nightclub stages a pageant devoted to the inexorable march of time. When Nick and Nora enter the club, Polly and the chorus, dressed in costumes decorated with a musical score, sing, "Father Time is marching on, marching to the rhythm of the band." According to the song's lyrics, even with the help of beautiful girls who try to keep him young, the best that Father Time can do is seize the moment and "blow in the new year, blow out the old, blow all [his] troubles out in the cold." This song echoes Nick's toast of "eat, drink, and be merry, for tomorrow we die" from *The Thin Man*, though with an emphasis on Father Time's advanced age as the old year ends.

Aging as highlighted in this performance in the Li-chee Club is relevant not only to Aunt Katherine and her clan; it is also the challenge to Powell and Loy who in the opening scenes of this film are subtly presented as older. The story would have us believe that Nick and Nora are just arriving from New York, days after the final scenes of *The Thin Man*. But Powell seems to have gained weight; he moves less gracefully, and his face and neck are jowly—evidence from his other 1936 films underscores that this look was created deliberately in support of the film's ideas. As Nick bends awkwardly to give Nora an affectionate yet hardly passionate kiss, his posture emphasizes his filled-out figure. A porter on the train platform wags a finger at them, causing Nora to announce, "It's all right, we're married." "Married" linked with heavier, older, and less glamorous is exactly the point—things have changed from the earlier film. The difference is immediately confirmed when Nora tells the newspaper reporters meeting the train that she no longer wants Nick to investigate crimes.

While foregrounding the passage of time, the Li-chee Club scene also explores the theme of jealousy. In this film, love triangles representing a threat to the monogamous couple replace the dysfunctional pairs that were used in *The Thin Man* to emphasize Nick and Nora's healthy relationship. The main triangle involves Robert, Selma, and David, but there are also

Polly, David, and Dancer; Phil, Polly, and Dancer; Lum Kee, his brother, and his brother's girl; Asta and an interloper who has taken up with Mrs. Asta; and, potentially, Nick, Nora, and the expected baby. Yet the kind of jealousy that drives David mad still seems to have no place in Nick and Nora's relationship. This is the point of the confusion at midnight: the lights go off, then on again to reveal Nick in the passionate embrace of a woman we presume to be Nora, only to discover it is another woman who had earlier greeted Nick with a warm "Hello, handsome" on his way into the club. Nick's recognition of his error does not diminish his apparent pleasure, and Nora is unfazed at the lipstick still smeared across his mouth. She merely says, "Wipe your mouth, you're bleeding," as if he has received a minor wound in battle. But this confusion of partners hits on two of the film's themes, the comfort of Nick and Nora with their partner's flirtations as well as the danger of the nightclub to a "respectable" family: in a place like this, anything can happen. Nora's adventuring into such a world—where she is appreciated as "hot" by one of the ex-cons that join their table—is what has allowed her to find Nick, and thus to bring in new blood to revitalize her dying family.

The killer revealed (*After the Thin Man*, 1936)

With jealousy at the heart of the crime in this film, David's role is central, and it provided James Stewart with an opportunity to show an emotionally explosive side of his screen personality that would remain important in his career. Before 1936, Stewart had made only two films, a short for Vitaphone in New York and a B-picture with Spencer Tracy entitled *The Murder Man* (Tim Whelan, 1935), in which Stewart had fourteen lines. Fortunately, however, his third film, *Rose-Marie* (1936), was directed by W. S. Van Dyke. *Rose-Marie* is a bizarre Jeanette MacDonald/Nelson Eddy vehicle in which MacDonald plays an opera singer who runs off in search of her criminal brother (Stewart) in the Canadian North Woods, only to fall in love with the singing Mountie (Eddy) who is pursuing the brother. In his brief appearance as the wanted killer, Stewart manages to express a weakness of character and psychological instability that make the brother unworthy of MacDonald's support.[18] As David in *After the Thin Man*, Stewart appears to be a gentle, most solicitous friend to Selma, until his entrapment by Nick brings out the fire of his hatred for her and for Robert. With David's emotional eruption, the film reveals a duality of calm and passion that would mark many of Stewart's most important roles, from Jefferson Smith in Frank Capra's *Mr. Smith Goes to Washington* (1939) to Lin McAdam and Howard Kemp in Anthony Mann's *Winchester'73* (1950) and *The Naked Spur* (1953) to L. B. Jefferies and Scottie Ferguson in Hitchcock's *Rear Window* (1954) and *Vertigo* (1958).

Asta's love triangle, like the confusion of partners at midnight in the club, comments on the issue of family in two ways. Returning to his mate only to discover that Mrs. Asta—as she is introduced in the film's opening credits—has found another partner, Asta suffers an agony of jealousy like that which drives David to murder. But the terrier love triangle is also a parable of enriching the family gene pool, dramatized in the color of the dogs. Asta is dismayed to find an additional, black offspring easily identified as having been fathered by the black terrier that repeatedly sneaks in under the gate to visit Mrs. Asta. Asta chases off the intruder, going so far as to push a lawnmower to cover the entrance of a tunnel into their yard. But in Asta's world, as in Nick's, the balance of power has shifted from the wandering male to the female who creates and maintains the family. In the beast fable, the screenwriters and Van Dyke are able to present a story of happy infidelity on the part of the matriarch that the Production

Code would certainly not have permitted for human characters. That the new puppy is black pushes the theme of crossing ethnic and class lines to include race. This interpretation might seem a stretch but for the obvious placement of a black newsboy who steps into the crowd of white ones surrounding Nick in a scene shortly preceding that with the puppies. The visual parallel cannot be coincidental.

Nora's announcement of her pregnancy as Nick and Nora are once again on the train, accompanied by the now-single Selma in the final scene, confirms Nora's triumph and the continuation of the Forrest family line. The clue that a child has been conceived occurs in an earlier scene, one of the few in which Nick and Nora are alone: Nora gets Nick to cook scrambled eggs for her in the middle of the night. Nick complies without understanding, any more than the audience does, that the craving signifies pregnancy. This annunciation once again represents the sequel's reopening and revision of settled material in the precursor. Hammett resisted this ending—in his view, the modern couple was fine without the responsibilities of family and children. Hunt Stromberg, however, insisted on it, no doubt with additional films in mind.[19] While in *The Thin Man*, the love story of Dorothy and Tommy seems grafted onto a core of materials from Hammett's novel, in the story for *After the Thin Man* overseen by Stromberg the idea of a birth and renewal suits not only the New Year theme, but also the focus of the film on Nora, on her family, and finally on the transformation of the couple into a family.

Hammett accepted the reviews of *After the Thin Man* with his usual self-deprecating objectivity. "Most of the lists of best pictures of the year, with which the papers are lousy nowadays, seem to include *These Three*," Hammett observed in a letter to Hellman, referring to William Wyler's 1936 film from her play *The Children's Hour*. "*After the Thin Man* got for the most part at least as good reviews as it deserved. Robert Garland, who hadn't seen the first one, had an orgasm, but then I always say an orgasm by Robert Garland is an orgasm by Robert Garland."[20] Apparently the public was also excited by the film. Building on the first film's reputation, *After the Thin Man* became the sixth highest grossing film of 1936, financially the most successful of the *Thin Man* series. Frances Goodrich and Albert Hackett were again nominated for an Academy Award.

Another Thin Man (1939)

As the title suggests, the third *Thin Man* film emphasizes the impact on the couple of the baby announced at the end of *After the Thin Man*. Yet while this film initially presents itself as another sequel, continuing the story where it left off and providing something substantially new to the reopened story, any novelty is quickly overwhelmed by repetition and variation of tropes from the preceding films. *The Thin Man* and *After the Thin Man* are genuine companion pieces, his story and hers. *Another Thin Man* emphasizes situations, character types, and jokes similar to those in the first two films.

With *After the Thin Man* a hit, MGM fully understood the value of Nick and Nora as a franchise, beyond any commitment by Hammett to create new stories. In February 1937, the studio offered $40,000 for "all rights in perpetuity, except radio serialization, to the *Thin Man* characters."[21] MGM still wanted Hammett to write for them if he was willing and able. On April 13, 1937, he signed a contract that would pay him "$5,000 for a synopsis, an additional $10,000 on acceptance of the story idea, and another $20,000 for a complete screen story."[22] Hammett was receiving other offers at this time, including $50,000 from William Randolph Hearst to write a script for Marion Davies, but he had realized that even working with Stromberg he was unsuited to writing for the studios. Hammett admitted as much to Hellman, citing a concurring opinion from his agent in a letter dated the month before committing himself to write *Another Thin Man*: "By this time everybody ought to know that if I want to work in pictures, I'll work for Hunt Stromberg, but even Leland Hayward agrees with me—against his pocketbook—that I've got no business working in pictures at all."[23] Stromberg had his own difficulties—he had become addicted to painkillers for a back injury. The result, as Layman recounts, was that Stromberg's "production unit was becoming more and more disorganized as his addiction to morphine increased. . . . He was incredibly moody, and his once prodigious powers of organization failed him."[24] Between Stromberg's difficulties and Hammett's own, the process of producing a story for *Another Thin Man* confirmed what "everybody" ought to have known. By December 1937, Hammett was writing to Hellman:

I'm in the middle of the usual so-the-script-is-done battles with my own dear producer, who insists that it's all right, but it's not exactly like the two previous scripts. The Hacketts sit on the sidelines and tremble while Hunt and I pace his floor and yell at one another. My latest line of attack is that since he doesn't seem to know what was good and what bad in the two previous pictures they were, so far as he is concerned, just lucky flukes. It's good clean fun and can't lead to anything more serious than blows.[25]

On March 23, 1938, as Layman and Rivett document in their collection of Hammett's letters, "Hunt Stromberg wrote a memo complaining that the Hacketts . . . were at a standstill 'owing to lack of knowledge of that last situation with its needed motivation for the whole treatment.' About seven weeks later, Hammett suffered his breakdown without having finished his work."[26] By then, after ten months sober, he was drinking heavily, and his weight had dropped to 125 pounds. Hellman flew him to Lenox Hill Hospital in New York.[27] He returned to Los Angeles and finished his final 144-page draft of *Another Thin Man*, but at that point he again needed help. Friend and film producer Charles Brackett paid Hammett's debts and put him on a plane, telling Hellman, "Dash is a very sick guy. He'll need some caring for. Can you handle it?"[28] Hellman took Hammett to a cottage on Tavern Island in Connecticut where she was working on her third play, *The Little Foxes*. Hammett slowly regained his strength while helping her with it.[29]

Just as *After the Thin Man* had been delayed by Loy's contract dispute with Mayer, the period before *Another Thin Man* stretched to three years because of Powell's health. He had suffered a personal tragedy with the death of Jean Harlow in June 1937, and then, early in 1938, he was diagnosed with rectal cancer, undergoing surgery on March 2 that left him with a temporary colostomy until a second operation ten months later. By the fall of 1939, he was recovering and ready to work. Powell seems vigorous in the film; though he was now forty-seven, his weight loss made him look younger. The marketing of the film focused on Powell's return to the screen, the trailer announcing over his image, "He's back!" followed by, "William Powell's return to the screen is the best news of the year!"

The original story Hammett was hired to write for *Another Thin Man* ended up being largely based on his *Black Mask* mystery "The Farewell Murder," published in February 1930. In this, the murder of an old man by his son-in-law is concealed behind an elaborate scheme throwing suspicion on a wronged business associate from years before. For *Another Thin Man*, Hammett added a considerable number of characters and plot twists, and he makes the murder victim the former partner of Nora's father. Nick and Nora return to New York City with their infant son, but they are immediately called to the Long Island estate of Colonel MacFay (C. Aubrey Smith). Some ten years earlier, an employee had gone to prison because of business he carried out for MacFay; now, as in "The Farewell Murder," the man has returned to "watch" MacFay die. The list of suspects is expanded for the film, and rather than unfolding entirely on the old man's estate, the story shifts back to Manhattan after MacFay is killed. The denouement of the mystery occurs at the Charleses' hotel suite where an ex-con friend of Nick has organized a birthday party for Nick Jr., inviting a whole crowd of Nick's disreputable friends, each bringing a baby for the party. As a sidelight to the party, the suspects have also been assembled, and after Nick has eliminated all the others, we learn that MacFay's daughter was behind the murder in order to inherit his estate immediately.

Rather than on its convoluted story, now as in 1939 audience interest in *Another Thin Man* depends on references to the previous two movies. Occurrences from the films are repeated, but in different form. For example, where in the first film Nick puts Nora into a cab and tells the driver to take her to Grant's Tomb so that he can go off investigating with Inspector Guild, in *Another Thin Man* Nick tells Nora that he hears the baby crying in the next room, then ducks out to investigate with Assistant District Attorney Van Slack (Otto Kruger). At the West Indies Club—like the Li-chee Club of *After the Thin Man*—a line of drinks reminiscent of Nora's martinis in *The Thin Man* is set up in front of Nick. The scene from *The Thin Man* in which Marion throws a frying pan at Nunheim is recalled in *Another Thin Man* when a woman named Smitty physically attacks a man named Vogel who spies on her for her imprisoned husband. *Another Thin Man* includes a character like David from *After the Thin Man*, MacFay's secretary Freddie (Tom Neal), the frustrated friend who is in love with Lois; Freddie's rival ends up dead like Robert in *After the Thin Man*, but in this instance Freddie is not the killer. As Nora and David in *After the Thin Man* are interrupted by a man on the fire escape before a policeman breaks in and arrests them, in *Another Thin Man* Nick is interrupted by thugs from the fire escape as he searches the apartment of MacFay's daughter—the police barge in, but this time they arrest the intruders from the fire escape, and they are led by Inspector Guild, the thick-headed cop from *The Thin Man* who makes more explicit comments showing his admiration for Nora. As Asta grabs a note tied to a stone in *After the Thin Man*, keeping it from Nick and Nora until some of the note is lost, in this film Asta grabs the murder weapon, a knife, and keeps it from the police, destroying fingerprints in the process.

Variations on jokes from the earlier films also punctuate *Another Thin Man*. There are Nick's references to Nora's wealth: "I'd hate to wake up some morning and find that the fortune I married you for is gone"; and when men crowd around Nora at the West Indies Club, "I knew there was only one woman in the world who could attract men like that . . . a woman with a lot of money." And there are inadvertent double entendres like that in *The Thin Man* when Nora tells the waiters at her dinner party that they may "serve the nuts," correcting herself to say, "I mean serve the guests the nuts." In *After the Thin Man*, Nick similarly corrects himself after saying to Aunt Katherine, "I recognize all the old faces." In *Another Thin Man*, when Lois MacFay's dog jumps up on Nick, Nora says, "Nick smells like a dog," correcting herself with, "I mean Nick smells like Asta." All these echoes and references draw much of their energy to entertain from the relationship among the films, also reminding viewers that they are watching something that they have loved before and are sure to enjoy again.

References to the earlier movies include the smallest things and the most important. The structure of *Another Thin Man* roughly duplicates that of *After the Thin Man* in that the film first shows us the family situation, with MacFay in Aunt Katherine's role, and then moves to the more diverse world of Manhattan and the West Indies Club. This parallel points up differences in the films: following the pattern of alternation set up between *The Thin Man* and *After the Thin Man*, *Another Thin Man* once again reverses ground. Set back in New York, and suggesting that Nora's family fortune was based on crime, this film undercuts her claim to social superiority, a point foregrounded when Nora defends her family saying, "My father was as honest as yours," and Nick replies, "Someday you'll find what a hot recommendation that is!" After the original film presented Nick and Nora as a free-spirited Jazz Age couple, the second film pulled them back under the authority of tradition with Nora's conservative family; now the pendulum swings once more toward Nick and New York. But little Nicky is the real focus of the threats in this film, which creates a feeling of parental vulnerability. The most important damage of losing Nora's fortune would be to undermine the baby's future. And the corruption of the parent foreshadows corruption of the child: the principal crime in this film is patricide—Lois murders her father, which, as in the case of Oedipus, dooms the child. Then there is the added specter of kidnapping—the 1932 Lindbergh kidnapping was the real-world event remembered by viewers in 1939. The film quickly shows that in this case it is merely another confusion of identities.

Van Dyke's key scenes in this film include that at the West Indies Club, one scene focused sharply on Nick, Nora, and the baby, and the thieves' baby party that provides the setting for the ending. Like the Li-chee scene in *After the Thin Man*, the West Indies Club setting carries through with the diversity theme of the series. Cairo and Morocco of "The Farewell Murder" become Cuba in *Another Thin Man*—the rhumba sets the tone for the music and dance. Furthermore, in addition to advancing the plot by providing Nick with a clue about Linda Mills, the nightclub scene presents a series of tableaux on the theme of dangers to the monogamous couple. First, when Nick arrives alone, he is surrounded by a bevy of available Latin beauties. Next, the floor show features a couple whose dance is a stylized performance of seduction, an elegant man in the embrace of a woman who turns him ever so slowly and gracefully on the pivot of his leather-soled shoes. While the man is the showier figure in the couple, the balance of power between the two—as with Nick and Nora—is open to interpretation. As this performance ends, we see a group of men surrounding a mysterious woman—again the theme of many potential lovers. Nora is the center of the group this time, and she attracts Nick's attention with a note signed with the name of an old girlfriend the police had used in trying to make her jealous—Nick the womanizer, a trope from *The Thin Man*, is played here both ways, as a threat to the couple, yet one that is always overcome by mutual trust. Nick quickly disperses the group by labeling Nora a mother and diseased, as if these are part of the same condition: "Now, Mommy,"

The West Indies Club (*Another Thin Man*, 1939)

he says, "you know better than to come to a place like this your first day out of bed. What if the health officers find out? They'll put you right back in quarantine." In the next instance, Nora, who is looking for Church's side-kick, instead finds an ardent Latin lover as a dance partner. As they had in the Li-chee Club in *After the Thin Man*, the lights go out; when they come back on, in a reversal of the Li-chee scene, we find Nora in Nick's arms. The pantomime is complete: the intruder has been driven off and the new family is safe.

The scene devoted entirely to the parents and infant is a nativity scene—the baby's manger is a dresser drawer safely close at hand, the animals of the stable in Bethlehem represented by Asta. When the baby is restless and Nick is asleep, however, Nora sets the baby on him, amused as Nicky pulls at Nick's mustache, gouges an eye, and drags his diapered bottom across Nick's nose. As if the new family dynamic were not clear enough already, Nora then wakes Nick to start him thinking about his responsibility to "tell the child about life." At first this scene stands apart, pure commentary on the family rather than advancing the story, but then Lois MacFay enters to look at the baby. In fact, she has set a gun to go off

Fatherhood (*Another Thin Man*, 1939)

in her father's room so as to falsely establish the time of his murder at a moment when she is with Nick, Nora, and the child—Lois's act of admiring the baby is only an alibi for the killing of her own father. The final birthday party scene multiplies the childcare issue exponentially, taking the film into a realm of screwball expressionism. When Creeps (Harry Bellaver) suddenly appears in the Charleses' hotel suite with fellow criminals from all over town, each carrying an infant and arguing over appropriate refreshments for the party, the world has been turned on its head. Petty criminals provide a safer environment for a child, apparently, than the wealthy—those such as MacFay who are considered respectable, whose daughter is now in the role of kidnapper.

Another Thin Man was successful, but less so than the previous *Thin Man* films. In the words of Frank Nugent in the *New York Times*, the film is "a trifle more forced in its gayety" and "some of the bloom is off the rose."[30] At the box office it was the weakest film of the series, most likely because of a labored complexity of the plot—what Layman refers to as a "too complicated climax."[31] Too many events in the straitjacket of a formulaic plot crowd out scenes between Nick and Nora that Van Dyke, when he was making the first film, had rightly identified as the crucial element.

The *Thin Man* Series after Hammett

Hammett's struggles with the story for *Another Thin Man* made it clear that he was unsuited to writing for hire in Hollywood, but he was also tired of the characters of Nick and Nora. In the early stages of his wrangling with Stromberg over *Another Thin Man*, he had written to Hellman:

> I should stop this [letter] and go to work on some changes in my charming fable of how Nick loved Nora and Nora loved Nick and everything was just one great big laugh in the midst of other people's trials and tribulations. Maybe there are better writers in the world, but nobody ever invented a more insufferably smug pair of characters. They can't take that away from me, even for $40,000.[32]

He had not only sold the characters to MGM, he clearly wanted to wash his hands of them altogether.

The disconnect with people's "trials and tribulations" was particularly an issue at a time when he and Hellman were so engaged politically; and once the United States was at war with Japan and Germany following Pearl Harbor, Hammett's patriotism pushed him to enlist, despite his age (forty-seven), his alcoholism, and the tuberculosis that had curtailed his military service in World War I. He joined the military in September 1942, remaining until August 1945, six months after the release of *The Thin Man Goes Home* (1945). Hammett thrived in the ordered life under military discipline, among other things editing a successful armed-forces newspaper while stationed in the Aleutian Islands. The period following the war, however, was among his most difficult. As Hellman wrote with considerable understatement, "The years after the war, from 1945 to 1948, were not good years; the drinking grew wilder and there was a lost, thoughtless quality I had never seen before."[33] The final film of the series, *Song of the Thin Man*, was released in September 1947.

From the first sequel on, of course, the series had belonged more to its stars than to Hammett, and to MGM, which focused on maintaining the profitability of the franchise. But however far the films moved from the world of Hammett's novels, they remained important to him. Not only did they provide significant income but, along with republications of his writing, films and radio shows from his novels, and the growing celebrity of Lillian Hellman, also worked to keep him in the public eye. Furthermore, while Hammett had no involvement with the last three films, the characters and their relationship were his creations—their history in the early films set parameters for their evolution, adapted within studio and filmmakers' goals as the basis of new narratives in the series.

Shadow of the Thin Man (1941)

Hammett wasn't the only one for whom writing about Nick and Nora had worn thin. Hackett later told Loy that, after *Another Thin Man*, "Finally I just threw up on my typewriter. I couldn't do it again. I couldn't write another one." "Perhaps," Loy adds, "we all should have concurred."[34] Yet the films continued to be successful. *Shadow of the Thin Man* was still produced by Stromberg and directed by Van Dyke, though Harry Kurnitz wrote the story and, with Irving Brecher, the screenplay. Loy and Powell continued to be embraced by a public that was aging along with them. The film was released on November 21, 1941, in New York, less than three weeks before the Japanese attack on Pearl Harbor. Yet this film's frame of reference remained the earlier movies in the series; in spite of the many signs that the United States would be entering the war, the only hints of it are the "Maj." preceding Van Dyke's name in the credits and military uniforms worn by Nick Jr. (Richard Hall), now about six years old.

The film's story is set in motion by the death of a jockey who was apparently killed to keep him from talking to the police about a gambling syndicate. Following the pattern of alternating between East and West Coasts, it is set in San Francisco and brings back Lieutenant Abrams (Sam Levene) from *After the Thin Man*. All the films had featured a damsel in distress: Dorothy in the first; Selma in the second; Lois—who turns out to be the murderer—in the third. Here the damsel is Molly Ford, played by Donna Reed in only her second film, employed by a racketeer, "Link" Stephens (Loring Smith). She has a boyfriend named Paul Clarke (Barry Nelson), a journalist working with notable citizen Major Jason I. Sculley (Henry O'Neill), who has been appointed by the state legislature to investigate Stephens and his gambling racket. Eventually Nick demonstrates that the frightened jockey accidentally shot himself when he dropped the gun he was carrying, and that the real villain is none other than Major Sculley, the state's investigator and the power behind the gambling ring. Most of the formulaic tale of corruption is told through Van Dyke's efficient "builder-upper" scenes, but he elaborates two moments in the film in rich detail in order to dramatize the film's concerns. One is set at the Arena where Nora has managed to drag Nick to watch a wrestling match. The second shows Nick accompanying his son on a merry-go-round at an amusement park.

At first viewing, the main subject of *Shadow of the Thin Man* seems to be Nora's hats. They leap to the viewer's attention in every exterior scene, making the point over and over again that Nora's high-fashion sensibility marks her as different from the ordinary people around her. All the hats are of a deliberately exaggerated design, but the one she is wearing at the Arena becomes part of the action. The wrestling matches are rigged, the combatants having "rehearsed," as an earlier comment by Nick makes clear. Nora's enthusiasm highlights her childlike naïveté, a quality she apparently shares with a majority of the ordinary spectators. The scene opens with a high long shot that shows a sea of heads of the people waiting to get in. All the men wear fedoras and the few women's hats are in the modest styles of the working class. Soon the viewer's eye finds Nora's designer sombrero with its enormous brim. The camera cuts to a medium shot as a man brushing by Nora knocks the hat crooked, commenting on how "screwy" it is, an observation made by three separate people throughout the scene until Nora has registered this note of popular rejection. The hat draws jeers not only because it looks absurd but also because it blocks the view. Even when Nora becomes completely absorbed, unconsciously grabbing Nick and putting him in a headlock in imitation of the action in the ring, her hat, again knocked askew, reminds us of her difference. The faces show wide diversity within the white working-class crowd. Only Nora stands apart, a fact underscored additionally by her manners: she thanks the vender "Meatballs" Murphy for his "wedding present" of a hot dog with the words, "I don't know what to say, Mr. Meatballs. You're too kind," and she pauses on their way out to politely thank one of the wrestlers in the ring. This entire scene is about Nora's not fitting in because of differences in social class, yet there is an ambiguity in whether being accepted by this group is a worthy aspiration.[35]

A wrestling match (*Shadow of the Thin Man*, 1941)

The merry-go-round scene once again showcases Van Dyke's ability to visually dramatize a film's ideas, in this case Nick's subjugation in the role of fatherhood. Nick has attempted to cling to the remnants of his former freedom, reading to his son from a racing form instead of from a children's book of fairy tales, but Nicky sees through the gambit—returning the favor by insisting that his father drink milk at dinner instead of a cocktail. Now the horses of the merry-go-round are a child's version of those at the racetrack—like Nicky in his sailor suit, all these children are dressed in emulation of adult roles. The scene is shot from the center of the whirling ride, a blurred image of the crowd in the background so that we feel Nick's disorientation. When one of the horses is vacant, Nicky wants his father to get on, but Nick resists. "Daddy [will] go so far, but no further," he declares, yet this attempt to draw a line and protect his dignity is a failure. To a chorus of "'fraidy-cat, 'fraidy-cat," from several awful children, Nick stumbles toward the horse. A boy in shorts, a tie, and jacket with round spectacles and his hair slicked back slaps Nick's hand with a strap when he attempts to steady himself on the tiger the boy is riding. An oversized girl with a rolled curl across her forehead and a long-haired boy in an argyle cardigan gouge at Nick's face when he leans too near them. But Nick can-. not simply dismiss them because he must support Nicky, whose sense of self is buoyed by confidence in his father's bravery. When Nick awkwardly tries to mount the horse, an eyeline match from his point of view shows the crowd in a kaleidoscopic fragmentation of the image, some of it rising, some falling, so that the viewer feels Nick's dizziness. Here he is infantilized and humiliated in a world where children, dressed as adults, are in command—he has never been so far removed from his role of independent man-of-the-world and detective.

Nora's fate is again to be called "Mommy" by her husband and to suffer the isolation from the world that comes with middle-class domesticity. Her new role is confirmed by her still elegant yet now somewhat matronly wardrobe. Adding racial difference to the class difference emphasized in the wrestling scene, Nora is given an African American maid, Stella (Louise Beavers), who struggles with words used by her more educated employers, such as "telepathic" to describe Nick's long-distance awareness when a cocktail is being prepared for him. Nora is still intelligent and can be useful to Nick, as when she recognizes that a laundry list with too many kimonos—elements of her women's sphere—must be a coded record of betting at racetracks. And she keeps up her banter with Nick. But when she attempts to investigate the crime at the racetrack, she takes pratfalls. In the final scene, she throws herself in front of Nick to protect him from the villain's gun, but the gun is not loaded and her action seems like the play-acting of a child in the grip of a fantastic story. Nick rewards her as one would a child, with a sparkling prize, in this case a diamond bracelet. Nora has become a trophy, a sign of the family's status, on display in her fashionable hats, gowns, and jewelry. She is no longer the new woman of the 1920s, but rather someone who looks "screwy" outside of her upper-middle-class domestic framework. Rather than critical of the class difference, this film accepts the superiority of people like Nick and Nora Charles, Nick helping to give his new class a façade of meritocracy.

The Thin Man Goes Home (1945)

If the 1941 *Shadow of the Thin Man* managed to avoid engaging the question of the coming war, *The Thin Man Goes Home* made patriotic defense of the homeland its central concern. So while the characters, the detective formula, and some of the humor repeat elements from the previous films of the series, the war theme and the film's attempt at relevance make it stand apart from the others. No one from the original *Thin Man* team except the actors was involved with the production. Robert Riskin, best known for the seven films he wrote for Frank Capra from *Lady for a Day* (1933) to *Meet John Doe* (1941), agreed to write the screenplay as a favor to his brother, Everett, the film's producer. According to Ian Scott, Robert's biographer, Riskin felt constrained by the preexisting characters, but his true interest at the time was to become involved in the war effort.[36] He had recently married Fay Wray, and "while he labored over the *Thin Man* screenplay during the early summer of 1942, Riskin, through Wray, [found] a route into institutional circles and to the offer of a government job in wartime propaganda."[37] Riskin would go on to produce a series of important documentaries for the Office of War Information (OWI), but *The Thin Man Goes Home* already fits their modus operandi, as described by the head of OWI, Elmer Davis: "The easiest way to propagandize people is to let the propaganda theme go in through an entertainment picture when people do not realize they are being propagandized."[38] Riskin, more than most involved, can be identified as the auteur of this film, though it was directed by Richard Thorpe, perhaps best known for his Tarzan movies with Johnny Weissmuller or *Jailhouse Rock* (1957) with Elvis Presley. Riskin's script and the film made from it are dominated by its focus on national defense and by a view of threatened small-town virtue similar to that in the films Riskin wrote for Capra.

The story is set in upstate New York, in a small town where people know and trust each other. Yet something has gone wrong—a man has been murdered because he was about to reveal that he was involved in the theft of secret defense plans from a local factory. The man was an artist, and the plans were drawn onto his canvases before he painted pastoral scenes to conceal them. Suspects include a banker, a doctor, another defense plant worker, and an art dealer, as well as the seditious organizer of the spy scheme and his wife. All these apparently upstanding citizens, for reasons ranging from petty greed to love, conspire to keep the treason hidden, thus corrupting the town and endangering the country and the Western world.

In order to elaborate this warning to viewers about dangers lurking within the heart of America, Nick and Nora first have to be reabsorbed into the heartland. For this Nick's past must be rewritten, making the title of the film somewhat ironic. No longer from a Greek immigrant family as in *The Thin Man*, novel and movie, now Nick is a simple WASP and his family are decent folk from the heartland. Nick's father is a doctor and even a teetotaler; contradicting one of his most defining personal characteristics, Nick will drink only non-alcoholic cider to please his father. In a slapstick scene at Grand Central Station, Nick sheds his previous agility for the clumsiness of an average guy. Once at home, in a house with a yard and a white picket fence, he lounges in a hammock, dressed down in a T-shirt and cardigan sweater that exaggerate his ordinariness, in part by showing off the heaviness and sag of his age.

The central metaphor of the film is the false bucolic painting which hides a sinister betrayal of the nation: Nick's genius is his ability to see through this camouflage just as the fluoroscope in his father's study allows the assembled group of suspects and the police to see through the paint that conceals the stolen defense plans. The formulaic detective plot and even the characters of Nick and Nora that Riskin found so intransigent to his creative interests are thus adopted in the service of Riskin's ideals and the national war effort.

Nora, in line with her advancing age and with the shift to a conservative, more rural context, continues to lose her independence and to become increasingly incompetent. Most expressive of her increasingly infantile quality is the scene in which Nick learns of a provocative statement she made to the press: he puts her over his knee and spanks her like a child, drawing a parallel to spankings he had received as a young boy from his father. This entire story of a return home, and to the foundational values of an earlier, more patriarchal period, is framed in Nick's desire, as repeatedly pointed out by Nora, to please his father. The final image of the film is Nick, after receiving his father's admiring pat on the back, swelling with pride to the point that the buttons pop off his vest as Nora had predicted they would. In this patriarchal setting, she is at her wisest in a traditional, wifely, supporting role.

Song of the Thin Man (1947)

In *Song of the Thin Man*, the aging of Nick and Nora is the only identifiable theme, which is explored by creating a setting for the murder that places the maturing couple in the company of young jazz musicians. Nora has arranged

The patriarchal order (*The Thin Man Goes Home*, 1945)

for them to attend a charity event held on a gambling boat, the SS *Fortune*, in order to strengthen their ties with the right kind of people. When a murder occurs that ensnares the fiancé of a young woman whom Nora is fond of, she encourages Nick to help out. The victim is band leader Tommy Drake (Philip Reed),who has made many enemies. The suspects include a songwriter and clarinet player named Buddy Hollis (Don Taylor) whose lover Drake has stolen; Fran (Gloria Grahame), a singer in the band whom Drake has now thrown over; Phil Brant (Bruce Cowling), the owner of the venue that Drake was quitting on short notice; David Thayer (Ralph Morgan), a wealthy patrician who doesn't want the owner of the club to marry his daughter; Al Amboy (William Bishop), a gambler to whom the band leader owed $12,000; and Mitch Talbin (Leon Ames), the band leader's new employer whose wife Phyllis (Patricia Morison) had been Drake's lover and who gave him a necklace to cover his debt to the gambler. Brant is accused of the murder and put in jail, Fran is eventually found dead with a knife in her back, and Hollis has been whisked away to a sanitarium in Poughkeepsie.

Powell and Loy were now fifty-five and forty-two, respectively, and as Nick investigates, taking the couple on a tour of the New York jazz underworld guided by "Clinker" (Keenan Wynn), the entire plot seems to have been created as a series of opportunities to show how out of sync with the times Nick and Nora have become. When Nick encounters the musicians retrieving their instruments from the SS *Fortune*, they drown him in slang that he barely understands, using words like "solid," "wacked up," "dig," "jam," and so forth. The next day when Clinker exposes Nora to the same impenetrable lingo, she stands amazed—echoing her difficulty in understanding Nick's shady friends in *The Thin Man*—so that Nick responds, "Mrs. Charles always wears her mouth open with this outfit." They are then led through a private party and five different jazz clubs, all emphasizing how little they fit in at this stage in their lives. Nick now prefers his pipe and slippers to going out on the town, and his acquiescing in Nora's attempts to raise Nicky in a mold of conventional middle-class respectability reinforces their shift in perspective on life since the original film. The most egregious example is when Nick, as the father, is prevailed upon by Nora to spank Nicky because he dared to run out and play baseball rather than practice the piano in order to impress Nora's friends. The younger couple of *The Thin Man* would have celebrated his streak of independence.

In contrast to the original *Thin Man*, New York is presented in *Song of the Thin Man* as an abstraction; the sets' stylized interiors and exteriors offer no sense of place. Nor is there a sense of the historical moment of New York in 1947. The music, for example, seems a deliberately dated swing, showing influences of Louis Armstrong and Count Basie rather than the more recent bebop of Charlie Parker and Dizzy Gillespie. Furthermore, all the jazz musicians are white. The movie seems made for an audience that, like Nick and Nora, has become befuddled by the rapid change and no longer wants to confront it. The filmmakers now point a judgmental finger at whatever Nick and Nora consider nonsensical, a world the audience can look down upon.

To understand the backward-looking qualities of this film we have only to compare it with a new trend of the period, the retrospectively identified films noirs including *The Maltese Falcon* (John Huston, 1941), *This Gun for Hire* (Frank Tuttle, 1942), *Double Indemnity* (Billy Wilder, 1944), *Laura* (Otto Preminger, 1944), *Murder My Sweet* (Edward Dmytryk, 1944), *Phantom Lady* (Robert Siodmak, 1944), *The Woman in the Window* (Fritz Lang, 1944),

Mildred Pierce (Michael Curtiz, 1945), *The Killers* (Siodmak, 1946), *The Big Sleep* (Howard Hawks, 1946), *The Postman Always Rings Twice* (Tay Garnett, 1946), and *Out of the Past* (Jacques Tourneur, 1947), among many others. We realize how the "charming fable of how Nick loved Nora and Nora loved Nick and everything was just one great big laugh in the midst of other people's trials and tribulations," in Hammett's words, could not embody the anxieties of the later period with its paranoia and the femme fatale's challenge to the wounded male psyche.

Hammett had concluded his involvement with the series of films in 1939, yet each successful release of a sequel fostered his reputation, particularly in the context of radio programs and other films from his writings. *Woman in the Dark* (Phil Rosen, 1934), from Hammett's novella, starring Ralph Bellamy and Fay Wray, appeared six months after *The Thin Man.* That was followed by *The Glass Key* (Tuttle, 1935) and a second version of *The Maltese Falcon* with Bette Davis, entitled *Satan Met a Lady* (William Deiterle, 1936).[39] *The Adventures of The Thin Man* radio series began a nine-year run in 1941, the same year that the best-known, third version of *The Maltese Falcon* (John Huston) appeared, followed shortly by a second version of *The Glass Key* (Stuart Heisler, 1942) starring Alan Ladd and Veronica Lake. In addition to adaptations and spin-offs of his own work, Lillian Hellman's play *The Children's Hour*—for which Hammett suggested the idea and provided detailed feedback on draft after draft—was produced six months after *The Thin Man*; it brought Hellman instant recognition during a period when she and Hammett were publicly recognized as a couple. After a failed second play, *Days to Come* in 1936, Hellman again triumphed with *The Little Foxes*, in February 1939. Her play *Watch on the Rhine* provided not only a third important Broadway hit for Hellman in 1941, but the 1943 film version earned Hammett his only screenplay credit and an Academy Award nomination as well.

4

Lillian Hellman

Woman in the Dark (1934) and
Watch on the Rhine (1943)

Hammett wrote the seventy-six-page novella *Woman in the Dark* shortly before *The Thin Man*, and it too reflects his relationship with Lillian Hellman. While not the only woman in his life in the early 1930s, Hellman was the person with whom he had the deepest and most enduring relationship. In the fall of 1930, as Diane Johnson writes,"they began an affair, which escalated into a love affair."[1] Hellman was married to Arthur Kober at the time; they would divorce early in 1932. In the meantime, Hammett, who had been separated from his wife, Josephine, for a number of years, frequently shared lodgings with Hellman when they were in the same city. His letters betray the continuing sense of attachment when they were apart, as in this note from May 4, 1932: "Sweetheart," he begins, "So after you left me I walked over to Broadway. . . . Then I sent you a wire—supposed to reach you at Washington, D.C., either as a good-night message or a good-morning one—bought a comb and brush, took on food at Childs, and came home expecting to find some such message as 'Mrs. Kober, who missed her train, phoned.' It wasn't here, though—there wasn't anything here but a bed you never slept in. I love you mugg!"[2] Hammett wrote *Woman in the Dark* shortly after this, during the summer of 1932.

In *The Thin Man*, as Johnson writes, "all the women . . . talked a little like Lillian, the banter of the hero and heroine was a little like talk between Lillian and Hammett, the drinking a little like their drinking, and the hero's cynical and depressed attitude toward society quite a lot like Hammett's own."[3] If *Woman in the Dark* reflects Hammett's experience with Hellman, it is less in the dialogue than in his experimentation with a woman protagonist, an independent female character whose decisive action determines the novella's outcome. But the Hellman connection goes beyond her influence in the creation of this character, Luise Fischer, to her shared interest with Hammett in theater. During this period he suggested that Hellman read William Roughead's *Bad Companions* (1930), which would be the basis of her play *The Children's Hour.* Hammett knew that the story would make a good theatrical piece; according to Johnson, "he had earlier said in an interview that he himself had thought of writing a play—perhaps based in this case."[4] The structure of *Woman in the Dark* is that of a play.

Hellman and the theater are also the reasons to take up *Watch on the Rhine* (1943) in conjunction with this period of Hammett's film career. His screenplay for *Watch on the Rhine* was based on Hellman's hit Broadway play. Like Hammett's earlier novella, Hellman's play explores the difficult course a woman must navigate in a world of masculine power.[ ]

Woman in the Dark (1934)

Woman in the Dark was published in three installments in *Liberty* magazine, on April 8, 15, and 22, 1933, and sold to Select Pictures Corporation for a $500 advance, $5,000 to be paid when the film went into production.[5] Each of the novella's three installments for publication—which became chapters of the book when it was eventually published in 1950—is staged in a different setting as in acts of a play: the simple cabin that is the home of the character named Brazil; the apartment in town of his ex-con friend Link; and Kane Robson's elegant house. Furthermore, the characters in the novella are largely presented as in stage and screen works—their motives must be inferred from what they say and do. Some of the action is viewed from Luise Fischer's perspective, but Fischer emerges as the protagonist mainly because of her action to take control of the situation in which she and Brazil find themselves, setting off the chain of events that brings the narration to closure.

In one respect the novella follows an old Hammett premise that a crime is not simply what has occurred, but rather what can be understood based on a reconstruction from known details. Because of information withheld throughout most of the story, the police no less than the reader suspect that Brazil, having knocked down Robson's sidekick after Fischer tries to escape the powerful Kane Robson, is responsible for the victim's lingering at death's door. More importantly, Brazil similarly misunderstands Fischer's leaving him as a self-serving desertion when she has, in fact, acted to save him. In his independence, Brazil is recognizably in the mold of earlier Hammett protagonists like the Op, Sam Spade, and Ned Beaumont, but this story focuses on Fischer and her survival in a world dominated by men who are rich and crafty like Robson or physically powerful like Brazil. The story is narrated sparely and objectively in the third person, yet Fischer's point of view is established in the opening scene as she stumbles out of the darkness to find Brazil's cabin.

Hammett would seem to have modeled Fischer as much on Marlene Dietrich as on Hellman and other women he knew. Dietrich had exploded on the American movie scene as Lola Lola in Josef von Sternberg's *The Blue Angel* (1930), followed rapidly by the same director's *Morocco* (1930), *Dishonored* (1931), *Shanghai Express* (1932), and *Blonde Venus* (1932); in three of these films Dietrich played a seductive entertainer, and she is frequently forced to make difficult choices like that between Robson and Brazil. In 1931 Hammett had been assigned by Paramount to polish the script of *Blonde Venus*,[6] and he had once written playfully to Hellman, "Your rival, Marlene [Dietrich], is back in town with her offspring and reputedly living in sin with that great, if somewhat stunted genius of the flickers and lisps, Joe Stoinboig."[7] Above all, Dietrich was the perfect embodiment of an independence of will and a decisiveness that Hammett wanted for Fischer.

Few people would have made any comparison of the film with Hammett's novella. In the wake of the success of *The Thin Man*, press notices leading up to the production refer to Hammett with every mention of the title, but the novella had only been available in serial publication, without the publicity of an Alfred Knopf novel. Furthermore, the film was a sixty-eight-minute B-project at a marginal non-studio, Select Picture Corporation. Its stars—Fay Wray and Ralph Bellamy—were third-tier actors, the film shot in eighteen days in the now obsolete Biograph studios in the Bronx,[8] and it was released by RKO with little advertising and without major reviews into second- and third-run theaters. What those few who might have seen the film with Hammett's novella in mind would have noticed was, above all, a shift away from Hammett's emphasis on the female protagonist.

Instead of beginning from the perspective of a fleeing woman who arrives out of the darkness to knock at the door of an isolated cabin, the film opens with Brazil, now called John Bradley (Ralph Bellamy), in prison where he awaits his release. Shots of the darkness of night in the prison show a man waiting anxiously, apparently on death row, though we are quickly disabused of this false assumption—he is about to be released. The prison warden (Frank Shannon) even praises him as a model prisoner, warning him against allowing his temper to make him a two-time loser. This warning foreshadows his vulnerability to the situation when Loring appears. Before Loring arrives, Bradley is shown at his cabin in dialogue with a pretty young woman named Helen (Nell O'Day), who happens to be the daughter of the local sheriff. Angering her father, she has a crush on Bradley, who treats her like a child. Hammett's story had taken advantage of this young woman to foreshadow the larger plot twist—in the novella Fischer finds Brazil alone, and when Helen comes out of the bedroom both Fischer and the reader jump to the false conclusion that she is Brazil's lover, once again emphasizing that the interpretation of events is frequently based on misleading information. The film, by contrast, establishes Bradley as the protagonist and adopts his point of view on Loring's arrival.

Wray, who had grown up in a Mormon family in Salt Lake City before attending Hollywood High, was cast as Louise Loring one year after her most famous role in *King Kong* (1933). Loring is unlike Fischer in the novella, a socially marginal cabaret singer in the mode of Dietrich's Lola Lola in *The Blue Angel* and Amy Jolly in *Morocco*. Instead, Loring is a middle-class American girl aspiring to a career as a concert pianist and trained in a European conservatory, a change that is part of a general orchestration of issues related to class and morality. Dialogue is inserted to make sure we understand that Bradley also comes from a respectable family and that Robson (Melvyn Douglas), regardless of his wealth, is not respectable. Furthermore, the Logans, the name given the unmarried Link and Fay of the novella, are morally good people in spite of their obviously lower-class manners and even lawlessness. Logan (Roscoe Ates) is generous and loyal in spite of a dishonest streak where jewelry is concerned; he is also made a broadly comic figure, with a debilitating stutter whenever he is put on the spot. Because of this, in addition to helping to define the class stratification in the film, his comic relief mitigates the unrelieved fatalism of the novella.

Despite its 1934 production date, *Woman in the Dark* seems more typical of films during the transition to sound in 1928 or 1929, a result of its production outside the major and even minor studios—it was the next-to-last film made by the Select Pictures Corporation, which had been a successful distributor and producer but was already in decline by the late 1920s.[9] The static framing suggests that camera movement was restricted by a soundproof cabinet, and while the dialogue is smoothly integrated into the performances, the sound texture remains thin, composed entirely of dialogue and an uncredited musical track. The lighting, developing a subtle play of many shades of gray, gives this film a tonal richness in contrast to the high-key lighting that emphasizes and isolates the stars in most 1930s studio films. Extreme close-up inserts of the characters' faces emphasize emotional states with a disregard for continuity, and when Loring recounts her past with Robson, there are two flashbacks introduced by pans that function as horizontal wipes. The camera pans slowly to the right until it seems to cross a timeline that allows us to see a scene from the past. When the scene is over, the camera pans left back to the present. This way of handling time creates an odd feeling of equivalency between the time periods, in contrast to the usual sense that the ongoing actions are more real than the material recalled from the past.

If the look of *Woman in the Dark* reminds us of silent film, perhaps one reason is that both director Phil Rosen and cinematographer Joseph Ruttenberg were veterans of the silent era. Rosen began in 1914 and filmed many of Theda Bara's most sumptuous pictures, with credit as cinematographer on some thirty titles up to 1920, and as director on thirty more before sound. Joseph Ruttenberg also shot nearly thirty silent pictures, followed by a long and distinguished career in the sound era.[10] In any case, the direction and cinematography of this film show an obsessive concern with the lighting and composition, which, along with the static framing, reinforces the allegorical simplicity of the story—Rosen and Ruttenberg stage nearly every shot as a tableau, with a portrait-photography composition that is balanced, static, and framed close so that the tableau imposes itself on the audience.

Each tableau is a frozen dramatic moment, as early in the film when Bradley discovers Robson's sidekick Conway standing over the dog he has just shot. Bradley is on the far left next to Conway, symmetrically balanced by Loring on the far right, with Robson positioned between her and the others. The crude chimney of the fireplace divides the shot vertically; it will be the instrument—the supposed murder weapon—that Robson uses in attempting to separate Loring from Bradley. At Logan's apartment, the camera lingers on an image that, in conjunction with the actors' talk and demeanor, dramatizes the power relations in the room—Logan's wife, Lil, and Bradley dominate the (apparently) weaker figures. Similarly, in the film's final scene at Conway's bedside when he is revealing Robson's ploy, the heads of the four characters form points in a harmonious curve from Bradley to Conway, with Loring's light-colored dress and the whiteness of the sheets and pillow leading the eye out of the darkness of the men's suits and furniture, visually underscoring, in effect, a moment of enlightenment conveyed in the narrative. The tableau is perhaps reduced to its simplest in the darkness of Bradley's car when he and Loring pause to sleep: only their two heads are revealed in

Friends—a tableau (*Woman in the Dark*, 1934)

The truth revealed (*Woman in the Dark*, 1934)

the darkness, emphasizing both their individual solitude and common situation within the black night.

The structured immobility within the fames of this film seems an extension of Bradley's quiet strength, which exploits a central quality of Ralph Bellamy as an actor. It would later be contrasted comically with Cary Grant's energetic quickness in films such as *The Awful Truth* (Leo McCarey, 1937) and *His Girl Friday* (Howard Hawks, 1940).[11] Even in this film as Bradley, he is presented as slow to understand Loring's actions, which in fact works against the shift for the film to his point of view. As a result, where the novella was clear in showing Luise Fischer as the agent of Brazil's rescue, in the film there is an ambiguity about whose perspective dominates, or who is rescuing whom. Nonetheless, Louise Loring is not Ann Darrow of *King Kong*, a helpless beauty in the grasp of a gorilla. Visually, the key to the film is the marriage of Bradley's stolid strength with Louise Loring's spark, the liveliness of her intelligence in rescuing the dull Bradley like the brilliance of her white gown piercing the darkness when she first arrives at his cabin—she stumbles out of a pitch-black night in a white silk dress, an apparition that would not be out of place in a horror film of the era.

The spark (*Woman in the Dark*, 1934)

Loring's deliberate action remains the key to the plot, even if in the film she cannot complete her rescue without Bradley's physical strength and stubborn unwillingness to let her go. Whereas the novella ends with Bradley's recognition of his error, the Hollywood film, even on the margins of the studio system, cannot allow the woman to remain so powerful and independent. Thus the film ends with Loring returning her sparkling jewelry to the hand of the unconscious Robson, and giving herself over to Bradley's strong embrace.

Watch on the Rhine (1943)

Nine years passed between *Woman in the Dark* and *Watch on the Rhine*, a period in Hammett's life that included momentous change. In 1934, he was celebrating the results of the most productive period of his literary career, with no clear sign that his oeuvre as a fiction writer was essentially complete. From 1935 though 1938 Hammett struggled with the stories for the first two *Thin Man* sequels, effectively ending—except for *Watch on the Rhine*—his career as a screenwriter and culminating in what Diane

Johnson calls his "crack-up."[12] The years following included some of the best time that Hammett spent with Hellman. They had vacationed together in Havana, and with the success of *The Little Foxes* in 1939, Hellman bought Hardscrabble Farm where she could write, Hammett could occupy himself with any number of activities, and friends could visit.

During the period from the mid-1930s until after *Watch on the Rhine*, Hammett was also more active politically than at any other time—friends such as Frances Goodrich and Albert Hackett were actively involved in forming the Screen Writers Guild, which became Hellman's primary initiation in political activism. In 1935, the Seventh World Congress of Communist Parties adopted its Popular Front policy, transforming narrower, more specific goals into a strategy of general resistance to fascism. As the Communist Party of the United States of America (CPUSA) worked with a range of other liberal groups, lines blurred and party membership swelled. According to a recent Hellman biographer, Alice Kessler-Harris,

> Dashiell Hammett most likely found a home in communism before Hellman did. Flailing a bit after completing *The Thin Man*, . . . he became increasingly committed to left-wing positions. His letters to his daughter Mary, written in the fall of 1936 in the midst of FDR's campaign for a second term and in the aftermath of the CPUSA's turn to the Popular Front politics, have the ring of an insider. "There is no truth to the statement that the Communists are supporting Roosevelt," he wrote to her disingenuously on September 11, "that's just the old Hearst howl."[13]

From 1936 to 1938, the Spanish Civil War absorbed attention of those in the antifascist camp—both Hammett and Hellman were involved in raising money for *The Spanish Earth* (1937), a documentary portraying the Republican defense of Madrid against the armies of Francisco Franco. In 1939 Hammett was involved with several magazines. At one, *Equality*, a "monthly journal to defend democratic rights and combat anti-Semitism and racism," Hammett joined Arthur Kober, Louis Kronenberger, Dudley Nichols, Dorothy Parker, and Donald Ogden Stewart.[14] At another, *PM*, he aided Ralph Ingersoll in founding a "liberal afternoon newspaper" for New York.[15] By the time of the Hitler-Stalin non-aggression pact, it became less "chic," according to Diane Johnson, to be a communist in Hollywood.[16]

During that period Hammett largely devoted himself to defending the rights of those, including CPUSA leaders, who dissented against active involvement in the war in Europe. With Hitler's continuing military successes, both Hammett and Hellman's views on the American role in the war changed: *Watch on the Rhine* called directly for Americans to assist Europeans who were fighting for democracy.

Hammett created neither the story nor the characters for *Watch on the Rhine*—the play was Hellman's, and along with its antifascist commitment it reflected her view of a woman's strength, just as *Woman in the Dark* reflected Hammett's view as formed in his experience with Hellman and others. Jacob Wilk, East Coast story editor for Warner Bros., initiated negotiations with Hellman and Herman Shumlin,[17] the play's producer and director on Broadway, and according to Deborah Martinson, "before agreeing to sell the film rights to Warners, [Hellman] insisted that Hammett write the adaptation and Shumlin direct."[18] She negotiated a good contract for Hammett—$30,000 and 15 percent of the gross—but his reputation for being unreliable was such that the film's producer, Hal Wallis, insisted that Hellman guarantee "timely delivery."[19] Hammett was given the contract on January 30, 1942. Since by then Hammett had largely stopped writing for publication, some have wondered whether Hellman herself wrote the screenplay for *Watch on the Rhine*, as she had for *The Little Foxes* (1941). In fact, Hellman would have liked to, but other commitments prevented her. As Bernard Dick reports, "There is ample evidence that the screenplay was indeed Hammett's" and "that Wallis acknowledged it as such, dubbing it 'Wonderful.'"[20] By mid-February Hammett had submitted a treatment for Wallis's approval, and by mid-April his work was finished.[21]

The extent to which Hellman's play was tied to its historical moment presented a challenge for Hammett and the filmmakers, for events and attitudes changed rapidly while she was writing the play and in the two years between the play and the film. When Hellman began the project in the summer of 1939, the country was evenly divided between isolation and involvement in Europe. During the German blitzkrieg, opinion began to change. By July 1940, polls showed that more than 66 percent of the public believed that Germany posed a direct threat to the United States.[22] The Farrelly family in the play represents an American public forced to recognize the danger of Hitler's expanding power and to respond. Fanny, the widowed matriarch, describes the impact of events on them, which is also the impact the play-wright hoped to have on the public: "Well, here we are. We're shaken out of the magnolias, eh?"[23] By April 1941 the play's message had already been embraced by a majority of the American public. This no doubt accounts in some degree for *Watch on the Rhine*'s extraordinary success.

Hammett understood the various roles of the writer in Hollywood. In this instance, rather than as an author of an original story, he was in the position of a film industry craftsman, charged with delivering Hellman's work in the way most likely to lead to a successful movie. He was mindful of being faithful to Hellman's ideas; he was also mindful of America's rapidly evolving posi-tion with respect to the war in Europe. Thus, Hammett's adaptation of Hell-man's play was respectful of its widely seen stage version while refocusing it to address the historical moment. Herman Shumlin, director of both the stage and screen versions, was mainly interested in replicating the stage produc-tion, though he was faced with the challenges of Bette Davis's influence as the film's powerful star and the constraints of the Production Code.

At the heart of Hammett's screenplay, as in the stage play, is a fam-ily melodrama; a sentimental family bond is magnified into an issue that, within its frame of international politics, sucks up all the dramatic oxygen of the film. As a father, Kurt Müller must take leave of his children, return-ing to Europe where he is wanted by the Germans in order to attempt the rescue of a comrade in the resistance. The children, without the depth of their mother's understanding, nonetheless grasp the danger of his going and do their best to accept it stoically. The emotional separation of Sara (Bette Davis) from Kurt (Paul Lukas), which defines the heroism of the decision, is the high point—two people, deeply in love, are saying goodbye forever and are fully aware of it.

The audience would expect no less of a film starring Bette Davis after her similar roles in films such as *Dark Victory* (Edmund Goulding, 1939), *All This and Heaven Too* (Anatole Litvak, 1940) and *Now, Voyager* (Irving Rapper, 1942). In fact, the casting of Davis caused Hellman some consternation; as Deborah Martinson writes, she knew that "Davis's fame would serve them well but [also] that she'd have to change the relatively minor character to fit Davis's larger-than-life presence. Neither Hellman nor Wallis was able to get Shumlin to control Davis, allowing her to push the character of Sara, they felt, from 'commitment' to 'saintliness.'"[24] The family receives more emphasis in the film than in the play, but not only because Davis makes the role of Sara more prominent.

Due to the evolution of events between the writing of the play and the film, the opening credits are followed by a scrolling prologue that looks back to the period of the play's gestation: "In the first part of 1940 there were few men in the world who could have believed that, in less than two months, Denmark, Norway, Belgium, Holland, and France would fall to the German invaders. But there were some men . . . who knew this mighty tragedy was on its way. . . . This is the story of one of these men." This prologue inadvertently highlights that with the country already at war, the film has lost much of the play's original raison d'être, while a significant new scene at the end seems designed to overcome this loss. Important in both the play and the film is Sara's sacrifice of the material well-being of her American family in order to support her husband, Kurt, as well as the even greater sacrifice on his part and theirs when he returns to Europe and almost certain death for the antifascist cause.

It was apparently at the insistence of Hal Wallis in response to Hammett's initial treatment that the argument in the film was given a further turn of the screw.[25] The play ends with Kurt's departure, but in the film a shot of falling snow then marks a passage of time with the changing seasons, and young Joshua Müller (Donald Buka) is shown at his desk with a map of Europe, plotting a path "home." When Sara discovers him making his plans, he tells her that if they have not heard from Kurt in five more months, by the boy's birthday, then he will leave to look for his father. Sara says, "I will not let you," but his answer shows that he is taking on the commitment of his father: "I believe that you will let me go. I believe that when my time will come you will want me to go. . . . I believe too . . . that you will tell Bodo [Joshua's younger brother] the things he needs to know and, if the world stays bad so long, you will send him after me when the time comes." Thus, in Bernard Dick's words, the "Müllers have formed a kind of apostolate in which the sons follow in their father's footsteps."[26] Sara, the mother, must prepare herself to send her young sons to die in the battle. There is a starkness of this realization reminiscent of Greek tragedy. It permits no equivocation and directly addresses a growing reality for many viewers in 1943, thus returning the film, in its final moment, to relevance.

Hammett's assignment was to make the drawing-room play more cinematic without losing the strengths of dialogue suited only to such a play. As Martinson writes, "He adeptly worked on a straightforward plot, and Hellman honed the speech."[27] So he used the dialogue, but wherever possible, he followed its suggestions to move scenes out of the Farrelly house. As Dick points out, the exposition is framed much more dynamically by creating the opening scene in Mexico and allowing fifteen minutes of cross-cutting between Fanny (Lucile Watson) and David (Donald Woods) in Washington and the Müllers' encounter with an antifascist Italian couple on the train. Similarly added by Hammett are a drive to the offices of the Supreme Court, where Joshua Farrelly had been a justice, and a Capraesque visit to the Washington Monument.[28] In the film we see Count Brancovis (George Coulouris) visit the German Embassy, whereas in the play this important event is only referred to in dialogue. Hammett also moves and reorganizes existing scenes to allow the story to gather momentum. Sara's quiet appreciation of the dresses her mother has bought for her, which allow exposition of her situation and attitude, falls earlier in the film than in the play, while a dramatic story that Kurt tells Fanny about raiding the home of a Gestapo officer occurs much later in the film as part of the escalation toward Kurt's killing of Brancovis to prevent betrayal of his plans to the Germans. But the words, for the most part, are Hellman's, even when placed in the mouth of a different character. In essence, Hammett is doing for Hellman what Goodrich and Hackett had done so masterfully for him in *The Thin Man*.

One change may have had more to do with the Production Code than with Hammett. In the film, the children are not present for the confrontation with Brancovis, whereas in the play Joshua helps his father dispose of the body—the PCA would be concerned about implicating young Joshua in a murder. We know that Joseph Breen also objected to dialogue implying that Marthe de Brancovis (Geraldine Fitzgerald) and David Farrelly are lovers, as well as requesting that Kurt be made to pay for his killing of Brancovis.[29] In response, the lovers' dialogue was removed, and a scene was shot in which Kurt is shown in Germany about to be arrested.[30] In it, as the ominous sound of boots approaches his shabbily furnished rooms, Kurt is giving instructions to a young man to pass on to Joshua. The scene was to be placed following Sara's realization that Joshua is planning to leave and preceding the final dialogue between Joshua and Sara. But the scene was eliminated from the film, and Kurt remained unpunished; a case could be made that by preventing Brancovis's treachery, Kurt is preserving his own life, one of the few reasons the Production Code Administration would accept for a killing without retribution.

If the new ending manages to lift the film beyond the historical circumstances of 1940 and 1941, Shumlin's direction ensures that it can only be seen as a footnote to the stage play. Shumlin, one of Hellman's lovers at that time, had produced and directed all her plays in New York, and *Watch on the Rhine* was dedicated to him. According to Martinson, Shumlin "saw a chance to work in Hollywood on a Hellman film . . . as a new career in the making."[31] But unlike some stage directors—Rouben Mamoulian, for example, whose first film, *Applause* (1929), is a masterpiece of innovation—Shumlin had difficulty shedding his habits as a stage director.[32] He imported Paul Lukas and Lucile Watson from principal roles in the stage production, and though he relied heavily on his directors of photography, he had them shoot *Watch on the Rhine* as he had staged it for the theater. According to Dick, "veteran cameraman Hal Mohr had to mark the camera positions for Shumlin and block the scenes with stand-ins so that, by the time the stars arrived on the set, Shumlin could go through the business of directing." Wallis "was constantly sending memos . . . recommending more dolly shots."[33] In spite of any and all assistance, the film divides awkwardly between the material lifted from the play and the scenes added for the film.

The early scene on the Farrelly patio provides a good example of Shumlin's approach to shooting the drawing-room material that dominates the play. He relies on dialogue, framed in medium shots that allow too much space around the characters, bright and even lighting, with obviously artificial painted scenery, all of which make the scene stagy. Editing is minimal, the passive camera positioning relieved only by a cut to an upstairs bedroom where Marthe and Brancovis are talking, and as they leave the room to come downstairs, a long tracking shot as requested by Wallis stands so markedly in contrast to the filming on the patio that it highlights the disjunction between stage and cinematic moments. Even dialogue in a car is framed as if for the stage, so the shock is greater when scenes are presented differently, as in Brancovis's evening at the German Embassy: from an opening shot showing the swastika outside the door, the camera insinuates itself fluidly among the guests, eventually panning to discover Brancovis and track him upstairs in the company of the editor of a "pro-Nazi" paper. In a card game that ensues, the characters are framed tightly, conversations presented using two-shots, tight close-ups, and a shot/reverse-shot pattern; the scene could not be presented more differently from that on the Farrelly's veranda, as if Mohr (or Merritt Gerstad, also credited as director of photography) shot them independently of Shumlin.

The contrast between Shumlin's inert direction and, say, that of William Wyler of similar scenes in *The Little Foxes* (1941) could not be more telling, yet because of Hellman's eloquence and the timing of the film's message of sacrifices required of a population at war, *Watch on the Rhine* was a hit at the box office, as well as winner of New York Film Critics Awards for Best Film and Best Actor, a Golden Globe for Best Motion Picture Actor, and four Academy Award nominations: Best Actor, Best Actress, and Best Picture, with Hammett nominated for Best Writing—Screenplay. *Casablanca* took the Oscars for Best Picture and Screenplay, but Paul Lukas received the award for Best Actor, perhaps partly in recognition of his stage success as Kurt Müller, which had defined a hero that Humphrey Bogart's Rick could only aspire to become.[34]

From stage to screen (*Watch on the Rhine*, 1943)

5

Sexual Politics

The Maltese Falcon (1931), *Satan Met a Lady* (1936), and *The Maltese Falcon* (1941)

The three films based on *The Maltese Falcon* span the most vital years of the cinematic response to Dashiell Hammett's writing. The novel was pivotal in his publishing career—after good reviews of *Red Harvest* and modest enthusiasm for *The Dain Curse*, its reception established him as the very best American writer in the genre. This new level of celebrity in turn encouraged further Hollywood interest in his novels and writing for hire. *The Maltese Falcon* (1931)—which to avoid confusion I refer to here by an alternative title, *Dangerous Female*—was one of the earliest of Hammett's eleven films in the 1930s and 1940s; *Satan Met a Lady* (1936) fell at the midpoint among these films; and *The Maltese Falcon* (1941) arrived toward the end, not including the last *Thin Man* films in 1945 and 1947. Like the novel, the third film version, directed by John Huston and starring Humphrey Bogart, became one of the principal vehicles for sustaining and prolonging Hammett's fame.

These movies—especially *Satan Met a Lady* and the latter *Maltese Falcon*—were important in the careers of their stars as well, and the casting, as always, was integral to the direction given the films—the first two were dominated by Bebe Daniels and Bette Davis, respectively, the third by Humphrey Bogart. Because all three were made by Warner Bros., successive productions began with a review of the studio's files from the previous version. There was an existing script to cannibalize or to react against, prior models for casting and for the interpretation of particular scenes, as well as for the handling of material deemed sensitive by industry censors. John Huston famously went back to Hammett's novel as his point of departure for the 1941 film, but not without a full awareness of the earlier productions.

One important factor in shaping all three versions was the Production Code developed under the supervision of Will Hays, president of the Motion Picture Producers and Distributors Association (MPPDA). Warner Bros. acquired the film rights on June 23, 1930, just three months after the Production Code was first published.[1] Compliance was largely voluntary at that point, yet *Dangerous Female* became the subject of extensive negotiations between the studio and the Studio Relations Committee (SRC), charged by the MPPDA with enforcing the Code. Between the first film, released in June 1931, and production of the second, a disguised remake, the SRC was converted into the Production Code Administration (PCA), its new head Joseph Breen instituting far more rigorous enforcement. *Satan Met a Lady* responded to this broader environment as well as being conceived within the framework negotiated for the earlier film. The 1941 picture similarly followed the understanding established in 1931, unable to sidestep the PCA's strictures on the representation of "illicit" sex.

The Production Code weighed so heavily on the development of these adaptations because the femme-fatale allure of Brigid O'Shaughnessy is central to the novel's narrative. Providing a challenge that would be handled differently in each film, the novel makes it clear that she and Spade sleep together. Early on, she taunts him with the line, "Can I buy you with my body?"[2] Later that night at his apartment, Spade tries to exhaust her store of lies by giving her coffee with brandy in it—the coffee to keep her talking and the brandy to weaken her resolve. Brigid counters his coffee and questions with a passionate kiss, and the chapter ends with Spade seeming to yield to her. "She . . . put her open mouth hard against his mouth, her flat body against his body. Spade's arms went around her, holding her to him, muscles bulging in his blue sleeves, a hand cradling her head, its fingers half lost among her hair, a hand moving groping fingers over her slim back. His eyes burned yellowly."[3] Spade wakes up with Brigid at his side—they have made love between chapters. Spade's relationship with Brigid is bracketed by his affair with Iva Archer, his partner's wife, and accompanied by his affectionate relations with Effie, his secretary. Iva offers a cautionary tale; Brigid poses the central test of Spade's character;

with Effie, Spade maintains a familial and comradely relationship that would be undermined by sex.

Like each of Hammett's novels, *The Maltese Falcon* defines for itself a unique subject of concern. In this case, it is the protagonist's resistance to being taken in by lies, no matter what the temptation. To develop this conceit to its fullest, Hammett folded a tale of adventure into the detective story, opposing the two genres, one that revels in the indulgence of fantasy, the other promoting skepticism of the delusions people fall prey to. On the one hand is the tale of the falcon, fantastic happenings that transpire in exotic locations. On the other hand is the mystery of Archer's murder, introduced by Brigid O'Shaughnessy. Stories of foreign adventure were common in the teens and early twenties, and Gutman's pursuit of the falcon roots itself in the very origins of Orientalist fantasy.[4] Juxtaposed with the adventure plot are Brigid's lies, from her initial claim that her name is Wonderly, later that it is Leblanc, followed by her claim that she and Spade are in love and that he should be willing to risk his security by lying to the police in order to save her—to "play the sap," in his words. Other lies include Iva's suggestion that Spade killed Archer in order to be with her—around which Dundy, the police lieutenant, constructs his own cracked theories—and Spade's various inventions, including his attempt to account for the facts of the case in order to deal with the authorities.

In *The Maltese Falcon,* challenges to Spade's clarity of mind can be described in terms that emphasize either the contest between Spade and Brigid or that between Spade and Gutman. Brigid can be described as merely one of several people assembled by Gutman to pursue the falcon; or Gutman can be understood as just another figure, along with Cairo, Thursby, and Jacobi, dragged into Spade's office by Brigid. Both Gutman and Brigid become Spade's partners and adversaries, as well as partner and adversary of each other. Hammett carefully balances against each other the tests faced by Spade—Brigid with her sexual allure and story of love; Gutman with his eloquence and imagination, his whiskey and promises of wealth. By contrast, each movie was shaped to emphasize only one of these strands: the first two films highlight Brigid, the third Gutman and his fantasy of the jewel-encrusted bird.

All three teams of filmmakers rejected various aspects of the novel, most significantly the Flitcraft anecdote that Spade recounts in chapter 7, the encounter with Gutman's daughter Rhea, and Iva's return at the novel's conclusion. Flitcraft, as Spade recounts, was a man who, after nearly being hit by a falling beam, reassesses his life, leaves his family to start over, then after creating a second family, changes course again to return to his initial home. From a cinematic perspective, there are obvious reasons not to include the tale—it is a long monologue and a digression from the action, and its meaning is ambiguous.[5] Censorship likely prevented the inclusion of both the episode involving Rhea Gutman and Iva Archer's return. The perversity of Gutman's using the "small fair-haired girl" to send Spade on a wild goose chase—drugging her, and having her mutilate herself with "a three-inch jade-headed steel bouquet-pin" to stay awake—would have been unacceptable to censors inside and outside of the industry, as would have been a continuation of the relationship between Spade and his partner's adulterous wife. Rhea is a minor character, easily dispensed with, but reconceiving Hammett's ending significantly undercuts his authorial vision.[6] In but a few lines describing Iva's return and ending with Spade's resigned words, "Well, send her in," Hammett drives home the message that anything promising freedom from the sordid web of the quotidian—whether dreams of wealth, adventure, or love—is unlikely to succeed. It was an idea as unwelcome in Hollywood films of the 1930s and 1940s as the adulterous relationship.

The Maltese Falcon (1931), a.k.a. Dangerous Female

Acquired for $8,500 in June 1930—shortly after publication and long before the resounding success of The Thin Man (1934)—The Maltese Falcon was handled by Warner Bros. with the usual Hollywood disregard for the novelist's ideas. This first version focuses on Ruth Wonderly, with the body of Bebe Daniels and her erotic appeal taking over the film. Sex as an antidote to declining box office was part of an industry-wide strategy as the 1920s passed into the 1930s. It was seen, along with violence, as certain to sell tickets. As Jason Joy, head of the SRC, wrote to Joseph Breen shortly after the release of Dangerous Female and at the end of a year that had seen the release of Little Caesar and The Public Enemy:

> The list of sex pictures we made up while you and the General [Will Hays] were here showed conclusively that we were in for trouble

because of the *number* of such stories. With crime practically denied them, with box office figures down, with high pressure methods being employed back home [in New York] to spur the studios on to get a little more cash, it was almost inevitable that sex, the nearest thing at hand and pretty generally sure fire, should be seized on. It was.[7]

By the standards of the time, *Dangerous Female* was a sex picture, which is reflected in its working title during production, *All Woman,* as well as *Dangerous Female,* appended later for TV release. Even without these explicit titles, however, there can be no confusion about the filmmakers' intentions. The opening scene suggests that Spade (Ricardo Cortez) has just been making love to a client on the floor of his office. He is a womanizer who lives for the moment, shallow and opportunistic. Furthermore, as James Naremore has pointed out, in this film "even Spade's womanizing is treated as little more than an opportunity for some cheerfully randy, pre-Code cheesecake."[8] While Spade's actions continue to dominate the narrative as they do in the novel, in this film his obsession with women, and the focus on Daniels/Wonderly's sexual allure, are such that Gutman's role is minimized.

When Hammett's novel was published by Knopf in February 1930, Warner Bros. was a relatively new studio in the throes of extraordinary expansion.[9] Roy Del Ruth had been a director there since his first feature film in 1925, and Daniels and Cortez were veterans as well. Cortez, born Jacob Krantz and raised in New York, had played in some forty-three films before *The Maltese Falcon,* frequently as the Latin lover, which explained his having changed his Jewish name to a Spanish one. Daniels had begun acting as a child and by age fourteen was hired by Hal Roach to work with Harold Lloyd in the series of Lonesome Luke comedies. More to the point, Daniels's roles had established her as a seductress. At eighteen she was given a part as "The King's Favorite" in Cecil B. DeMille's *Male and Female* (1919). In two other DeMille films—*Why Change Your Wife* (1920) and *The Affairs of Anatol* (1921)—she played, in Eve Golden's words, a "cheap tart" and a "baby vamp" named Satan Synn. Golden writes that although "Bebe was never a sex symbol like Clara Bow," she was "striking rather than beautiful, adept in both comedy and drama."[10] Yet because of an offscreen incident in which she was arrested for speeding and spent ten days in jail, a film was written for her entitled *The Speed Girl* (1921), and her allure was such that she was cast opposite Rudolph Valentino in *Monsieur Beaucaire* (1924). Daniels made some fifty-one films at Paramount between 1919 and 1931, including *My Past* with Del Ruth immediately before *The Maltese Falcon.*[11]

Casting Daniels as Wonderly made the character less mysterious than Hammett's O'Shaughnessy, as did the script. She no longer has several aliases, and she does not change her address after her initial encounter with Spade. When the issue of her duplicity does arise, it is transformed into a question of her appearance: while Spade and the others await the dawn so that Effie can deliver the falcon to them, Spade plays with a card that presents the image of a woman in outline. Shaking it allows the thread of the line drawing on the card's surface to move, changing the contours of the woman's face. Spade compares the image to Wonderly, then shakes the card until he seems satisfied that the new outline resembles her.[12] This focus on Wonderly's visual profile is an extension of the film's accentuating her body as the source of her powers, also found, for example, in the language used toward the end of the film as Spade confronts her about killing Archer. The dialogue in the novel reads, "You could have stood as close to him as you like in the dark and put a hole through him";[13] in *Dangerous Female* Spade says, "Then you could have stood with your body up close against his and he would have grinned from ear to ear." Her body disarms Archer as she would have it disarm Spade.

Daniels's costuming in this film follows this emphasis. Restrictions on costume were included in an outline of what were called "Particular Applications" of the 1930 Production Code, which proscribed the "use of liquor in American life," "adultery and illicit sex," vulgarity, and obscenity. Further specifications included the following:

1. Complete nudity is never permitted. This includes nudity in fact or in silhouette, or any lecherous or licentious notice thereof by other characters in the picture.
2. Undressing scenes should be avoided, and never used save where essential to the plot.
3. Indecent or undue exposure is forbidden.[14]

Yet these points read like a recipe for the film that Roy Del Ruth delivered to Warner Bros. Visually, the central theme became the progressive disrobing of Bebe Daniels—a montage of her dresses is a study of the plunging neckline.

She first appears with a cape-like jacket, a V-neck revealed when the jacket is open. A pendant draws the eye downward in this and in the following scene in her hotel room, where she is costumed in a diaphanous dress with sleeves that open and flow from the elbow. From the waist up, the dress has two layers, a transparent V to the waist superimposed on a visible undergarment cut in a wide V from her shoulders to a spot between her breasts. In this scene, where she is actively working at seducing Spade, she leans toward him, a high camera angle looking down into her dress. She begins her plea with a shake of her breasts to emphasize the word "can't" in the phrase "I *can't* explain," implicitly offering her body in place of the explanation. Spade's praise of her performance—"It's chiefly your eyes, I think"—only emphasizes the real terms of her offer. In the novel and in all of the films, the Wonderly/O'Shaughnessy character gives Spade money at the end of this scene to continue working with or for her. In the novel, O'Shaughnessy gets the money from her bedroom and then, only when Spade asks for the rest of the $500, does she "put her hand inside the neck of her dress and [bring] out a slender roll of bills."[15] In *Dangerous Female*, Wonderly takes the entire $500 from between her breasts. In this film she is also lying to Spade about this being her only money: when he has left—a rare moment with Spade offscreen—she pulls up her dress to reveal her legs and another wad of bills tucked into her stocking, an image that emphasizes the relationship between her body and her deceit.

For the third costume, she appears in a coat with a V-neck, peeling off the coat to reveal a dark dress that has slit openings from the shoulder to the elbow and a wide neckline. A more complicated necklace, emphasizing the new exposure, replaces the simple pendants. From this dress she progresses to a dressing gown, left open to reveal her slip, the final costume of the evening. Morning finds her in Spade's bed, apparently covered only by the sheet, though when she responds to Spade's reentry into the room we see the shoulder straps of her nightgown. When Iva (Thelma Todd) arrives and makes a scene, Wonderly throws off the kimono that Iva has left in Spade's apartment. Next she is seen in the bathtub, apparently naked, hidden from her breasts down by the edge of the tub, a scene

"*I can't* explain" (*The Maltese Falcon*, 1931)

that was at the center of negotiations with the SRC. She is shown to us three times, the last time washing her back with a brush and teasing Spade about having "trouble with your women."

Late in the novel, in Spade's apartment where he forces O'Shaughnessy to strip to be searched for Gutman's $1,000 bill, she is given a line that pushes her sentimental claims on Spade to the limit: "I'm not ashamed to stand naked before you but—can't you see? Not like this. Can't you see that if you make me you'll be—you'll be killing something."[16] There the focus is on Spade's ruthlessness; in *Dangerous Female*, it is on Bebe Daniels's nakedness. Hammett has her undress showing "pride without defiance or embarrassment,"[17] while in the film she is defiant, in the posture of a stripper throwing her gloves at Spade, beginning a recapitulation of the unveiling which is central to the film. Although this scene too was a product of intense negotiating with Jason Joy and the SRC, there are no fewer than five medium-close shots of Bebe Daniels clutching her dark dress to her breast, intercut with the action in the other room as Gutman tells Spade about her past. Wonderly's veiling of her nakedness emphasizes what is left uncovered while inciting a desire to see what is hidden, in counterpoint with

Gutman saying, "Miss Wonderly's admirers have been many, sir, and she has used them all to her great advantage."

The costuming of Thelma Todd as Iva dramatizes Spade's shift of attention from her to Wonderly. At the beginning of the film, Iva, on the phone with Spade, is shown in revealing intimate wear. But she is then covered up as Wonderly is gradually unwrapped, as if the costume of the women is directed by Spade's desire. In the scene where Wonderly appears in Iva's kimono, for example, soon to be seen naked in the tub, Iva arrives wearing a blouse closed tightly at the neck and wearing a helmet-like hat and armor-like cape similar to Wonderly's first outfit. Her line, "Who's that dame wearing my kimono?" underscores the displacement of Iva by Wonderly. By the next-to-last scene of the film, the neckline of Effie (Una Merkel) is also plunging, though hers is bordered by a broad Pierrot collar that underscores her innocence relative to Iva and Wonderly. Effie is young and sexy in this film, contrasting with the dizzy blonde called Miss Murgatroyd (Marie Wilson) in *Satan Met a Lady* and the more matronly Effie (Lee Patrick) in *The Maltese Falcon* (1941). In *Dangerous Female* she is kissed and caressed by Spade between clients and is complicit in arranging his

"Miss Wonderly's admirers have been many, sir" (*The Maltese Falcon*, 1931)

affairs. She tweaks Spade when she announces Joel Cairo as another possible conquest, withholding the fact that Cairo is male while describing the
as yet unseen client as "gorgeous." In fact the women in this film promote a
comfortably permissive environment. Wonderly is untroubled by Iva, Iva is
untroubled by her faithless marriage to Archer, and Effie is untroubled by
any of Spade's liaisons. Until the tacked-on ending, there is little sense of
judgment or disapproval—the world is full of sexual relationships of many
varieties, and Spade is at home in such a world.

Warner Bros.'s negotiations with the SRC over these scenes began with
the screenplay and continued until the release of the film. When Darryl
Zanuck first submitted the script in early 1931,[18] Jason Joy responded with
a list of four Production Code concerns, and four additional suggestions
with an eye on "official censorship," by which he meant state and foreign
censors outside of the industry. These included moments such as Wilmer
deliberately kicking Spade in the head while he is lying on the floor, which
would be cut from this version. With respect to the Code, Joy was concerned with the amount of drinking in the script, and with two scenes that
would remain bones of contention: a line calling for a "sexy shot of the girl
bathing in the tub," and the scene in which Spade forces Wonderly to strip
as he searches her. Of most concern, however, was the handling of Wonderly's spending the night at Spade's apartment: "While we believe the
idea that the girl stays all night with Spade is not objectionable," Joy wrote,
"we feel that the details of the script suggest this too broadly."

Joy suggested that the filmmakers account for Brigid spending the
night in Spade's apartment by showing that she was afraid to leave because
Wilmer, the gunman, was waiting outside; this would be followed by Spade's
lines, "It will be all right, though. You can sleep in the bedroom—I'll spend
the night here on the divan."[19] When the film was made, however, instead
of addressing Joy's complaint, Zanuck and Del Ruth emphasized Wonderly's deliberate seduction of Spade: Wilmer is neither mentioned nor
shown, a series of lines emphasize Wonderly's intentions, and finally, with
Wonderly in her nightgown, Spade dims the lights, they kiss, and the scene
fades to black as the camera focuses on a skipping record that the lovers
ignore. As if to leave no room for misunderstanding, in the morning when
Spade returns from searching Wonderly's apartment, three wide shots allow
us to see her lying in a double bed with the imprint of another head on the

pillow next to hers. If in working around the Production Code, filmmakers tried to maintain a certain deniability with respect to facts unacceptable to the censors, Zanuck and Del Ruth made no such effort.

Joy seems to have reconciled himself eventually to the film's logic of highlighting Bebe Daniels, including the scene of the night spent in Spade's apartment. In an April 7 summary of the completed film for Carl Milikin, secretary of the MPPDA, Joy even takes the trouble to rationalize the film's opening scene, which he describes as establishing how Spade is "absolutely irresistible to women, including his secretary."[20] But Joy was not satisfied with the bathtub shots and the later strip search. About the bathtub scene, created for this film based on the modest phrase in the novel "while she bathed and dressed,"[21] Zanuck responded immediately to Joy, writing, "I wish to advise you that I have complied with this suggestion by FADING OUT sooner on Daniels—not showing her breasts in the tub." Several shots in the release print still show the upper part of her breasts, but the scene fades out as she begins to stand. And rejecting Joy's reading of the later strip scene, Zanuck becomes a logician of deniability, showing the kind of casuistry such negotiations invited. Joy thinks of Daniels as completely naked, Zanuck claims, only because of language in the earlier script, arguing that the strip scene is no longer a problem: "We leave her in her stockings, underwear and brassiere. While we do not see her dressed in this, which would be impossible to photograph because of the censor requirements, we can only assume that she is thusly dressed, because of the fact that she does not take off her stockings, underwear or brassiere. Therefore, she must still have them on."[22]

Joy was not convinced. According to the procedure in place at the time, he requested that Hays convene a jury of studio heads to rule on the film's suitability for release.[23] The fact that Warner Bros. released the film without the changes required by Joy and the jury of studio heads shows the limits of the MPPDA's ability at this time to impose the policy agreed upon by its members. And Joy perceived this instance of rebellion as emblematic—in a letter to Hays on June 9, 1931, his principal point is that Warner Bros.'s ignoring the jury's decision, for whatever reason, "is important for the future development and the security of the system which has been put into effect by the producers in Hollywood."[24] But what the case also shows is how intent the filmmakers and Warner Bros. were—in spite of the pressure from the powerful trade organization—on remaining true to their conception of *Dangerous Female*. In fact, during the negotiations one sees Darryl Zanuck and the filmmakers clarifying and strengthening the film's initial direction.

Since the relationship with Brigid and the sex theme as a frame for showcasing Bebe Daniels entirely dominate, Spade's contest with Gutman is reduced to almost nothing. In fact, this Gutman is not even a worthy opponent—he is so dull-witted that Cairo (Otto Matieson) is made to interrupt Gutman's dialogue, explaining to him that he has no need of Spade. The two adversarial meetings of the novel are telescoped into one, therefore, in which Gutman immediately signals to the Asian butler (uncredited) to drug Spade's drink.

With Gutman's account of the falcon drastically truncated, the film introduces a generalized Chinatown motif. In the novel, the only suggestion of this was a mention of Archer being killed where "Bush Street roofed Stockton before slipping down hill to Chinatown."[25] In the film, however, when Spade arrives at the scene, a lighted sign announcing "Chopsuey" looms in the background. Then, as Spade leaves after speaking with Tom Polhaus (J. Farrell Macdonald), an Asian man (uncredited) speaks to Spade in Chinese from a doorway and Spade answers in the same language. No further reference to this occurs until newspaper accounts are shown on the screen toward the end of the film after Miss Wonderly has been arrested: the article tells us that a man named Lee Fu Gow, a Chinese merchant, the only eyewitness to Wonderly's killing of Archer, was produced by Spade as a surprise witness at her trial. Spade's knowledge of the city and of the Chinese language provides him with a key that he holds throughout the story, though his motivation for withholding it when the police accuse him of killing Thursby is unclear. Significantly, then, rather than being associated entirely with Gutman through his tale and his Asian butler, the "Oriental" references expand into a general characterization of the mystery to be dispelled by the detective. Cairo's homosexuality, in the novel linked to exoticism and transgression, has little echo in this film beyond Spade's repeatedly calling Lieutenant Dundy "sweetheart" as a challenge to his masculinity.

Unique to *Dangerous Female* is the final scene showing Wonderly in jail, where Spade visits her. Ilsa Bick has lucidly described the image of

Wonderly behind bars as part of a pattern of containing the "dangerous female" within the "all-encompassing umbrella of patriarchy and the law," a description accurate in some degree for the novel and at least two of the films.[26] In this version, however, Spade has also accepted employment in the D.A.'s office. Throughout Hammett's writing, legal institutions are compromised—the private detective maintains his integrity by remaining insulated from them, and *Dangerous Female* seems to maintain that position until the final scene. While inconsistent with the rest of the film, Spade's crossing over to join the law has the effect of emphasizing his opportunism. But a more obvious reason for such a last-minute shift in the story is as a gesture to the Hays Office: the fallen woman is punished, the law triumphs, and the D.A.'s office reclaims a rogue investigator. Why, after all, should Warner Bros. resist making the narrative more pleasing to the censors when the story is no more than, in Naremore's phrase, an "opportunity . . . for cheesecake."

Satan Met a Lady (1936)

The second film version of *The Maltese Falcon* seems to have been made in reaction to the first, motivated largely by the climate of stricter Production Code enforcement. Pre-approval of scripts was now required by the PCA under the leadership of Joseph Breen rather than voluntary, and films needed a certificate of approval or they could not be released in theaters owned by member studios of the MPPDA, which is to say the first-run exhibition venues in the United States where most of the money was made. No studio could afford to invest millions of dollars in films that could not be shown. So from the decision to acquire a property until the final cut in the editing room, everyone involved in the filmmaking process was aware of the need to pass through the filter of the PCA. Brigid's nudity and spending the night with Spade had raised red flags in the script for the 1931 film. Brown Holmes, who had worked with Maude Fulton on that screenplay, was fully cognizant of the earlier history as he reworked the same material for what would eventually be titled *Satan Met a Lady*.

Though much of the dialogue, originally from the novel, was used again, and *Satan* retains much of the plot structure from *Dangerous Female* and the novel, the studio went to great lengths to hide this film's origins.

Along with the title, the names of the characters were changed—even the falcon of the novel and first film was replaced by the Horn of Roland, stuffed with jewels by the Saracens who took it from Roland after he fought to prevent them from overrunning Charlemagne's army as it retreated from Spain through the Pyrenees.[27] But the most important distancing of *Satan Met a Lady* from *Dangerous Female* concerns the removal of any focus on the sexuality of Wonderly, now called Valerie Purvis (Bette Davis). After showcasing Wonderly's body in *Dangerous Female*, attention in *Satan* shifts to Purvis's mind—her competition with the detective, now called Ted Shane (Warren William), is now a battle of wits.

As early as 1932 a strategy was being suggested to prevent audiences from being "offended" by the representation of sex: make a joke of it.[28] As Andrew Sarris imagines the development of the screwball cycle, "Frustration arises inevitably from a situation in which the censors have removed the sex from sex comedies. Here we have all these beautiful people with nothing to do. Let us invent some substitutes for sex. The aforementioned wisecracks multiply beyond measure, and when the audience tires of verbal sublimation, the performers do summersaults and pratfalls and funny faces."[29] This describes the transformation of *Dangerous Female* into *Satan Met a Lady*, full of pratfalls, funny faces, and other farcical exaggerations.[30] The script for *Satan Met a Lady* was developed throughout 1935; both its screwball side and the battle of the sexes between Purvis and Shane were also no doubt a response to the box office success of *The Thin Man* the previous year.

At a moment when eroticism was to be removed from the story in favor of wit and spirit, Bette Davis must have seemed a logical casting choice to Zanuck and Jack Warner. From the beginning of her career— according to Hollywood folklore—she had been considered ugly in contrast to the typical screen beauty, and whatever sexual heat Davis was able to generate derived more from a portrayal of passion than from her appearance. On the set of *Cabin in the Cotton* (1932), in which she showed a seductiveness that would become an important part of her screen persona, the film's director Michael Curtiz reportedly described her within earshot as a "no good sexless son of a bitch," which gives a sense of the image against which she was struggling.[31] Davis achieved recognition in the role of Mildred in *Of Human Bondage* (1934) and even an Academy Award the following

year, and so resisted the role of Purvis, feigning illness until a studio sus-
pension forced her to appear on the set.[32] And to the end of her career
she considered *Satan Met a Lady* among her worst films. Yet one reason
beyond the script for Davis's resistance was most likely the casting of Warren William in the role of her lover/competitor. Lawrence Quirk describes
their interaction in the making of an earlier film, *The Dark Horse* (Alfred E.
Green, 1932):

> Davis was having problems with Warren William, a notorious ladies'
> man who reportedly had an erection ninety percent of the time and
> had to wear a special crotch support to disguise the fact—not always
> successfully. She had dodged all his passes all through *The Dark Horse,*
> and then, to her horror, found that Warners expected her to go to
> New York with William on a personal appearance tour. She suspected
> that Zanuck had cooked this up as a favor to William, who was his
> friendly rival in the cocksmanship sweepstakes. . . . "If William has the
> hots for the dame. I'll make it easy for him," he told Alfred Green.[33]

According to Quirk, William dreamed up a sketch that Warner approved
for Davis to perform with him before a screening at New York's Capital
Theatre. Afterward, back at their hotel, "Davis heard the patter of little
feet . . . and heard the inimitable sexy Warren voice calling out 'Room
service!'" Davis telephoned her fiancé, telling him she was in "imminent
danger of being raped," after which he called and threatened William, who
finally desisted in his pursuit of Davis.[34] If the anecdote helps to explain
Davis's resistance to the role, it also suggests a secondary motive for the
decision to cast Davis as Valerie Purvis—the story of the film re-creates William's relentless pursuit of Davis during the two films they had previously
made together (the other was a promotional short, *Just Around the Corner,*
1933). William's returning to scratch at her hotel room door is reenacted
onscreen, and one reading of this film is as an inside joke for Jack Warner
and others at the studio familiar with the earlier occurrences.

Beyond references to offscreen Hollywood lust, however, *Satan Met a
Lady* remains fundamentally a film shaped by the addition of wisecracks
and pratfalls in place of erotic seduction. There are four key moments in
the novel that a director with his mind on the erotic might exploit: Spade's
first encounter with O'Shaughnessy in her rooms; the night spent together

in Spade's apartment; the morning following their night together; and the strip scene after she is accused by Gutman of taking the $1,000 bill. In sharp contrast to *Dangerous Female,* none of these are used in *Satan Met a Lady* to emphasize Purvis's sexuality. The encounter between Purvis and Shane in her rooms focuses on her wit and skill as a pickpocket. The suggestion of their spending the night together is turned into broad comedy with Shane caricatured as "King Kong"; no motive except sex explains his return to her door, yet the scene is located in Purvis's rooms rather than in Shane's apartment—the scene lampoons his male animal dominance, emphasizing Davis's power to admit or reject him rather than what might take place in her bedroom. There is no morning-after scene to confirm that he stayed the night, and the fourth opportunity for eroticism, the strip scene, is also eliminated.[35]

As a battle of wits, the competition between Shane and Purvis is fully engaged when he goes to her hotel to see what she knows about the death of his partner—named Milton Ames in this version—a key scene in Hammett's novel and in all three films. Where in *Dangerous Female* it had emphasized Bebe Daniels's physical attributes, here it plays out as a chess game. Surprised as she is hurriedly leaving, Purvis at first pretends not to know that Ames is dead, then claims she is moving out of the hotel because the house detective has been forcing his intentions on her. At her new rooms, Shane's first move is to look in Purvis's purse, taking a gun he discovers there as well as money, as we will later learn. The camera frames him in a medium shot while he puts the gun in his pocket, then cuts to a shot of Purvis at the vanity mirror in her bedroom: in the glass we see her face and through the open door Shane, whom she is watching as he robs her. She tells Shane that Farrow was supposed to be helping her, but she won't say how. Shane threatens her with the police, and she keeps him from leaving by standing close to him, touching him with her hands. We know she is making an impression, because even though he keeps questioning her, he interjects in a voice that expresses his feeling: "You really do look gorgeous." Yet this moment of physical contact is unusual, and Davis's costumes, unlike those of Bebe Daniels in the earlier film, entirely hide her body. Where Bebe Daniels seemed to offer her body as the reward for Spade's assistance, the scene here remains a duel of wits between con artists. When Shane again prepares to leave, Purvis offers to hire him and looks for money in her purse. She pretends to be surprised that the money is missing, and he admits with an air of triumph to have taken it. She then turns the tables, however, by showing that she has picked his pocket of both the money and her gun. She has won the first round.

In the second major encounter, Purvis surprises Shane in her apartment when he thought a telephone call from Murgatroyd had lured her away. Pointing a gun at him, Purvis has him put his hands above his head so that she can frisk him. Shane playfully swings from the door jamb, and Purvis jokingly calls him "King Kong." As Murgatroyd tells him on the phone, "I guess Little Miss Innocence didn't fall for the mastermind's tricks." But he answers that she should not worry: "No woman ever made a chump out of Papa Shane." The competition continues until he shows he is more interested in the valuable Horn of Roland than in Purvis—she goes into her room, shuts the door, and he starts to leave. But he returns to scratch on her bedroom door, and when she asks who it is, he answers, "King Kong." Fade to black. This is the night they spend together, but for this film it transpires in her apartment, the decision to admit him is entirely hers, and she yields no ground in their struggle.

Deceptions (*Satan Met a Lady*, 1936)

The final scene of the film confirms the reversal of power from *The Maltese Falcon* and *Dangerous Female*. After a shootout, Purvis manages to escape in Shane's car; then, on a train headed north—in an ending to match the arrival scene at the beginning of the film—he forces her to admit that she shot Ames. But Shane's goal is now the reward of $10,000 that he will get for turning in Purvis to the police. Once again, she outwits him. Overhearing him talking with the police, she manages to have an African American maid employed by the railroad company bring her to the police so that the maid, rather than Shane, can claim the reward. After Shane's line, "I won't play the sap for you," Purvis delivers her summation: "But for me you'll go through something that will be worse than death. Because you'll always remember me, the one woman you couldn't take for both love and money. The one woman who handed you double-cross for double-cross right up to the end. 'Cause now you found a woman can be as smart as you are. Someday you'll find one who'll be smarter. She'll marry you!" Even though Shane has had Purvis arrested, he cannot win, which is the final word in this film. Murgatroyd steps forward to accompany Shane on a holiday—she appears to be the "smarter" woman taking possession of Shane, like Iva Archer's return at the end of the novel, but in a very different key.

The extent of the dominance of the film by the women is evident in the transformation of the Gutman figure into Madame Barabbas, and her role underscores the emphasis in the film on intelligence rather than on physical beauty. When Shane is taken to see the master criminal, he immediately says he knows that "we're after something really big," emphasizing the magnitude of her reputation. "So, you recognize me," she says. To which he replies, "It's a face that haunts every detective and copper in the world, in his worst nightmares." The "only sort of compliment this old physiognomy deserves," she responds. Like his relationship with Purvis, Shane's interaction with Madame Barabbas is a battle of wits and, in essence, Hammett's two tests of the detective, represented respectively by Gutman and O'Shaughnessy, have been merged into one—as a competition between one man and various clever women.

However transformed this version of the novel, Purvis still ends up in jail, though she will not be shown there, and the apparent feminism of her character is hedged by the emphasis on marriage in her closing line, that a "smarter" woman will marry Shane. In fact, all of Purvis's resistance to

"This old physiognomy" (*Satan Met a Lady*, 1936)

Shane is explicitly displayed within the patriarchal social framework that film scholar Ilsa Bick has described so well. Shane's libertinism is given an exaggeratedly paternal or patriarchal spin. In the opening scene, where he is being put on the train by some town officials, Shane is misidentified by photographers as the father of sextuplets who is also on the train; this suggests momentarily to the audience that Shane is being run out of town for his sexual potency. Throughout the film he calls himself "Papa Shane," and as the representative of patriarchy he competes with a committee of "City Fathers," who in a late scene pay a visit to Shane and threaten him. Thus "Papa Shane" is faced off against "City Papa," as he addresses one of the men. Murgatroyd, after showing them out, tells Shane she hopes he's "not going to become a father," and he is, effectively, rendered impotent in his standoff with Purvis. Shane's final partner in the film, Murgatroyd, seems entirely infantile. In the framework of screwball comedy, nothing escapes absurdity—if the triumphant woman must pretend to be a child, patriarchy is emphasized only to be discredited.

    This film does not restrict itself to Shane's point of view, a shift related to the screwball tone that transcends Shane's—and any individual character's—mindset. Thus we see Travers search Shane's rooms when he is absent, slashing all the furniture with an enormous knife, this exaggeration a running joke evoked by a similar destruction in Shane's office, and again when Shane takes a knife to Purvis's sofa. Further distancing the narration from Spade/Shane's perspective, an odd graphic display is inserted after Madame Barabbas offers Shane money for the Horn of Roland: an image of a Sunday magazine supplement fills the screen with images of Roland and a hunting horn under the headline, "The Trumpet Calls—and only unto death." Below Roland, after a one-sentence summary of the story of the jeweled horn, another headline announces, "These have died," with four pictures labeled respectively "a vampire," "a prince," "a pawnbroker," and "an international thief." These are followed by the question: "Who will be next?" and elaborately framed pictures of Purvis, Barabbas, and Travers are shown, with a large question mark in the otherwise empty fourth frame, suggesting that one of the three is the next likely victim. This graphic seems to exist in an uncomfortable limbo between public awareness of the crimes within the story and the filmmakers' narration. Shane—like Nick Charles in *The Thin Man*—has achieved a tabloid celebrity, but this summary seems aimed more directly at the audience, a rhetorical tactic to reframe the story as it moves toward a climax.

The Maltese Falcon (1941)

If *Dangerous Woman* and *Satan Met a Lady* were developed around their differing constructions of the detective's female adversary, *The Maltese Falcon* (1941) is dedicated to Sam Spade, especially in relation to Gutman and the other male characters. Beyond the novel's suitability to the national mood of 1941, John Huston and the film's casting—especially of Humphrey Bogart—are the principal factors that shaped the film. But first came Huston's interest in making a third film version of *The Maltese Falcon*, for the side of the novel that appealed to him was underrepresented in the earlier films. "Huston was known as a 'man's man,'" writes William Luhr, "and he probably worked with more male action stars than any other director."[36] In James Agee's words, Huston was "leery of emotion—of the 'feminine' aspects of art,"[37] a description that might be applied equally to Hammett, even from *The Glass Key* on, where women characters are accorded more agency. And Huston no doubt responded to the fact that Spade's point of view dominates the narration. Then, to play Sam Spade, Huston found an extraordinary interpreter in Bogart, who would become the preeminent male star of the 1940s, an important model of masculinity for the era. In all, Bogart played the male protagonist in six of Huston's films between 1941 and 1953. *The Maltese Falcon* is among the most important for both men's careers, and, in part because of his association with them, for Hammett's as well.

Huston became known for making films from literary texts,[38] and this, his first film as director, was his most direct transposition. William Nolan presents one version of an oft-repeated anecdote: "Huston gave the book to his secretary and told her to recopy the printed text, breaking it down into shots, scenes, and dialogue. A copy of this fell into the hands of Jack Warner, and he thought that Huston had adapted the Hammett story into a final screenplay. 'I just read it and it's great,' Warner told him. 'You've really captured the flavor of this book. Now go shoot it with my blessing.'"[39] If Nolan's account is marked by a conversational vagueness, the extent to which the film's plot and dialogue follow the book lends it credence.

The Maltese Falcon, Huston's first film as director, leans heavily on Hammett's story and dialogue, but it also depends for its success on Bogart's performance, and on the supporting cast of Mary Astor, Sydney Greenstreet, Peter Lorre, and Elisha Cook Jr. Huston grew up watching his famous father, the actor Walter Huston, give voice to ideas in the cogent sentences of literary works. In one interview, he even traces his impulse to direct films to watching his father at work: "I would attend rehearsals of plays he was doing and I'd see what he would do with a scene. It was mostly his creation of a role, how he went at it, that was a lead into direction."[40] About working with actors, Huston invariably makes the same two claims: the key moment of directing a film is the casting; once selected, actors are best given a clear sense of the character they are playing and then allowed to work without undue interference from the director. "I choose an actor for his kinship to a role. I cast personalities rather than actors,"[41] he once said. And, "in a given scene, I have an idea what should happen, but I try not to tell the actors. I think they should follow their own hunches. I just tell them to do it their own way, and sometimes they improve on it, add something by accident."[42] Acting and theater are referenced throughout

The Maltese Falcon (1941), most obviously in the closing line echoing Shakespeare's *The Tempest*, but also in Spade's critiques of O'Shaughnessy's dissimulations as performances, and when he smiles after breaking off the first meeting with Gutman, apparently in anger.

The importance of the film's casting has been widely recognized. As Bosley Crowther in his review for the *New York Times* wrote, "Sydney Greenstreet, from the theatre guild's roster, is magnificent as a cultivated English crook, and Peter Lorre, Elisha Cook Jr., Lee Patrick, and Barton MacLane all contribute stunning characters."[43] Casper Gutman was Greenstreet's first movie role, but Peter Lorre would have been known to filmgoers from the Hitchcock films *The Man Who Knew Too Much* (1934) and *The Secret Agent* (1936), as well as from his eight appearances between 1937 and 1939 as Mr. Moto. Thus Peter Lorre brought to Joel Cairo a screen persona grounded in his abilities to convey the sinister, the exotic, and, above all, the comic. But as James Naremore pointed out, Huston's "casting against type" was also among the most important alterations in an otherwise famously "faithful" adaptation[44]—Naremore particularly emphasizes the extent to which Bogart does not resemble Hammett's Spade, who in the book is described as a "blond Satan."

Mary Astor, an established star, defines Brigid O'Shaughnessy through a reserved performance, in marked contrast to those of Bebe Daniels and Bette Davis. One of Astor's recent roles had been opposite Davis in *The Great Lie* (Edmund Goulding, 1941), an implausible story about a high-living concert pianist named Sandra Kovac (Astor) who gets pregnant during a brief affair but who gives up the child to another woman (Davis) until she thinks she can use the child to win back Davis's husband, the child's father.[45] Astor would win an Oscar for Best Supporting Actress for her role in the film, which was released a few months before *The Maltese Falcon*. Audiences seeing both films might have felt that the character of Kovac perfectly represented the side of Brigid that remained hidden in *The Maltese Falcon*. Bosley Crowther found Astor's performance as Brigid "well-nigh perfect as the beautiful woman whose cupidity is forever to be suspect."[46]

Bogart, however, dominates *The Maltese Falcon*, and indeed, in a film told from his character's perspective, is onscreen in every scene. He had already achieved some recognition as Duke Mantee in *The Petrified Forest*, first on Broadway, then—when Edward G. Robinson lost the part by holding

Sam Spade (*The Maltese Falcon*, 1941)

out for top billing with Leslie Howard—in the 1936 film. Yet Warner Bros. continued to consider him, as Stefan Kanfer writes, "a journeyman . . . decently salaried but never a star,"[47] so that he appeared in secondary roles in twenty-four films before his 1941 breakthrough with *High Sierra* and *The Maltese Falcon*. In *Angels with Dirty Faces* (Michael Curtiz, 1938), Bogart played Jim Frazier, a cowardly, dishonest lawyer whom Rocky Sullivan (James Cagney) kills to protect his childhood friend, a crusading priest. In *The Roaring Twenties* (Raoul Walsh, 1939), he is George Hally, who betrays his partner Eddie Bartlett (Cagney) in the bootlegging business, the film highlighting Hally's weakness and dishonesty. In *They Drive by Night* (Walsh, 1940), Bogart plays Paul Fabrini, the weaker brother of Joe (George Raft). These roles include fear, indecision, and cowardice that can be read into his later characters as unexpressed vulnerabilities, human weaknesses for him to rise above.

The success of *The Maltese Falcon* confirmed for the public Bogart's promise in *High Sierra*. But his "sudden rise in status" also depended, as Robert Sklar argues, on "the continuing impact of *The Maltese Falcon* on the nation's reviewers." In Sklar's words:

Following its initial release in October 1941, the picture was opening in a second tier of cities in December, and in such places as
Baltimore and Dallas the praise for Bogart was more striking than
ever. John Rosenfield in the *Dallas Morning News*, for example, called
Bogart's Sam Spade "one of the more elegant performances of his
eminent career." . . . Each new batch of reviews confirmed what
any open eye could see: Bogart's doubleness, his hardness and his
humor, his ambiguity, leaving the spectator in doubt until the very
end, his sudden, powerful bursts of temper.[48]

Hal Wallis finally understood Bogart's value apparently—he quickly assigned
Bogart to *Across the Pacific* (1942), directed by Huston, and to *Casablanca* (1943).

As a beginning director, Huston sketched out the scenes as he
wanted to film them, sharing his drawings with veteran William Wyler,
who had no official role in the film's production, to be certain that the
shots would work.[49] Huston's cinematographer was Arthur Edeson, whose
nearly thirty years' experience included *All Quiet on the Western Front*
(Lewis Milestone, 1930) and *Frankenstein* (James Whale, 1931), as well as
Red Dust (Victor Fleming, 1932) with Mary Astor, *Satan Met a Lady,* and *They
Drive by Night* with Bogart. Robert Haas, the art director, created a set with
echoes of his work on *Dangerous Female* ten years earlier.

As we could expect from Huston as a "man's man," this version of *The
Maltese Falcon* amplifies the role of Casper Gutman and—in Huston's direct
reliance on the novel—the drinking motif important in Hammett's writing, both aspects that were reduced in the previous two film versions. The
sensual power of Brigid O'Shaughnessy, on the other hand, is suppressed
in Spade's contest with her. In this respect, the goals of the film worked in
harmony with those of Joseph Breen and the Production Code, as had the
screwball direction of *Satan Met a Lady;* by 1941 there was a loosening of
the constraints on ideas, but sex remained as rigidly restricted as in 1934.
In this film, even jokes about sex are absent. The idea of O'Shaughnessy's
physical attractiveness remains important—Effie describes her as a "knock-
out" and Archer offers his silent wolf whistle before following Brigid up a
dark alley to his death. But modesty and feigned respectability dominate
Astor's performance, even when she admits to having been "bad." Rather
than strip O'Shaughnessy in this film, Spade simply accepts her word that

she has not taken Gutman's $1,000 bill—Jason Joy's suggestion for dealing with the scene back when *Dangerous Female* was being developed.[50]

Spade claims at the end of the film that "all of him" wants to ignore his common sense and "play the sap" for her, but the vague motive cited is "love," with little evidence of sexual desire. Brigid's costumes are all designed to conceal: a blouse open only to the first button and covered by a jacket, a dressing gown with heavily padded shoulders that covers her from head to toe, a dress clasped near the throat. There is only one loosening of this protective cover, when she physically attacks Joel Cairo. After she and Cairo have been separated, she carefully pulls up a zipper that had slipped a few centimeters down from her throat. Brigid's costume during the final scenes conceals her more than ever, behind a blouse with an abundance of ruffles in front like some kind of chest protector. Her costumes throughout the film reinforce her role as someone who can never be open or transparent, rather emphasizing good taste and a feigned middle-class decency. The fact that Spade too is only pretending to have completely fallen for O'Shaughnessy further removes any idea of a romance developing between them.

In this film, because of the intervention of Breen, there is even considerable ambiguity as to whether Brigid and Spade have sex. In Spade's apartment, Spade makes the coffee while Brigid tries out versions of her story, and she soon lies back so that Bogart can kneel and kiss her. As in the novel and the previous two films, this is the moment that should lead to the bedroom. But as early as the first assessment of Huston's "temporary" script in a letter dated May 23, 1941, Breen wrote that "the fade-out of Spade and Brigid is unacceptable because of a definite indication of an illicit sex affair. There must be no indication that Brigid and Spade are spending the night together in Spade's apartment. Otherwise it cannot be approved in the finished picture."[51] Four days later, after reviewing pages of changes, Breen repeated his warning and added as a note to page sixty-seven: "This fade-out on Brigit is still indicative of an illicit sex affair, which could not be approved in the finished picture. Some other business must be substituted, in order to make the story conform with the provisions of the Production Code."[52]

The result is evident in the film: just as Bogart's lips are about to touch Brigid's, his eye is drawn to a moving window curtain and through the open window he sees Wilmer (Elisha Cook Jr.) in the street below. In the novel, Spade is deliberately lying to Brigid when he tells her that Wilmer is still there. Here, the camera lingers on Wilmer until the screen fades to black.

The consequence is that this sequence of shots poses difficulties of interpretation: after being momentarily distracted, will Spade lead Brigid to bed? The blowing curtains suggest a cinematic convention for sex that cannot be shown, but Spade's movement is away from the kiss, toward the gunman. In fact it leads us away from the sexual contest with Brigid and back toward the wider mystery plot and Gutman. The irresolution of the scene is so awkward that it suggests the adjustments to address Breen's demands were made, late in the process, in the editing room. It is likely that informal meetings took place at that time between representatives of Jack Warner and Breen or his staff. The film was finished in July 1941 and, as we can see—in contrast to the release of the 1931 film disregarding the MPPDA mandate—Breen had his way. Jack Warner was notified of the film's certificate of approval, number 7457, on August 18.[53]

Beyond the fadeout, since there is no morning-after scene in this version of *The Maltese Falcon,* we hurry forward in the story, as if, with or without sex, the relationship between Spade and Brigid is the same. Yet this suppression of her sexuality and persisting doubt about Brigid's true identity exhibit a pattern identified by feminist critics as frequent in film noir. In the words of Mary Ann Doane, "The femme fatale is situated as evil and is frequently punished or killed. Her textual eradication involves a desperate reassertion of control on the part of the threatened male subject."[54] The parallel here between the noir strategy of "eradicating" the dangerous female and the actions of the PCA lays bare the relationship of its politics to the malaise of threatened patriarchy.

Eliminating Brigid as a physical presence in the mold of Bebe Daniels or as a combative intelligence as played by Bette Davis conversely strengthens the idea of her as fundamentally unknowable, a mystery related to others such as the story of the falcon. In fact, the renewed prominence of the Orientalist fantasy and of Gutman's role in this film is announced by the fact that before everything else, especially before the introduction of O'Shaughnessy and her first lie, the story of the falcon is scrolled up the screen to be firmly established as a framework of reference. This opening statement is matched to the film's final line of dialogue in which the counterfeit falcon, made of lead instead of being encrusted with jewels, is described as "the stuff that dreams are made of," a line which according to various accounts was suggested by Bogart when Huston was not satisfied with Hammett's return of Iva for closure of the narrative.[55]

In conjunction with the emphasis on Gutman and the falcon, if the film goes further than the novel in suppressing sex, it follows the book closely in using alcohol to measure and represent the competition between the adversaries. Reflexively, Breen—as he and Joy had with respect to *Satan Met a Lady*—again complained to Jack Warner about the drinking in the script. He cites at least seven different instances in the "temporary" script and mentions among his three overarching points about the "final" script that "there is a great deal of unnecessary drinking."[56] After the corrections reviewed on June 1, only a few instances are cited. But a principal reason that so much drinking remains in the story is no doubt that in this version, Spade's primary struggle to maintain his independence and self-dominance plays itself out among men. As sex mediates competition between men and women, drink is central to the ritual mediating rivalries among men.

In Spade's relationship with Polhaus and Dundy, for example, having a drink marks an understanding between them. Once Spade understands that Polhaus and Dundy have reasons for suspecting him, he offers them a drink in order to demonstrate his acceptance of their justifiable behavior. Polhaus, a closer acquaintance, accepts without reserve; Dundy accepts grudgingly—the ritual can barely varnish over the adversarial relationship. But it is in the two scenes between Spade and Gutman that we see not only Hammett's careful calibration of the drinking with the competition between the men, but also Huston's method of using the detail of Hammett's novel. When they first meet, Gutman leads Spade directly to the whiskey and praises him for being unafraid to drink during this type of confrontation: "I distrust a man that says when. If he's got to be careful not to drink too much, it's because he's not to be trusted when he does."[57] Thus, Gutman labels alcohol as a dangerous substance for a man with secrets. Following this there is an obsessive focus on their whiskey glasses—the word "glass" is used more than a dozen times in the first encounter alone, and Spade is described as actually bowing over his glass. The emptiness of Spade's glass in the first encounter becomes a metaphor for Spade's being empty of the information Gutman wants. In the second encounter, Gutman empties himself, pouring out his story of the falcon, then refilling his glass as a way of refueling so that he can continue to spin out his tale: drink enables both Gutman's telling and his belief in the fantastic story. Just at the moment that Gutman fills Spade's glass, Hammett has Gutman say, "You begin to believe me a little?"[58] The whiskey will help Spade to believe. At one point drink is even referred to as "nourishment"; it nourishes Gutman's dreams and his "talk." Twice drink appears as medicine: during the first encounter Gutman says, "This kind of medicine will never hurt you";[59] in the second encounter, of course, Gutman drugs Spade's drink in order to deliver the medicine that will hurt him. In these scenes drinking is ostensibly an opportunity for bonding, a gesture of trust or agreement bordering on a seduction; to break off the first meeting, therefore, after mocking Gutman's toast to "plain speaking and clear understanding,"[60] Spade throws down his glass, shattering both it and the bond of which drinking is a part. In the second encounter, Gutman stops the conversation by putting the bottle on the table with a "bang." This confrontation is a more subtle and sophisticated version of the "drinking contest pure and simple" from "The Golden Horseshoe" (see chapter 2), both part of the faceoff and a way of indexing the strength of the adversaries.

As in the novel, in Huston's film Gutman leads Spade to the drink, and praises him for being unafraid that the whiskey will influence what he says. Replacing Hammett's verbal emphasis on the glasses, the mise-en-scène foregrounds the table with bottle, glasses, and siphon, like an altar in the center of the room. Appropriately it stands between the characters in most shots. As in the novel, the action underscores the thematic use of drink: the timing of Gutman's pouring whiskey and drinking from his own glass is coordinated with Gutman's narrative. When they reach a standoff, Spade shatters his glass to break off the dialogue as in the novel. And in the second meeting, again as in the novel, Gutman refills Spade's glass after his story reaches the point where the falcon is in the hands of the Greek Charilaos Konstantinides. "No thickness of enamel could conceal the value from his eyes and nose," says Gutman in the novel.[61] His speculation on how the Greek might have thought to get the most money for the falcon is eliminated for the film. But as Gutman finishes his sentence, he stands to refill their glasses, and precisely as in the novel asks,

"You begin to believe me a little?" The coincidence of filling the glass and asking this question emphasizes the role of the whiskey in helping Spade to believe the wild tale. Yet as in the book, Gutman's smooth performance covers his deeper scheme. Gutman is taking his time and watching with great interest to see exactly when the drugged drink he has given Spade will take effect.

Added to the standoff in the film is further visual commentary. While Spade and Gutman perform the drinking ritual, the phallic nature of their competition is underscored visually: in two-shots where the men face each other, the siphon is repeatedly positioned to stick up directly in front of Sydney Greenstreet, echoed by a similarly phallic cigar in front of Bogart. For the second meeting the camera films the men from the opposite side, but the use of siphon and cigars is repeated. While drink and the masculine Spade/Gutman competition were played down in the first two films—*Satan* even transposing the Gutman figure into Madame Barabbas—here, to some extent as in the novel, the sexual theme is displaced onto the relations among the men. Thus, once the femme fatale has been stripped of her sexuality, a detail such as the mention of Cairo and Brigid's past competition for the affections of a boy in Istanbul gains significance; it reenacts the idea of her reduced sexual power as well as its displacement to the men. Thomas Leitch has described how beyond the femme fatale in films such as *The Maltese Falcon* (1941), "the private eye's manliness must constantly be confirmed through conflicts with asexual or bisexual characters—or, far more often, with female or gay male characters—whom the film leaves demystified, disempowered, defeated and dehumanized."[62] Cairo and Wilmer—whom Gutman loves "almost as if he were his own son"—are humiliated; in spite of his sophisticated seduction of Spade, Gutman, when the falcon turns out to be made of lead, is proven to be a fool.

As to the phallic iconography in the drinking scenes between Gutman and Spade, does it represent what separates them or what draws them together? The question is in some degree beside the point, in that sex of any kind, for Huston as for Hammett, must be managed as a threat to clearheadedness and self-possession. In the wide spectrum of men in the film, only those who stay clear of sex survive, Spade through his own peculiar strength of character, Polhaus and Dundy through their allegiance to social law as embodied in the police department. Gutman is Spade's principal

Phallic confrontation (*The Maltese Falcon*, 1941)

adversary in this film, and if the challenge for the detective is to resist Gutman's fantasy of exotic luxury, in the process fending off or enduring the weakening influences of sex and drink, Greenstreet's Gutman embodies complete surrender to such luxury. He has given his life over to unrestrained indulgence in every area: an obsessive pursuit of money, acceptance of baroque fantasies and fictions over reason, physical indulgence in the luxury of his accommodations, clothing, food, drink, cigars, and, apparently, sex.

Huston's favoring of writerly texts and his emphasis on actors and their performances converge in the final confrontation between Spade and O'Shaughnessy, in which Bogart recites Spade's speech from the novel explaining why he will not "play the sap" for Brigid. Although he has delivered other set-piece monologues, such as those to Dundy and to the district attorney, this one is the longest and is meant as a summation that will allow the audience to resolve questions about Spade's character. He is, finally and fundamentally, honest. And just as he has not been taken in by Gutman's dream, refusing to believe it fully until he sees the bejeweled falcon with his own eyes, he will not be blinded by "love." Huston's script for this culminating moment lifts long passages verbatim from the novel and includes others with minor editing: "Listen," says Spade. "This won't do any good. You'll never understand me, but I'll try once and then give it up. When a man's partner is killed he's supposed to do something about it. It doesn't make any difference what you thought of him. He was your partner and you're supposed to do something about it. Then it happens we were in the detective business. Well, when one of your organization gets killed it's bad for business to let the killer get away with it. It's bad all around, bad for every detective everywhere."[63] Bogart delivers these now famous lines as if in a trance, the camera alternately showing him head-on and in profile to catch Astor in the background watching fearfully. A moment later he stands, and as in the novel takes her by the shoulders for the final statement: "If all I've said doesn't mean anything to you, then forget it and we'll make it just this: I won't because all of me wants to, regardless of con-sequences, and because you've counted on that with me the same as you counted on that with all the others."[64] Bogart/Spade's monologue goes on for a long four minutes, its theatricality emphasizing his lack of connec-tion with Astor/O'Shaughnessy.

But this exacerbates the audience's sense that the film has presented little or no evidence of love, or—discouraged by Breen—sexual excite-ment, to the point that today's undergraduates not steeped in the lore of Hammett, Bogart, Huston, and film noir react dismissively, finding this performed absence of a connection between Spade and O'Shaughnessy unsatisfying. Furthermore, theirs seems to be in some degree a gendered response: if Gaylyn Studlar could argue that male critics slighted Huston because his "anxious vision" of masculinity emphasizes failed undertak-ings, responses to the film articulated by students in this instance echo James Agee's observation that Huston is "leery of emotion."[65] Inadver-tently, Huston's emphasis on the text, on the actor, and on the man is yet another way to carry out the process of eradicating the femme fatale in conjunction with O'Shaughnessy's being ushered out the door to jail and, perhaps, execution.

As William Luhr has written, "*The Maltese Falcon* would forever be seen as the turning point in both Huston's and Bogart's careers: before it, they were minor figures in Hollywood; after it, they became industry legends."[66] Their working together produces a synergy, the celebrity of each continu-ing to bolster that of his partner in the body of work their reputations is

"I won't because all of me wants to" (*The Maltese Falcon*, 1941)

based on. This mutually sustaining interplay of reputations includes Hammett to some extent. Just as Hammett's biographical persona and those of the Op and Sam Spade bled together in public perception, Sam Spade in turn infused the Bogart persona, an amalgam of Spade, Rick Blaine from *Casablanca*, Philip Marlowe from *The Big Sleep* (Howard Hawks, 1946), and others. This constellation of star images, overflowing the boundaries of Hammett's, Bogart's, and Huston's individual profiles, moved forward through popular culture of the 1950s and 1960s, part of the intellectual environment of many who came of age in that era.

6

Ethnic Politics

The Glass Key (1935 and 1942)

The films based on *The Glass Key* bear the imprint of industry censorship at least as much as those from *The Maltese Falcon*, though the objectionable content in this novel was political rather than sexual. The direction the *Glass Key* films would take was set from early on—in March 1931, almost a year before U.S. publication—when the book was reviewed by Jason Joy for the Studio Reslations Committee (SRC). Joy identified the principal challenge of *The Glass Key* as having a story too "mixed up with the politics and administration of municipal and State government,"[1] and in a meeting between Joy and the authors of a first treatment, Lloyd Sheldon and Bartlett Cormack, the "elements involving the municipal and State office holders were eliminated."[2] The full screenplay by Kathryn Scola and Kubec Glasmon for the 1935 film, while very different from that early treatment, followed Joy's recommendations. "By looking over the file," a 1934 review of the screenplay under Joseph Breen states, "you will see that they have gone a long way themselves to change the picture from the condition which earned Col. Joy's condemnation three years ago."[3] Yet the politics and social underpinnings of city government were as important to the novel as the love triangle among Ned Beaumont, Paul Madvig, and Janet Henry. In fact, the characters only gain meaning through their class and political affiliations. Without the political context, an entirely new sense of purpose would have to be invented for the films. Thus in the 1935 film Paul Madvig's "big heart" would become central to the narrative, as well as Beaumont's willingness to defend him because of the love he inspires. The 1942 film, while restoring some detail from Hammett's novel, would emphasize the love story between Beaumont and Janet Henry, pursuing the studio's goal of establishing Alan Ladd and Veronica Lake as a romantic screen couple.

The Glass Key was the culmination of a thee-year burst of activity between 1927 and 1930 that produced all of Hammett's novels except for *The Thin Man*. He had just finished six months of steady employment writing advertising copy for Albert S. Samuels's jewelry business, a job that ended suddenly on July 20, 1926, when he collapsed after hemorrhaging from the lungs. Richard Layman describes the remarkable turn that followed Hammett's recovery: "In those three years he wrote nearly sixty book reviews, two novelettes, and four stories in addition to four novels, of which three—*Red Harvest, The Maltese Falcon*, and *The Glass Key*—rank among the best detective fiction ever written by an American."[4] There are readers, reviewers, and critics who have preferred *The Maltese Falcon*—Dorothy Parker among them—but from the beginning there have also been those who, along with Hammett, considered *The Glass Key* his best novel. He had long looked down on the murder mysteries he produced for pulp magazines, aspiring to write what he saw as a higher form of literature. The more complete social context of *The Glass Key* was a further step in that direction.

Machine politics was hardly fresh material in March 1930 when *The Glass Key*—set in an unnamed city frequently assumed to be Hammett's native Baltimore—began to appear in *Black Mask*. The machine and the political boss had arisen in the mid-nineteenth century to fill a power vacuum during a period of explosive urban growth. In the absence of government-run social services, bosses and their political organizations were able to respond to and exploit the needs of the immigrants whose background and situation made them receptive to the personal style of the bosses and their representatives. Wielding the voting power of large immigrant communities on the one hand and the power of patronage on the other, the boss profited from his role as intermediary. But New York's famously corrupt Boss Tweed had been locked away in 1871, and muckrakers had been attacking patronage in cities across the country for a half-century. While evolving, however, the urban political machine was an enduring reality, and two struggles of the 1920s brought it into the headlines: both the battle over Prohibition and that over Al Smith as a candidate for national office set rural nativist conservatives against urban voters. Smith's career began in the streets of New York City's Irish Fourth Ward, and even when he was governor of New York the buzzwords "Tammany Hall" and "gang rule" linked him to the teeming immigrant city, a refrain taken up again by adversaries during his run for the Democratic presidential nomination in 1924 and when he became his party's candidate against Herbert Hoover in 1928.

In *The Glass Key*, the power of Paul Madvig extends to municipal contracts, illegal businesses, control of the police, the district attorney's office, and masses of voters, and thus to public officeholders. We learn of Madvig's sources of income mainly thorough cryptic phrases in the dialogue between Madvig and Beaumont. One of his offices is in the East Side Construction and Contracting Company.[5] In the past, he profited from a "street-car franchise."[6] He skims money from a "sewer contract" and will profit from "street work next year when the Salem and Chestnut extensions go through."[7] Among the illegal businesses thriving with the blessing of the machine are gangster Shad O'Rory's speakeasies and gambling houses, for which he pays protection money to the police; their dependence on Madvig becomes evident when he closes them with one phone call to the police chief, Rainey. One might think of Madvig's organization as a shadow or parallel government, but that is not the case. Rather, the political machine weaves together the lawful and unlawful, bringing government organizations and criminal gangs under a single, hierarchical organization. When his speakeasies and casinos are closed, O'Rory thinks of himself as a wronged member of this organization: "Business is business and politics is politics," he says. "Let's keep them apart."[8] Madvig's "no" to this is unequivocal—he rejects what he sees to be a false dichotomy between government and O'Rory's illegal activities. District Attorney Farr clearly takes orders from Madvig, as we see when Farr deputizes Madvig's political fixer, Beaumont, or discusses with him what steps should be taken in investigating the murder of Taylor Henry, the son of Madvig's political rival. Judges who fall under Madvig's control include the one who will handle the estate of publisher Hal Matthews, whose newspaper *The Observer* Madvig needs to silence. Ultimately, Madvig's control of the city resides in his power to put his candidate in office; as we learn from references in conversation, he is marshaling the vote from the Third Ward, as well as the "votes on the other side of Chestnut Street," from the old Fifth Ward where Madvig had been shown the ropes by Packy Flood, and the "railroad vote" with the help of someone named M'Laughlin.[9] For this election, Senator Henry is to be the beneficiary of Madvig's power, at least until Taylor Henry's murder and O'Rory's rebellion undercut Madvig's ability to deliver votes.

The urban political machine was synonymous with the masses of immigrant voters who by the early twentieth century had become an overwhelming majority in many cities—87 percent in Chicago, for example, 80 percent in New York, 84 percent in Milwaukee and Detroit.[10] This predominance of immigrants and the growing power of the cities inevitably produced a backlash. One sign of it was legislation in 1921 and 1924 to curtail immigration; a more general response was the development and spread of an ideology promoting assimilation, most aggressively advocated by conservatives, yet so widely accepted that it became a cultural master narrative of American identity shaping novels and films ostensibly concerned with other issues.[11] Ella Shohat describes the effect on American cinema of the period as creating "a tendency toward ethnic 'allegories' . . . of texts which, even when narrating private stories, managed to metaphorize the public sphere."[12] Hammett's novel creates just such an allegory through a three-tiered structure of Senator Henry, Paul Madvig, and Shad O'Rory, a structure ultimately dismantled by Beaumont.

The senator is a "gentleman," "one of the few aristocrats left in American politics" according to a supporting newspaper, the *Post*. As Beaumont tells Madvig, from the Henrys' perspective Madvig is "the lowest form of animal life and none of the rules apply."[13] But while the class difference between the Henrys and Madvig is so clearly announced, the ethnicity allied with it is barely expressed. The Henrys are coded old-stock Anglo-Puritan by their name, by the description of the senator as an "aristocrat," by his daughter Janet's blondness and her manner of speaking. The Madvigs are also light-haired and blue-eyed and thoroughly assimilated. Their name, however, suggests Danish roots.[14] O'Rory has gray-blue eyes and prematurely white hair, but his name and the "faintest of brogues" mark him as Irish American,[15] most likely having immigrated to the United States as a child. Beaumont, with his French or French Canadian name, is difficult to place in one category or another, perhaps from long-established North American stock, but not from the Anglo-Puritan group in the United States.

He is established as Madvig's tutor when he coaches him on a proper gift for Janet's birthday. But he has no past, and his story to Janet that Madvig "picked him up out of the gutter," a way of lampooning her view of Madvig, underscores the obscurity of his origins. Beaumont's whole persona is an embodiment of classlessness, or of the invisibility of class and ethnicity, making him comfortable with everyone.

Hammett is indeed "metaphoriz[ing] the public sphere." Over the course of the novel, his allegory shows the WASP elite crumbling as Senator Henry, the aristocratic father, murders his own degenerate son, Taylor. Madvig will not be permitted to join the elite as kingmaker at the top of the pyramid. Rather, at the end of the novel he merely survives, maintaining his place in the hierarchy, allowed to rebuild his political machine on his verifiable strengths of character. His Irish American challenger O'Rory, meanwhile, is eliminated, and with him the most directly expressed ethnicity in the text. The ethnically colorless Beaumont brings about the resolution of the conflict represented in the allegory: after he has supervised the execution of O'Rory, the ethnic upstart, he rescues Janet from the crumbling WASP aristocracy. His pairing with her elevates the two of them as a meritocratic elite: the two smartest, best-looking, and most refined people, regardless of origin. Their departure for New York, a modern hub of the ethnic mingling detested by nativist groups such as the Ku Klux Klan, seems to make them emissaries to the future. Beaumont and Janet can represent the new generation permitted by Beaumont's Oedipal triumph over Madvig, his surrogate father, for the hand of Janet, Madvig's would-be wife. Hammett's variation on the master narrative of Americanization attacks the idea of an old-stock elite while it nonetheless expels O'Rory, the least assimilated character, still a stock figure in this social comedy, the ethnic gangster.

Beaumont's personal qualities, of course, embody ideas beyond those of ethnicity and class, above all a mental toughness and willpower that prove superior to physical and political force. And in the end, Beaumont is shown to be single-minded in his pursuit of loyalty, or its equivalent—a trusting relationship. The kiss-off between Madvig and Beaumont arises precisely because Madvig fails to trust him, lying in order to protect the senator and Madvig's dream of marrying Janet. However understandable, the lie is a betrayal, and Beaumont cannot forgive it. Significantly, and perhaps explaining Janet's late appearance in the novel—halfway through, in chapter 5—Beaumont only becomes close to her as his relationship with Madvig dissolves. His pairing with Janet is confirmed with their agreement to join forces in order to prove or disprove that Paul is the murderer. Beaumont's trust is expressed by his openly giving Janet information about the case. "But no tricks," he warns her, to which she replies: "If you only knew how happy I am to have your help . . . you'd know you could trust me."[16] This trust will ultimately be the reason they can go off together at the end of the novel. Yet the book's final sentences create ambiguity: "Janet Henry looked at Ned Beaumont. He stared fixedly at the door." Beaumont's sadness at the loss of Madvig seems more compelling that any excitement at pairing with Janet.[17]

The Glass Key (1935)

Without motives arising from political and class affiliations, loyalty and the affection between Beaumont (whose first name here is changed to Ed) and Madvig are made the heart of the movie directed by Frank Tuttle, though the mise-en-scène ultimately undercuts the narrative's buoyant tone. Although the basic story is the same as in the novel, the seventy-seven-minute film alters the trajectory to highlight the strength and durability of sentimental bonds like that between Beaumont (George Raft) and Madvig (Edward Arnold). While the novel ends with a definitive break between Beaumont and Madvig, Beaumont leaving town paired with Janet Henry, the daughter of Madvig's rival, this film ends by affirming Beaumont's friendship with Madvig, coupling him instead with Madvig's daughter Opal (Rosalind Keith).

The film could have been called "The Boss with a Heart of Gold," for it is a quality of enthusiastic innocence in Madvig that inspires Beaumont's support for him, and it is Beaumont's affection for and belief in Madvig that inspire Opal's love for Beaumont. The flashpoint creating this emotional chain reaction occurs two-thirds of the way through: as in the novel, Opal believes that her father killed Taylor Henry (Ray Milland) because Taylor refused to stay away from her. To bring Madvig to justice, Opal has been working with Janet (Claire Dodd), who is feeding information to a newspaper, *The Observer*, that is under Shad O'Rory's control. In the back of a taxi just after he has snatched her away from Janet and a reporter, Beaumont explains why he is protecting Madvig: "That guy could never kill anyone. He's all heart." In Beaumont's faraway, tear-filled eyes, Opal sees his love for Paul; recognizing Beaumont's heart, she cannot resist him. "And you're just a tough guy," she says gently. Opal's epiphany and conversion here also provide the key moment of revelation for the audience— Beaumont's openness and sentiment in response to Madvig are the basis of goodness in the world of the film.

Madvig's superiority, rooted in his innocence and generosity, is established by many details that frame him, for example, as a loving son who takes care of his mother (Emma Dunn, who already had forty-two similar roles to her credit, including her first film in 1914, a short entitled *Mother*). Mom likes wholesome pleasures such as the circus, to which Beaumont as a surrogate second son invites her. She tells Beaumont that Madvig is a "good boy," and hers is the good family in the story, in contrast to the wicked family of Senator Henry. Opal Madvig, blinded by the appearance and social position of Taylor, will ultimately be reclaimed for the family

"He's all heart" (*The Glass Key*, 1935)

by being paired with Beaumont. And the conclusion of the film brings Madvig's leadership full circle, placing it once again under the sign of his mother. Beaumont suggests half-seriously that Mom is the one responsible for selecting Doherty—an "honest man" whom Paul won't be able to manage—to replace the corrupt Senator Henry on the reform ticket. While Madvig has run the city based on sentimental bonds with individuals, he will now have to do it according to the rule of law.

If Madvig's goodness of heart is a quality inherited from his mother, it is incorporated into his role as political boss by emphasizing one aspect of the boss, that of gift giver, or the person who helps out individual constituents. The opening scene of the film has Walt Ivans (Frank Marlowe), who has just killed a man in a car accident, requesting that Madvig be told so that he can "get me out of it." The scene actually shows Madvig's goodness in two ways: not only his history of doing favors for others but also in his rejection of Ivans's request for having crossed a line. Ivans had ignored Madvig's frequent advice that he not drink and drive, and through his irresponsibility Ivans has caused harm for which justice demands that he pay. Even in Madvig's standoff with O'Rory, Madvig is placed on the right side of the law, in the reformer's position of closing the gambling houses.[18]

The pared-down story of the film enhances the importance of its fewer characters—and thus of its stars—relative to the background, part of the shift in focus from the political machine to a story about individuals. Madvig's political organization, therefore, is seen only in brief visits to his clubhouse, where men smoke, drink, dine, tell stories, and occasionally play a game of poker. But the boss is also made a less powerful figure. District Attorney Farr, for example, a terrified political hack in the novel, is now an authoritative presence, independent and responsive to public opinion as represented by articles in the press. PCA guidelines insisted that the law and public officials not be mocked—in this film, Farr (Charles C. Wilson) is even elevated to the role of judge in the all-important penultimate scene, determining whether Senator Henry will remain a candidate for office and whether Madvig will be tried for murder.

The power of the boss and his organization are also reduced relative to the press, which in this film replaces the personal interaction of machine politics with public opinion as mediated by news. In fact, one reading of the film is as part of the cycle of newspaper films including *The Front Page*

(Lewis Milestone, 1931) and at least fifteen other titles before *It Happened One Night* (Frank Capra, 1934) and *Front Page Woman* (Michael Curtiz, 1935). The opening credits of *The Glass Key* (1935) are framed as an advertisement for *The Observer* on a billboard, placing the entire story under the banner of the newspaper. After the long introductory sequence, major transitions in the film are framed by shots of headlines. Taylor Henry's murder becomes one such headline in the *Daily Times Herald*, after which O'Rory is shown telephoning *The Observer*, which leads to a montage of shots showing ordinary people reading the news. The attacks on Madvig surprise them because of his image as fatherly and good-hearted—O'Rory's claim that *The Observer* has "evidence" against Madvig is the key to turning people against him. Later, a similar transitional montage shows groups of people now in agreement that Madvig is the killer of Taylor Henry; in each shot a newspaper is conspicuously visible as the inspiration for their changed opinions.

By removing the sociopolitical background and emphasizing the sentimental, the film converts Hammett's hard-boiled social allegory into something reassuring. The three classes in the novel are reduced to two, a fading WASP elite and the people, who divide not along class or ethnic lines but based on goodness. Emphasis from the beginning is on the social-climbing aspect of Madvig's interest in the senator, and significantly, when the Henry family falls, the "honest" candidate who replaces him has the Irish surname Doherty, marking him as one of the people. And the new Opal/Beaumont pairing keeps him within Madvig's political family. Beaumont already calls Mrs. Madvig "Mom" and treats her with a son's affection and respect. Of course, this represents a considerable reordering of the Oedipal relationships in the novel. As in the book, Taylor Henry has rebelled unsuccessfully against his father, for which he has been killed. Beaumont, Madvig's surrogate son, after quarreling with Madvig, is transformed into a potential son-in-law, while Madvig is reunited with his mother. Opal, formerly the prisoner of an authoritarian father, becomes the prize of the surrogate son, while Janet, never paired with Beaumont in this film, is excluded from the resolution: as a member of the declining Anglo-elite, she has no future. It is important to note that violence in the film cannot be directly attributed to Madvig or Beaumont. Internal corruption ruins the Henrys, and O'Rory's criminal family similarly self-destructs when the henchman inadvertently betrays his boss. O'Rory's thug Jeff (Guinn Williams) kills him, for which he is arrested as he should have been for the murder of Sloss, a witness in the Taylor Henry killing. Thus, the big heart, represented by the Madvig clan, will triumph over two forms of evil, the ineffectual aristocrat who falls into self-pity after killing his degenerate son, and the lower instincts represented in the criminal behavior of O'Rory and Jeff.

At least partially expressed in the allegory of power and politics in Hammett's novel, ethnicity was deliberately minimized in the film, especially through the casting, an ethnic scrubbing typical of Hollywood in the mid-thirties. In an industry where immigrants played such an important role, as Ella Shohat has pointed out, filmmakers' "agility in expressing, and more often repressing and sublimating America's multiethnic dimension offers a barometer for the sociopolitical context within which these images were produced."[19] Sound had made ethnicity difficult to ignore, especially in the cycle of films most famously represented by *Little Caesar* (1931), *The Public Enemy* (1931), and *Scarface* (1932). Accents and vernacular speech became defining characteristics of the gangster, linking their immigrant status to their identity as enemies of society. Ethnicity was linked with criminality such that, in Jonathan Munby's words, "in stigmatizing the ethnic urban poor as criminal, the gangster genre betrays its origins in a nativist discourse which sought to cast 'hyphenated' Americans as 'un-American' and in need of 'Americanization.'"[20] Yet the violent, antisocial figure of the ethnically identified gangster attracted attacks not only from nativist Protestants, but also from immigrant Catholics and audiences in foreign markets, an important source of film industry revenue.[21] Gangster films were banned the same year this version of *The Glass Key* was released, but the MPPDA's response went further. Stories that dealt with ethnic bigotry were censored wherever raising the issue was seen as "provocative and inflammatory,"[22] and, as Ruth Vasey has documented, "industry policy" led to blurring the ethnicity: "'Foreignness' became less clearly associated with particular ethnic and national groups . . . so that specific interest groups could find fewer grounds for complaint."[23]

If this version of *The Glass Key* is not a gangster film, it is a near cousin, and the casting of George Raft, a veteran of gangster roles such as Guino Rinaldo in *Scarface*, must have encouraged viewers to imagine a past for

Beaumont that is not supplied in the film. Raft was a street kid from Hell's Kitchen in New York who made his way into film by way of dancing and whose reputation included real-world underworld connections. Materials in Paramount's pressbook for *The Glass Key* not only recommend that Raft's reputation be at the center of promotions for the film, but that they specifically mention his role in *Scarface*.[24] The two films share specific parallels. As Beaumont is Madvig's sidekick, Rinaldo was Tony Camonte's (Paul Muni). Like the Beaumont/Opal relationship, Rinaldo had fallen for Camonte's kid sister (Ann Dvorak). Camonte has a close relationship with his mother (Inez Palange)—who represents his Italian immigrant home life—just as Madvig has with his. Interestingly, Camonte and his mother have heavy accents, while Rinaldo and Camonte's sister have none—they represent a step toward Americanization, away from the ethnic immigrant past. Yet when Rinaldo and Camonte's sister rebel against Camonte's authority as boss and family patriarch, the result is the opposite from that in *The Glass Key:* Camonte shoots Rinaldo down, while Madvig, entirely assimilated himself, accepts Beaumont as a member of his family. From Rinaldo to Beaumont is a short step, for Raft and for the audience, particularly as framed by the extreme contrast between Muni's machine-gun-happy gangster and Edward Arnold's avuncular political boss.[25]

Raft brought the assimilated gangster to Beaumont's character in *The Glass Key*; Arnold, without a hint of immigrant ethnicity, brought a history of representing the rich and powerful, which firmly locates Madvig as a member of the establishment. Madvig's most important quality in the film is an ability to shift from expressing grave concern over his affairs to radiating pleasure at seeing Beaumont. Yet the innate human generosity embodied in Arnold cannot be disentangled from his screen history of playing the rich and/or powerful. A comic version can be seen in Mae West's *I'm No Angel* (Wesley Ruggles, 1933) where he plays Big Bill Barton, or his role as a financier in *Thirty Day Princess* (Marion Gering, 1935). Dramatic embodiments include alcoholic millionaire Jack Brennan in *Sadie McKee* (Clarence Brown, 1934), the secretary of war in *The President Vanishes* (William Wellman, 1934), and, immediately before *The Glass Key*, King Louis XIII of France in *Cardinal Richelieu* (Rowland V. Lee, 1935).[26] As Paul Madvig, his portrait of power skews toward the benign, but even as the common-man son of his circus-loving mom in *The Glass Key*, Arnold cannot shed an aura of already belonging to the establishment without a hint of the upstart or "foreign" interloper.

Casting Robert Gleckler as O'Rory completed the job of eliminating the ethnic allegory from *The Glass Key* (as the chief of police in *Mister Dynamite* the same year, Gleckler was even a part of the governing establishment). In fact, all the male characters look like successful white businessmen, speaking without a trace of a foreign accent in correct English at a time when vernacular speech was a way of coding the ethnic.[27] The effect is to flatten the implied ethnic stratification of Hammett's novel: in the melting-pot society of the film almost everyone is entirely assimilated. The Henrys are a neo-aristocratic elite marked only by formal manners and the grand architecture of their house. More significantly, O'Rory is no longer a scapegoat for the unassimilated, except insofar as the criminal might be assumed to be a disguise for an unmentionable ethnicity.

Such near-complete erasure of class and ethnicity markers encourages us to look at the two African American characters in the film. One is the gentle doorman at Madvig's Voter's League headquarters (George Reed), used to highlight the monstrous aspect of O'Rory's henchman who crushes the man's glasses. The second is the singer (Herbert Evans) in the bar where Beaumont finds Jeff hiding out; as an entertainer, this man is outside the regular social circle of the saloon. The balance of placing one African American on each side of the power equation, however, one in O'Rory's territory, one in Madvig's, appears deliberate. The only other group given separate treatment in the film is the normative, and therefore ethnically invisible, WASP Henrys, marked for extinction and excluded from the Madvig family as definitively as are the criminals.

Minimizing references to ethnicity—remarkable when the Tammany Hall setting was notoriously dependent on immigrant ghettos—reinforced the effects of Jason Joy's elimination of politics, further removing motivation for the conflicts among the characters. Yet the film requires conflict, which if not evident in the dialogue or casting must be compensated for by the director's use of mise-en-scène. From Beaumont's dialogue with Madvig, for example, we would be justified in believing that Madvig is separated from the Henrys by issues as trivial as selecting the right socks to wear. And the distance between them is further minimized in casting Arnold as a very respectable political boss. Visually, however, director Tuttle creates a line between them that can never be crossed, as when Madvig first visits the Henry mansion and he is shown listening to Janet play the piano. The camera moves in from a long medium shot, closer and to the right until the post holding up the top of the grand piano is positioned perfectly as a dark diagonal line separating the images of Madvig and Janet, a visual representation of the class barrier that has otherwise been reduced.

Similarly, Tuttle frequently introduces shadows more common to films noirs, here representing a doubling and concealment that competes with, even contradicts, the sentimentalized story. During an early conversation between Beaumont and Madvig, for example, their silhouettes are projected onto a bare wall by a bright lamp low in the foreground: the conversation is about Madvig's socks as he dresses for dinner with Janet and Senator Henry. But Beaumont is not thinking about Madvig's wardrobe; he is sorting out Madvig's motives and the implications of Madvig's visit, which in turn Madvig is concealing from Beaumont. One possible inspiration for Tuttle's visual design is Hammett's language, as in the scene where Madvig falsely confesses to Beaumont that he has killed Taylor Henry.

Class divisions (*The Glass Key*, 1935)

Arrière pensée (*The Glass Key*, 1935)

Beaumont has told him he must take steps to clear up the murder: "Madvig stopped looking at Ned Beaumont. He looked at a wide vacant space on the wall. He pressed his full lips together. Moisture appeared on his temples. He said from deep in his chest, 'That won't do. Think up something else.'"[28] Concealed from Beaumont at this moment is the false confession Madvig is about to make in order to protect Senator Henry.

Beyond mention of the bare wall, the novel's motif of imprisonment is frequently reflected by the shadows throughout the film. During the sequence where Madvig falsely confesses to Beaumont, he is sitting against a bare wall on which are projected the vertical lines from the shadow of Venetian blinds, the shadow of imprisonment in Madvig's thoughts. And later, as Madvig continues to ponder his fate, he paces against a wall with this same expressionist background. The most literal imprisonment in the film is Beaumont's when he is confined and repeatedly beaten by Jeff on O'Rory's orders. We view the room through the bars of the brass bed in which he lies unconscious, shadows of the two thugs across the room projected high on the wall behind them, images of their black souls.

Their black souls (*The Glass Key*, 1935)

Sometimes the images derive directly from the novel's dialogue, as when Janet refers to Opal as "a prisoner"—when Beaumont takes Opal home to Madvig's house, she climbs the stairs trapped between the row of heavy posts of the railing and their shadows projected on the wall. Later, as she talks with O'Rory, Janet is filmed through the bars of the railing for the stairway at her house, apparently imprisoned in their plot to use Opal. But Tuttle's images go well beyond those suggested directly by the novel, as in the climactic scene of the movie when all the players are assembled in Farr's office. A medium shot shows the senator to the right, while Madvig is on the left visually imprisoned by a grid of shadows from the Venetian blinds. This is the moment when Madvig is about to be liberated, and in fact, as Senator Henry confesses and the danger to Madvig is lifted, the bars fade and disappear.

Mark Winokur has argued that where ethnicity as an evident element of the social dynamic is repressed, we should expect "a displacement of ethnic tension onto other issues that allow these tensions to emerge in disguised form."[29] Such a displacement is most obvious in the killing of O'Rory, who is treated as the scapegoat after having been stripped of his markings as the less assimilated upstart.[30] In one sense, O'Rory's killing is merely a

Opal Madvig ascending the stairs (*The Glass Key*, 1935)

Madvig about to be liberated (*The Glass Key*, 1935)

vestige of the novel that complies with the PCA rule that murder must not go unpunished.[31] But it ultimately concentrates, and still manifests in disguised form, a concentration of what the PCA found unacceptable in the source material, ethnicity in relation to politics and sex. The principal sex scene in the novel is Beaumont's seduction of the wife of the newspaper publisher, which drives him to suicide; it is not in the film. The only other encounter exhibiting sexual tension is that between Beaumont and Jeff, who seems to look on Beaumont as a perfect sadomasochistic partner. Jeff calls Beaumont a "tough baby" who likes to be beaten, saying, "I never seen a guy that liked being hit so much or that I liked hitting so much."[32] He calls Beaumont a "massacrist," inadvertently making him a Christ figure as well as a masochist,[33] and he announces to the bar, "Excuse us gents, but we have to go up and rehearse our act, me and my sweetheart."[34] This scene is included in the 1935 film, though even with the hints of brutality to come, the relationship is played as comedy. In the film Jeff calls Beaumont "Cuddles," which draws a laugh from those at the bar. Shortly thereafter, when Jeff strangles O'Rory under Beaumont's steady gaze, however, there is no comedy—the moment conflates the repressed sexual tensions with those of the film's ethnic cleansing. A bare bulb under a shade is set swinging as Jeff grabs O'Rory and the line of darkness swings just to Beaumont's eyes as he coldly watches the murder. This degree of violence questions the Pollyanna storyline in a film that has otherwise eliminated ethnic, class, and sexual material. In the allegory of Americanization in the novel, the killing of O'Rory is a performance of "assimilation," an acting-out of the expulsion of ethnicity itself through the elimination of the only character openly marked as ethnic. In Winokur's terms, we can see in the visual expressionism of this scene a displacement or release of tensions that could not be permitted more direct statement through the events and dialogue. Ruth Vasey has argued that film industry censorship frequently led to "visual and narrative incoherence";[35] in this film we cannot reconcile Beaumont's brutality with the sentimental goodness that wins Opal's heart.

The Glass Key (1942)

If the adaptation of the 1935 film turned on reducing the social and political content of the novel, the 1942 film was shaped first and foremost by Paramount's interest in promoting Veronica Lake and Alan Ladd as a romantic screen couple. The new production relied not only on the novel as its source but on the studio's earlier script, sets, cinematography, and agreements with the PCA. The ethnic allegory from Hammett's novel survives in this film, but only as a platform for the promotion of Ladd and Lake as a couple, with an eye to box office returns.

Screenwriter Jonathan Latimer drew heavily on material created for the 1935 version. After the opening scene in which Janet (Lake) slaps Paul Madvig (Brian Donlevy), replacing the car accident scene of the earlier film, the narrative closely tracks that of the 1935 movie. As Madvig prepares for dinner at the senator's house, his plan to marry Janet is introduced and the confrontation between Madvig and O'Rory—now named Nick Varna (Joseph Calleia)—takes place. When Varna arrives, Jeff (William Bendix) repeats the business from the earlier film of grinding the doorman's glasses into the floor with his heel, though in this case the doorman is not African American. Once again, Opal Madvig (Bonita Granville) borrows money from Beaumont (Ladd), who then follows her to the apartment of Taylor Henry (Richard Denning) where, as in the earlier film, he disposes of Taylor with a kick in the shins that demonstrates the distance between the characterless rich kid and Beaumont, a hardened man of the world. Varna approaches the senator to offer an alliance as O'Rory did in the earlier film, though this time the scene is set at the cemetery after Taylor's funeral rather than at the senator's house. Once again a character named Sloss (Dane Clark) is a witness whom Madvig tries to keep away from the district attorney and who is murdered. Some news headlines are used to convey information to the viewer, and in the basement bar, one of the melodies played by the black entertainer—this time a woman (Lillian Randolph)—is from the song "Walking the Floor" in the 1935 movie. Significant stylistic details are also borrowed: the idea of an expressionistic set for the scene of Beaumont's beating (Hans Drier was ultimately responsible for the art direction of both films); the shadow of bars on the wall behind Madvig when the district attorney holds him in jail; and, above all, the swinging light fixture with its naked bulb in the violent murder scene where Jeff strangles Varna under the steely gaze of Beaumont.

Some elements from the novel that were eliminated for the 1935 script have been restored for this film, which again elevates the power of the political boss and machine. A simple explanation for this is that the PCA, under pressure of an antitrust suit filed in July 1938, was narrowing the scope of its censorship. As Richard Maltby writes, "The affairs of the late 1930s suggested that mechanisms for the control of content had become too extensive, so that [the Production Code] could not so effectively fulfill its function as the currency of negotiation among parties who felt that the movie business was their business. Rather, the censorship of the movies—as opposed to the movie content—was in danger of becoming the issue."[36] "Content" was a code word for political ideas or social criticism as opposed to sexual morality—government and the police could once again be criticized. Thus Farr (Donald McBride), the district attorney, can be presented as a pawn of the boss and treated comically. As in the novel, Madvig is a force: he can impose his will on the district attorney, the police chief, the hospital staff, and everyone else. Donlevy makes him more of a roughneck than the benevolent patriarch played by Edward Arnold.

Among the most important restorations to the story is the scene at the house of the publisher of *The Observer*, Matthews (Arthur Loft), where Opal has gone, eventually followed by Beaumont: in that scene from the novel, the publisher's wife, Eloise, turns away from her husband, who is not only corrupt but broke. Beaumont openly seduces Eloise, driving the jealous and despairing publisher to suicide. Matthews provides an obverse image of Beaumont and Madvig; his is a riches-to-rags story, the reason Eloise scorns him. Clearly by 1942, the industry had less difficulty with this material. In the film Eloise (Margaret Hayes) throws herself at Beaumont, who accepts her advances in order to drive Matthews to suicide. In fact, to make sure the blame for what occurs falls on Eloise rather than Beaumont, she is made more predatory than in the novel by her costume and flirtatious manner. "Your lead, Ed," the PCA advised Luigi Luraschi, an executive at Paramount Pictures, "must not be shown kissing Mrs. Matthews, although it will be acceptable to show her as playing up to him."[37] Beaumont does in fact kiss Eloise, though only after she clearly invites him to. He is unquestionably only feigning interest in her; when she asks in distress if the shot they have heard from upstairs has to do with her husband, Beaumont merely nods with satisfaction and says, "Dead as a mackerel." This scene not only helps create the image of Beaumont as attractive to women, but, more importantly, puts the press once again under the thumb of the all-powerful political machine. In this film, unlike in the novel, the scene ends with Madvig's surprise entrance, after which he knocks Jeff to the floor with a punch.

The power of the boss is elevated in the 1942 film above the power of the law and the press, but the love story has been expanded to the point that the political machine gets very little screen time. It is presented solely through the sets of the campaign offices, background for few of the scenes. The political in this film is entirely subsumed in Madvig, the individual, who is more powerful than in the 1935 film, yet with a diminished role—Donlevy received top billing though with less screen time than Alan Ladd or Veronica Lake.

The Ladd/Lake focus of the film is set up by an opening scene which establishes with a single gesture that, as in the earlier film, all motivation will be personal. Madvig enters campaign headquarters in a hotel lobby, and when he comments that the reform party's candidate for governor, Senator Ralph Henry (Moroni Olsen), should start by reforming "that son of his," he is slapped by a woman in the crowd who turns out to be the senator's daughter, Janet. This slap has the magical power of making Madvig fall in love with her, which in turn motivates his political shift to support Senator Henry.[38] Beaumont will yield to Janet's charms more gradually, eventually to be torn between his growing relationship with her and his loyalty, based on principle but also deep personal affection, for Madvig. The emphasis in this film is on Beaumont's struggle and on his growing entanglement with Janet.

Veronica Lake was seen as a rising star on the slender basis of two films when she was cast in *The Glass Key*—*I Wanted Wings* (Mitchell Leisen, 1941), which also included Donlevy, and *Sullivan's Travels* (Preston Sturges, 1941). Born Constance Ockleman in Brooklyn, she had a disastrous screen test but was given a second chance by Paramount producer Arthur Hornblow Jr., Myrna Loy's husband. He cast her in *I Wanted Wings*, in which she was billed seventh, right after Constance Moore, the only other woman in the film. The film was a box office success in spite of a "B" rating by the Legion of Decency, based, according to Cecilia Agar of *PM*, on Lake's "splendid bosom, unconfined and draped ever so slightly to make the current crop of sweater girls look like prigs by comparison."[39] *Sullivan's Travels* was shot in May 1941, when Lake was six months pregnant. But it was on the set of *This Gun for Hire* (Tuttle, 1942), in production when *The Glass Key* was being cast, that the chemistry between Lake and Ladd was recognized.

One reason for pairing Lake with Alan Ladd was their height: she was just under five feet tall, while he was barely six inches taller. Unlike Lake, Ladd had been struggling for some time in his efforts to get an important part—between 1932 and his role as Raven, the hit man in *This Gun for Hire*, he had bit parts in some forty-three films (including *Citizen Kane* [1941], where his voice can be heard in the smoky screening room of the opening sequence). Raven is a hired killer who wins the sympathy of Ellen Graham (Lake), employed by the man Raven is hunting. When he is injured, she nurses him, and her touch creates an electricity in the potentially trans-gressive relationship that upstages her supposed love for a police detective she is engaged to. Seeing their potential together, Paramount cast them as Beaumont and Janet Henry, with *The Glass Key* having finished shoot-ing before *This Gun for Hire* premiered in New York on May 13, 1942. Per-haps through the lens of her disappointing career trajectory, Lake cynically described their effort on *The Glass Key*: "Alan and I attacked the project with all the enthusiasm of time clock employees, a pretty cocky approach for two people without acting credentials and only the instant star system to thank for our success."[40] But Paramount's strategy was successful—*This Gun for Hire* was a hit, leading to a profitable run at the box office for *The Glass Key*, though reviewers felt the latter was a weaker film.

Beaumont and Janet are brought together earlier and more often in this film, for she is no longer merely a representative of the Henry family as in the 1935 movie, to be purged in favor of Opal Madvig. Rather, the relationship is developed persistently over seven scenes placed through-out the film, from their first introduction when Beaumont and Janet size each other up as people who understand more than those around them, through a tug of war in which Janet declares her liking for Beaumont while he resists, until the final scene in which Madvig realizes that they are in love and gives Beaumont permission to pursue the relationship. Their banter reflects the competition between them, a bristling style of dialogue that remained current in film noir, bitterly sarcastic and showing the defensive isolation of frightened people in a dangerous world.

Their relationship is developed in calibrated steps. When they first meet and Janet shows contempt for Madvig, Beaumont tells her: "I get along with

Paul, because he's on the dead up and up. Why don't you try it sometime?" Their next encounter continues to develop the idea that they are worthy adversaries; then, after scenes establishing that the Taylor Henry murder is a problem for Madvig, Janet shows up at Beaumont's apartment for a longer exchange that directly explores the major themes of her mistaken, class-based sense of superiority, of Beaumont's core value of independence, and of his belief in that forthrightness. "You're slumming," Beaumont tells her, "and I don't go for slummers." They come together again at the hospital after Beaumont has been beaten. She flirts with him but conceals it from Madvig. "Do you hate me for this?" she asks once Madvig has left, and Beaumont confesses his developing feelings: "I don't want you around because I'm liable to start making passes at you." By the time of their next scene, in the apartment Opal had used for her affair with Taylor, they are ready to kiss, but they must still address the fundamental issue between them, trust, which requires that Janet give up loyalty to her father. Only with the senator's confession is this last barrier removed and the arc of their relationship complete.

After Ladd's role as the killer in *This Gun for Hire*, Paramount was promoting him to romantic lead, so even more than the novel this film frames Beaumont as irresistible. The nurse in the hospital flirts with him, and where in the novel a second nurse who tries to restrain him is simply ignored, in this film the only nurse looks delighted when he kisses her as a way of sidestepping her authority. Eloise Matthews pays special attention to him from the moment of his arrival at their house in the country, seeing him as some kind of treat delivered for her entertainment, something to make up for her disappointment in Matthews. Even Opal is drawn to him. So in the relationship with Janet, Beaumont is cast as the prize. Ladd carried some of the hard edge of Raven over to Beaumont, a toughness and physicality that we see in the way he puts himself in front of Varna and Jeff when they want to go upstairs in the campaign headquarters to see Madvig. Similarly, he is tough in his dialogue with Janet, as he had been when Raven held Ellen hostage in *This Gun for Hire*. In fact, a great deal of Ladd's appeal in *The Glass Key* seems to assume that honesty entails toughness and abuse, a quality admired in the world of this film by both men and women.

There is a contradiction in Beaumont's claims throughout the film that his friendship with Madvig would not keep him from being with Janet if that is what he wanted, for in the final scene he clearly needs Madvig's permission before he and Janet can go off together. That comes as a surprise to the viewer mainly because Ladd's performance allows no hint in Beaumont of uncertainty or fallibility. The issue does not arise in the novel—Beaumont does not require Madvig's approval. In fact in the book, their final conversation at his apartment emphasizes the cruelty that accompanies his honesty. After Madvig asks him to stay and work with him, Beaumont tells Madvig that he is leaving and that Janet is going with him. She appears from the other room and begins an apology that Madvig cuts short. Then: "[Madvig] looked dumbly at Ned Beaumont and as he looked the blood went out of his face again. When his face was quite bloodless, he mumbled something of which only the word 'luck' could be understood, turned clumsily around, went to the door, opened it and went out, leaving it open behind him."[41]

The film, unwilling to break a sentimental bond so easily, has Madvig bless the couple with his approval, especially because this is the correct couple, as the entire narrative has worked to establish and as Paramount hoped would continue as a successful pairing of actors in many movies to come. In place of Beaumont's staring "fixedly at the door," the last sentence of the novel that leaves us focused on Beaumont's sense of loss, the final statement of the film is a celebration of this couple—the characters and the actors.

The ethnicity of the characters, so noteworthy by its absence from the 1935 version, allows this film to offer an allegory very much like that of the novel. Here, Janet, Taylor, and Senator Henry remain the WASP elite, and the actors look the part. The main coding of Madvig as ethnic or immigrant is simply his identification with the political machine and crime, and his heavy reliance on vernacular speech.[42] Among the first things we hear about and from him are that he's a crook and his phrase "Why don't he start on that son of his." Donlevy typically played an energetic tough guy of indeterminate ethnicity, as in *Union Pacific* (Cecil B. DeMille, 1939), where he was Sid Campeau, and *Beau Geste* (William Wellman, 1939), where he played Sergeant Markoff, a brutal Russian in command of a corps of the French Foreign Legion. His most significant part with respect to *The Glass Key* was as Dan McGinty in Preston Sturges's *The Great McGinty* (1940), a role that cast him as a pawn for a Tammany-style political machine that

The love triangle (*The Glass Key*, 1942)

over the course of the film helps him rise from a ballot box stuffer to a governor elected on a "reform" ticket. The progression from McGinty to Madvig is nearly seamless. In *The Great McGinty*, the political boss coded as ethnic is played by the Armenian actor Akim Tamiroff with a vaguely Russian accent; he even speaks briefly on the phone in a foreign language. The boss takes a liking to McGinty because he recognizes himself in McGinty's tough insubordinate way of being. "He thinks he's me!" the boss proclaims, and in *The Glass Key*, Donlevy has indeed become the boss, though he is more assimilated than Tamiroff's portrayal. Released by Paramount on August 23, 1940, *The Great McGinty* would inevitably have come to mind for studio executives and with regular moviegoers considering *The Glass Key*.

The ethnic gangster in the 1942 version of *The Glass Key* is newly emphasized. In the novel Shad O'Rory was coded as Irish American; now, as Nick Varna, he is, in Madvig's derisive term, a "spaghetti bender." Varna is played by the Maltese actor Giuseppe Maria Spurrin-Calleja, better known as Joseph Calleia, and the character's surname echoes that of a seaside city in Bulgaria. But the point, as Vasey has observed generally, is that he is foreign. In Munby's words, "For the gangster to be recognizable as such, he must be specifically demarked as an 'ethnic' outsider (which, in this context connoted someone of Irish, Southern or Eastern European, Catholic or Jewish stock)."[43] Transforming O'Rory and his light brogue into the dark-haired Varna with a thick accent adds visual and auditory confirmation of his status as a more recent and more identifiable immigrant. Calleia was well established with audiences as both a gangster and a foreigner. John T. McManus had described him in a review of *Tough Guy* (Chester M. Franklin, 1936) as "probably our favorite public enemy."[44] As Donlevy's movement to the role of Madvig from the role of McGinty builds directly on the previous film, Varna in *The Glass Key* is a direct continuation of Calleia's role as Italian gangster Eddie Fuseli in *Golden Boy* (1939).

So in this film the plot presents an Italian gangster confronting a more assimilated Irishman (with a Danish name) who seeks to marry the princess who is daughter of the WASP king. As in Hammett's novel, Taylor Henry stands for the degeneration of the line and of the WASP elite's hold on power. Furthermore, the women in the film reflect the WASP-to-Italian spectrum of Senator Henry to Varna: in this black-and-white film, Janet's hair is Lake's almost silvery blond, while Opal's hair and that of Eloise Matthews is darker, more like Paul's. The color-coding is complete when we add the black-haired nurse with whom Beaumont flirts in the hospital, who, while attractive, is of the working class. The African American entertainer, outside the spectrum of women Beaumont encounters directly, must be seen as either entirely marginal or as a step farther from blondness than the dark-haired nurse.[45]

The narrative action of the film carries through on a message of assimilation as healthy for society. While Madvig rigs the election, he represents a man who has risen from the people, a man of loyalty and generosity, even though he is a criminal. Senator Henry is finished, to be replaced by whomever Paul nominates, and his son is dead. The veiled Oedipal story here is similar to the one set up in Hammett's novel. One son rebels against the father (Senator Henry) and is killed for it. Madvig tries to marry another woman but is returned to his mother. Beaumont, who has no other known family, rebels against his father figure Madvig and takes the woman (Janet) who would have been this father's wife. Out of this, a new generation might come from the pairing of Beaumont and Janet. The Henry male line (Taylor) has failed, as has the Madvig female line (Opal). Varna, the recent immigrant stereotyped as an Italian gangster, is eliminated. Madvig maintains his power, but he is not quite assimilated enough to join the nativist elite, and when he blesses Beaumont's departure with Janet Henry, he is, in a sense, sacrificing himself for his friend.[46] Only Beaumont, because of his perfect assimilation, can take away the blonde princess.

7

Hammett in Retrospect

Miller's Crossing (1990)

Half a century after the second film version of *The Glass Key* there would be a third, *Miller's Crossing* (1990). The passage of time, however, ensured that this adaptation, not only of Hammett's novel but also of the two earlier films as well as other sources, would produce a categorically different kind of work—different because it was made for a changed world, and different by the very fact of its retrospectivity. Hammett's stories and novels were set in the present. As they were remembered or sought out rather than newly popular, they triggered a sense of the past, at first the recent past, then a time across the great divide of World War II, the Cold War, the civil rights era, space flight, and personal computers. Whatever forces shaped the development of these new projects, the first challenge was to position new films with respect to the differences between then and now, and to take into account the degree to which some Hammett books and films were now thought of as "classics."

Echoes of his work kept Hammett in the public eye long after he stopped writing for publication. Radio and television series based on characters from his work persisted into the 1950s. *The Adventures of Sam Spade* and *The Fat Man* radio series were broadcast from 1946 to 1951, the second inspiring a movie, *The Fat Man* (William Castle, 1951). *The Adventures of the Thin Man* radio series was broadcast from 1941 to 1950, followed by seventy-two episodes of a television series, *The Thin Man,* aired from 1957 to 1959, starring Peter Lawford and Phyllis Kirk as Nick and Nora Charles.

But Hammett's name was also in the headlines for less positive developments, such as his imprisonment in 1951.

Hammett was one of three trustees of a bail fund for a group called the Civil Rights Congress, which had been declared subversive because of links to the Communist Party of the United States of America (CPUSA). When four of the men for whom the fund had posted bail failed to appear at their hearing, the trustees were called to testify. Hammett refused and was cited for contempt of court; he was sentenced to six months in prison, "or until he purged himself of the contempt."[1] Because of Hammett's reputation, the hearings were covered by a series of articles in the *New York Times*, and on the day following his sentencing a full-length photograph appeared on the front page over the caption, "Dashiell Hammett going to Federal House of Detention last night."[2] On December 9, 1951, after serving twenty-two weeks at the West Street detention center in New York and the Federal Correctional Institute near Ashland, Kentucky, he was released. Less than two years later, he was again summoned to testify, this time before Senator Joseph McCarthy's Permanent Investigation Subcommittee of the Senate Committee on Government Operations. At a hearing on March 26, 1953, Hammett refused to answer questions from McCarthy's lead counsel Roy Cohn about any communist affiliation. This time he was not imprisoned, but, as the *New York Times* wrote in his obituary eight years later, "Hammett's novels were plucked from the shelves of seventy-three of the 189 American libraries overseas as a result of State Department confidential directives, based largely on testimony before the McCarthy committee. This continued until President Eisenhower said at a news conference that 'he would not have removed the books.'"[3]

Both of these incidents firmly located Hammett among writers blacklisted and otherwise persecuted during the Red Scare, and Hammett's past CPUSA affiliation continued to affect his reputation in complex ways throughout the Cold War and beyond his death. Meanwhile, he emerged from prison with his health broken and little income. As Richard Layman writes, "His radio shows were cancelled, his books were out of print; and all his income was attached by The Internal Revenue Service in lieu of more than $10,000 in back taxes from 1943. By 1954, the total amount of tax liability thorough 1950 was $111,008.60."[4] He would spend the last five years of his life as a houseguest dependent on Lillian Hellman, whom he named in his will as his literary executor.[5]

Because of their long association and shared politics, Hammett's reputation remained intertwined with Hellman's and indirectly suffered when she was branded an unrepentant Stalinist in the later years of the Cold War.[6] But by the mid-1960s, with the rise of the New Left and an appreciation by feminists of Hellman's accomplishments, as Alice Kessler-Harris writes, her "star once again rose. Requests for rights to perform her plays in both the United States and foreign countries poured in."[7] Hellman's social and political activity of the 1960s and 1970s helped sustain Hammett's reputation, as did the three memoirs that brought Hellman to the peak of her popularity. The last section of *An Unfinished Woman*, a best seller that won the National Book Award in 1969, was entirely devoted to a celebration of Hammett. This was followed by *Pentimento* (1973), which drew as much praise, and when the chapter entitled "Julia" was made into a successful film in 1977, directed by Fred Zinnemann and starring Vanessa Redgrave and Jane Fonda, Jason Robards won an Academy Award for Best Supporting Actor for his portrayal of Hammett.

While frequently linked with Hellman, Hammett was never the lightning rod for resentment that she was, particularly after her third volume of memoirs, *Scoundrel Time*, in which she attacked liberals whom she felt had betrayed their friends and allies during the McCarthy years.[8] In contrast, Hammett remained a less narrowly defined figure of resistance to government, to the "establishment," and to the fashions of the mass market. In a long tradition of artists in conflict with prevailing manners and ideas, his ignoring the conventions of marriage, sexual restraint, sobriety, and employment all resonated in the era of counterculture. This independence, a quality of his fictional protagonists, was compounded by his personal reputation and epitomized by his willingness to go to jail rather than give in to government bullying. His death in 1961 spared him from the attacks that Hellman's argumentative activism in the mid-1970s would draw.

But if Hammett and his work were not forgotten, he was no longer viewed as contemporary, rather as someone to be memorialized. He had received this treatment in Hellman's memoir, and even more so in Zinnemann's *Julia*. Indicative of his standing in the 1970s was Joe Gores's homage, *Hammett,* a novel deliberately conflating the celebrity author with his most famous creations. "I wanted to write a novel about Hammett the detective," wrote Gores, "because his experience *was* so seminal to his art. But it is not Hammett the detective who fascinates readers; it is Hammett the detective-turned-writer."[9] Further evidence of Hammett's cultural cachet was the film produced from Gores's novel by Francis Ford Coppola, who hired New German Cinema director Wim Wenders for the project. The resulting film, *Hammett* (1982), goes even further than Gores in using the author's fiction to animate his biography, citing aspects of Hammett's Pinkerton apprenticeship while creating scenes that evoke *The Glass Key* (in which the fictional Hammett's imprisonment replays Beaumont's) and *The Maltese Falcon* (a fat man à la Gutman appears and the fictional Hammett's hands shake like Bogart's in the 1941 film). The sense of the film's memorializing a lost past is underscored by its use of old Hollywood faces: Sylvia Sidney, Samuel Fuller, Hank Worden, and especially Elisha Cook Jr., Gutman's "gunsel" in *The Maltese Falcon* who now, forty years later, plays Hammett's taxi-driving sidekick; referring indirectly to Hammett's politics, he explains himself as "an anarchist with syndicalist tendencies."

That Hammett would become a figure of the past was inevitable, of course, and even by the late 1950s the *Thin Man* television series was given a contemporary setting rather than being set back in the 1930s. Filmmakers now interested in adapting Hammett's work had to choose between reproducing the earlier period or updating the material to the present. The challenges of each strategy are clear from the 1978 television miniseries based on *The Dain Curse* and the film *No Good Deed* (2002) from Hammett's story "The House on Turk Street."

The Dain Curse was the only Hammett novel not to be adapted for a feature film, most likely because of its episodic structure, its complexity, the exposition needed to recount the Leggett family history, and subject matter that included the cure of a young woman's morphine addiction. It was only seized upon for television as part of the neo-noir revival in the 1970s and Hammett's renewed visibility after the release of *Julia,* resulting in a three-part, six-hour series starring James Coburn, broadcast by CBS in two-hour segments over May 22–24, 1978. The exigencies of the television venue shaped the adaptation in significant ways, as did the miniseries format, but for our purposes the most significant aspect of the project was its emphasis on "pastness"—understanding Hammett as a historical artifact or museum piece through décor, music, and a vague confounding of the detective protagonist with popular recollections of Hammett the man.[10]

Casting James Coburn as the Continental Op—named Hamilton Nash in the TV show—was important in restyling the protagonist. The actor, whose breakthrough to stardom had come as a comic James Bond-like figure in the box office hit *Our Man Flint* (Daniel Mann, 1966), was known for playing a singular man who exhibited a perfectionist's mastery, his performances displaying more than a hint of narcissism, and his tall, lean physique—not to mention the image of Flint as a man irresistible to women—transforms the self-described short, fat Op into a character more like the celebrity author—lean, handsome, fashionably dressed, and a womanizer. But this iteration of the detective, a product of Bogart's Spade and Marlowe and forty years of film and television, was also framed as retrospective through a voiceover narration imitating films such as *Double Indemnity* (1944) and *Sunset Blvd.* (1950), through period décor that relied heavily on antique cars as props, and through a score of generic polyphonic jazz that crowds every transition. In many ways, the show reflects a cycle of nostalgic classic-novel adaptations, films that, as Fredric Jameson writes, frequently "reinvent the feel and shape of characteristic art objects of an older period."[11] Reviewing the miniseries for the *New York Times,* John J. O'Connor wrote that "the individual ingredients turn out to be more interesting than the whole, [but] when noticing Mr. Coburn's smart hat and raglan overcoat begins to take precedence over the story, the project is obviously in trouble. Style is indeed something, but it can't be all." In fact style was all, along with a vague evocation of the detective of another era, and with it came the presumption that we should remember Hammett's work and value it regardless of its irrelevance to the world we live in. In terms of its share of the television audience, *The Dain Curse* was moderately successful.[12]

Twenty-four years later, Bob Rafelson's *No Good Deed* attempted a very different strategy, reframing the contest between a femme fatale and masculine protagonist of a Hammett story in the present. Samuel L. Jackson, Milla Jovovich, and Stellan Skarsgård starred in the film. Jovovich had taken on increasingly prominent parts on her way to popular recognition in *Resident Evil* (Paul W.S. Anderson, 2002), released earlier in the same year as *No Good Deed,* but Jackson was the bankable star. Internationally

Hamilton Nash (*The Dain Curse*, 1978)

known after playing Jules Winnfield in *Pulp Fiction* (Quentin Tarantino, 1994), by 2002 he was on his way to becoming one of the largest-grossing movie actors in history.[13] The strategy for this film was to rewrite the plot of Hammett's story for the new millennium—the crime now involves shutting down a bank's computer system—while making the film's climax turn on a choice echoing the famous moment in *The Maltese Falcon* when Spade hands Brigid O'Shaughnessy over to the police rather than "play the sap" for her. *No Good Deed* reworks several themes of Hammett's story, such as the role of accident or coincidence in disrupting lives, and race as a social determinant of behavior. Without any knowledge of Hammett's story and *The Maltese Falcon*, however, an audience has no way to understand Rafelson's manipulations and the plot consequently becomes nonsense. In spite of its stars and director, *No Good Deed* failed to find U.S. distribution, and a film with a production budget of $12 million had a domestic gross of a mere $181,600.

The Coen brothers' *Miller's Crossing* faced similar challenges to those of *The Dain Curse* and *No Good Deed*. On one hand it is a period film exploiting nostalgia in numerous ways; on the other, understanding the film depends

Temptation (*No Good Deed*, 2002)

on a knowledge of its source and references. But the film addresses the potential difficulties directly: nostalgia is always tempered by irony, the past viewed through the lens of the present even while the present offers a pastiche of the earlier works. The Coen brothers, withholding attribution of the film's sources, insist on identifying them through a deliberate excess of narrative, visual, and verbal citation. Among other things, *Miller's Crossing* becomes an important document for the present study because it offers a reading of *The Glass Key*, novel and films, that underscores ethnicity and the allegory of assimilation, Hammett's almost prudish sublimation of sex, and the gangster subtext suggested in the casting of George Raft and Alan Ladd in 1935 and 1942. But *Miller's Crossing* is also more than that. Fredric Jameson's words about *Body Heat* (1981) and its relation to *Double Indemnity* could not be more accurate if he were writing about this film: "The word remake is anachronistic to the degree to which our awareness of the pre-existence of other versions (previous films of the novel as well as the novel itself) is now a constitutive and essential part of the film's structure: we are now, in other words, in 'intertextuality' as a deliberate, built-in feature of the aesthetic effect and as the operator of a new connotation of 'pastness' and pseudohistorical depth, in which the history of aesthetic styles displaces 'real' history."[14]

The multi-layered nature of *Miller's Crossing* did make it a difficult film for audiences. The Coen brothers had a bigger budget for this film than they had had previously—the box office success of *Raising Arizona* (1987) allowed them to raise $14 million from Twentieth Century–Fox based on a "two-line pitch."[15] But the film was a financial disappointment, taking in only $4.7 million (Martin Scorsese's *Goodfellas* earned ten times as much the same year).[16] And reviews point to its complicated intertextuality as the reason for the film's cool reception. Vincent Canby wrote that "*Miller's Crossing* wants to be both fun for the uninitiated and for those who are hip to the conventions of the genre that is being recalled."[17] Roger Ebert suggested, "It is most likely to be appreciated by movie lovers who will enjoy its resonance with films of the past,"[18] and Garry Giddins argued that "Joel and Ethan Coen may represent the apotheosis of classroom cinema. [*Miller's Crossing* is] so clever about its sources . . . that it has little life of its own."[19] The failure to credit Hammett and *The Glass Key* as sources would be more puzzling if the Coen brothers' entire project were not about emphasizing what had been at once unstated and fundamental.[20]

Set around 1930, *Miller's Crossing* recounts the story of *The Glass Key* but with pieces of the puzzle rearranged and the characters assigned somewhat different values. The main figures are still the political fixer, the boss, the gangster who challenges the boss, and a woman, love for whom distracts the boss from conducting his affairs with his customary ruthless efficiency. And a love triangle among the fixer, the boss, and the woman is still central to the plot. But now there are three love triangles—in addition to Reagan (Gabriel Byrne), Leo (Albert Finney), and Verna (Marcia Gay Harden), another is formed by Bernie (John Turturro), The Dane (J. E. Freeman), and his lover Mink (Steve Buscemi); the third comprises Verna, her brother Bernie, and Reagan (to Verna's suggestion that they leave town together, Reagan quips sarcastically, "Where would we go, Niagara Falls?"). As for Madvig in all versions of *The Glass Key*, behavior that is predictable on the basis of greed and other forms of self-interest is redirected by desire, or as Reagan voices explicitly to Johnny Caspar (Jon Polito), "There's always that wild card when love is involved."

Hammett's characters are redesigned for *Miller's Crossing* in ways that replicate, alter, and comment on the originals. Caspar, for example, is still the gangster who challenges the boss, but now he harps on "ethics." Leo is still the object of affection—as in the 1935 film—because he has, as Verna tells Reagan, "a big heart." Bernie Bernbaum in *Miller's Crossing* is an elaboration of Bernie Despain from Hammett's novel, who had a significant role in running off with Beaumont's winnings and thus allowing Hammett to establish important aspects of Beaumont's character—his intelligence and force of will. The chapter devoted to the pursuit of Bernie Despain is entitled "The Hat Trick," the point of origin for the many hat references in *Miller's Crossing*. Yet Bernie also parallels the role of Sloss, the missing witness in *The Glass Key* films who was named after another minor character in the novel. Everything and everyone are recognizable yet changed; the problem is that the Coen brothers had no reason to redeploy these characters except for the playful enjoyment of opening up the text to include earlier ones.

Tom Reagan as substitute for the Beaumont role is the most complicated character. The Coens' working title for the film was "The Big-head," their nickname for Reagan,[21] and, like Ned Beaumont, he is smarter than everyone else. The word he is most associated with is honesty, and throughout the film he tells people difficult truths they don't want to recognize, such as informing Verna that her brother does not deserve her

Bernie Bernbaum (*Miller's Crossing*, 1990)

support and telling Leo that Verna is unfaithful. Based on a lucid evaluation of evidence and probabilities, he tells Leo that protecting Bernie is a "bad play" because it will erode his power. At another point he insists that people should only do things when they have a "reason." Reagan and Bernie discuss their reasons in terms of selfish motivation, without malice toward those who inadvertently suffer the consequences. Thus, he has "no hard feelings" when he is beaten for failing to pay his gambling debts. But Reagan's behavior ultimately has no rational goal and he frequently lies to Caspar and to Verna, who at the end claims that lying rather than honesty defines him, as does, in contrast to Leo, his absence of a heart.

Key scenes from Hammett's narrative and the earlier films are reworked with layers of reference and revision, especially those in which O'Rory confronts Madvig, Beaumont's meeting with O'Rory after pretending to break with Madvig, and the kiss-off, the definitive break with Madvig over the issue of trust (undone in the 1935 and 1942 films). The scene where Reagan approaches Caspar after breaking with Leo is a good example of how the Coen brothers transform the material. In *The Glass Key*, O'Rory offers to set Beaumont up with his own gambling casino for changing sides. In *Miller's Crossing*, the money is specifically to pay off gambling debts and the cooperation begins with turning Bernie Bernbaum over to Caspar, but, as in Hammett's novel, Caspar offers a deal; Reagan seems to play along, learns what he can, then refuses to cooperate. For this he is beaten. But unlike all versions of *The Glass Key* in which Beaumont is held and tortured for days, in *Miller's Crossing* Reagan is rescued almost immediately by a police raid. The Coens pass up what the earlier filmmakers took as a prime opportunity for violent spectacle, replacing that with Leo's tour de force with the Thompson machine gun. Meanwhile, the chair that fragments when Reagan hits the oversized Frankie (Mike Starr) before being quickly subdued by the much smaller Tic-Tac (Al Mancini) is a playful reference to the chair in the novel and earlier movies that Jeff effortlessly rips apart with his hands. Here, the chair is used to highlight the comic odd-couple of thugs, adding yet another reversal of events from *The Glass Key*: just as the big man is not tough, and the imprisonment of Reagan will not lead to a harsh beating, The Dane (in Jeff's role) will not kill his boss. The way the police submerge Reagan in water directly references Jeff's method of bringing Beaumont around for more interrogation in the earlier versions. In the novel and those films, as revenge for his torture, Beaumont uses Jeff to kill O'Rory (Varna in 1942), then turns him over to the police for trial and, we can assume, execution. Since in *Miller's Crossing* the torture does not occur, the revenge scene is also reconfigured: Reagan sets up Bernie to kill Caspar, then personally executes him for his earlier double-cross. In *Miller's Crossing* the cops ask Reagan if he wants to "scrap a knuckle" on the thugs; but "skin a knuckle" is a phrase given to Jeff in the novel and in the earlier films. This kind of verbal echo, insistent and unnecessary to the story, helps interweave the narrative and visual citations of earlier material into this film.[22]

Miller's Crossing's open citation goes beyond the novel *The Glass Key,* of course, to the 1935 and 1942 films, to other Hammett writings, and to the gangster film genre, especially *The Godfather* (Francis Ford Coppola, 1972). *Miller's Crossing*'s final farewell scene, set in a cemetery, for example, transforms a scene from the 1942 film where they gather to bury Janet Henry's beloved brother and Opal Madvig denies her own brother the opportunity to take her home; in *Miller's Crossing* they are burying Verna's brother, and Verna takes the car, making the men walk home. And the slap that sets off Madvig's love for Janet in the 1942 film is parodied in *Miller's Crossing* when Verna punches Reagan, after which Reagan falls for Verna, losing her to Leo just as in the earlier film Madvig lost Janet to Beaumont. The raid on the Sons of Erin Social Club in *Miller's Crossing* echoes *Red Harvest,* while also showing an awareness of films inspired by *Red Harvest, Yojimbo* (Akira Kurosawa, 1961), and especially *A Fistful of Dollars* (Sergio Leone, 1964), by copying the way members of the opposing gang are shot as they emerge from the burning building; in this instance the Coen brothers emphasize the path that leads from Hammett to their film.

But nothing shows *Miller's Crossing*'s complicated referencing of other texts better than its opening scene, which replicates the crucial "Cyclone Shot" chapter of the novel while also offering, in Ronald Bergan's words, "a pastiche of the opening monologue of *The Godfather.*"[23] In that film, the camera shows the undertaker Bonasera (Salvatore Corsitto) facing the camera, light reflecting off his bald pate and highlighting the tips of his white shirt collar and cuffs, the camera ever so slowly pulling back until Don Corleone (Marlon Brando) begins to be seen at the edge of the frame. In *Miller's Crossing,* during his interview with Leo, the Irish godfather, Caspar is in

Deceptions? (*Miller's Crossing*, 1990)

the spotlight, bald pate gleaming, but the camera movement is reversed—instead of pulling back, it moves forward from a medium shot until Caspar's animated face crowds the frame. The stylistic contrast between *Miller's Crossing* and *The Godfather* is as important as the similarities, of course, but there are numerous elements of Coppola's film that allow the Coen brothers to triangulate among it, their own film, and the various versions of *The Glass Key*. Tom Reagan is cold and calculating like Michael Corleone, for example, and his name echoes that of Tom Hagen, the don's consigliere in *The Godfather;* but beyond these and the gangster element, especially important is the attention to ethnicity and assimilation. Citing the opening scene of *The Godfather* highlights a crucial intent of *Miller's Crossing,* to turn *The Glass Key* inside out by bringing to the foreground elements that Hammett and the early versions of *The Glass Key* had left in the background: the gangster elements, ethnicity, and sex.

Ethnicity in *Miller's Crossing* represents the film's the most profound engagement with Hammett's novel and the two earlier films. Whereas Hammett's critique of society, explicit and implicit, was contemporary, the Coen brothers place their viewers in the comfortable—or, more likely, uncomfortable—position of judging that world though a post–civil rights era lens in a time in which concepts of multiculturalism have challenged assumptions of the rightness of assimilation, the melting pot, as a national ideology. With the passage of time, ethnic bigotry that once passed as

Johnny Casparo (*Miller's Crossing*, 1990)

normal or invisible now leaps to the eye and ear, while at the same time the ethnic difference that it signals is no longer assumed to be something that should be stamped out. Recognizing this, the Coen brothers have Leo refer to Johnny Caspar as "the Guinea," the "Itai," and "that dago." Caspar refers to Tom Reagan as a "potato eater," as does The Dane, whose surname refers to his ethnicity. Bernie Bernbaum is nicknamed "the Schmatta Kid," or just "Schmatta," and is variously referred to as "sheeny," "Hebrew," and "hymie," while Tom Reagan tells Verna that if he had known they were going to cast their feelings into words, he would have "memorized the 'Song of Solomon.'"

But the definition of their characters as ethnic grotesques goes well beyond derogatory verbal stereotyping. *Miller's Crossing* follows the 1942 film in adopting the stereotypical Italian gangster rather than the Irish O'Rory of Hammett's novel, though as we have seen, Leo, the Irish boss, clearly developed out of the Irish gangster. Leo and Reagan were originally conceived as assimilated Irish Americans, apparently, offering the layers of progressive assimilation that we find in Hammett and in *The Glass Key* (1942).[24] But this layering is maintained by the relative exaggeration of Jon Polito's playing of Johnny "Casparo," with his spoiled son and an overfed, operatic wife who speaks volubly in Italian. And the Coens, Jewish themselves, are as comfortable magnifying Jewish stereotypes—both Bernie and Verna—as they are with the Italians and the Irish.[25] In Bergan's words, "The

Irish and Italians don't come out too well, both being equally corrupt. The Jews, as represented by Bernie Bernbaum, come off worse."[26] Instead of the novel's use of stereotypes as a shorthand to provide a social background, *Miller's Crossing* pushes Bernie's character to that of an extreme outsider, because of his ethnicity, but also as part of the homosexual love triangle with The Dane and Mink.

The already exaggerated ethnic coding is then pushed to an extreme by Carter Burwell's musical score, most obviously in the maudlin rendition of "Danny Boy" to accompany Leo's triumphant performance with the machine gun. "Danny Boy" was in place from early in the project, but Gabriel Byrne recommended some of the songs Burwell would ultimately use. "When we were finishing the movie we started listening to a lot of Irish music," Ethan Coen noted in an interview. "The song on which Carter Burwell based the main theme is an old ballad suggested by Gabriel . . . called 'Come Back to Erin.'"[27] This is complemented by the singing in Italian during the Miller's Crossing sequence. The performance of "Danny Boy" by Irish tenor Frank Patterson was "paced to fit the finished scene." Patterson "was able to watch the action and match the rhythm of his vocal to the unfolding violence."[28] The result is that the music in the film comes to the fore, as in a music video, rather than being relegated to the background as is the theme of ethnicity itself in *The Glass Key*. Byrne reports Ethan Coen saying that he and Joel "got mugged by the whole Irish

"An artist with the Thompson" (*Miller's Crossing*, 1990)

concept," but this statement must be understood in the context of a film based on a book and earlier adaptations that already revolved around the issue of ethnic stratification.

Sex, like ethnicity, is pulled from the background in *The Glass Key* to the foreground in *Miller's Crossing*, developing ambiguities that include queer and straight readings of the film. In Hammett's novel the attraction between Beaumont and Janet is so understated that their going away together at the end almost comes as a surprise—their relationship is finally solidified by a very rational pact without a hint of sexual passion. This plays out in *Miller's Crossing* as the voracious coupling of Reagan and Verna, in contrast to Leo's prudish modesty. The Coen brothers address the Jeff/Beaumont relationship, which reaches its climax when Jeff strangles O'Rory while his eyes are fixed on Beaumont, by making the equally brutal Dane openly homosexual, and his relations with Mink and Bernie a central plot element.

Furthermore, there is what we might call the central "bromance" between Madvig and Beaumont, which over the course of the novel gives way to Beaumont's pairing with Janet. The Coens take up this ambiguity, not only with the suggestion that Verna and Reagan are competing for Leo's affection, but through Albert Finney's performance in the last scene dramatizing Leo's anguish just after he has told Reagan that he and Verna are getting married. Leo pleads, "Jesus, Tom, I'd do anything if you'd work for me again. . . . I need you, and things can be the way they were." And when Reagan refuses Leo's forgiveness, Leo's face shows an extraordinary sense of loss. In Erica Rowell's words, "As with so much in the film, there is a straight way to read things and a 'queer' way," but the Coens, deliberate in their play with gender roles, retain an ambiguity from the Madvig/Beaumont relationship in that between Leo and Reagan.[29]

The difference between Janet Henry in the novel and earlier films and Verna in *Miller's Crossing* helps us understand the ways in which the Coens have turned the allegory of *The Glass Key* inside out. Janet is blond, a member of the WASP elite, her mind rather than her physical presence capable of challenging Beaumont's; by contrast, Verna is dark, coded as ethnic, and able to take care of herself physically, either in a fight or in bed. Hammett portrays Janet as redeemable in spite of her class position because she is genuinely superior—she has the intelligence and beauty to match Beaumont's. Verna is believed by everyone except Leo to be a treacherous whore, potentially a femme fatale. And yet here, too, there is ambiguity: little evidence is offered to show that Verna is not what she pretends to be, a women concerned about her brother who finds Leo's honesty and good heart attractive. Reagan's belief that she shot Rug Daniels (Salvatore H. Tornabene) turns out to be unfounded, and The Dane's labeling Verna a whore seems a product of his hatred of all women. Her concern for Bernie is genuine, and when she comes to see Reagan after Leo has broken with her, Verna is crestfallen—nothing in her manner suggests a grifter looking for a new angle. Reagan is the one seeing an angle and taking it: he gets Verna to give him Bernie's address, not in order to help him but to resolve Leo's problem by turning him over to Caspar. Perhaps because as viewers we are under the spell of Reagan's skepticism, we too are unable to get beyond the fiction he spins out of his own inner darkness, to see Verna for anything other than a grifter and whore.

However we understand her, Verna is central to the allegory of *Miller's Crossing*, which at its simplest is that of *The Glass Key* with the top layer eliminated: there is no longer a Senator Henry figure, no WASP elite. Instead Leo, the political boss, is at the top of the food chain. In this version, he is unquestionably Irish American, while the Beaumont figure is thoroughly Irish, foreign rather than entirely assimilated. The challenge to the boss's power comes from an Italian racketeer, who in turn—adding a lower layer to the allegory in this case—is challenged by a bookmaker who is Jewish and homosexual. As the suppressed material from the novel and earlier films has now been emphasized by the Coen brothers, however, the ethnic allegory has also been reformulated ironically to fit the times: Caspar with his "ethics," rather than Reagan or Leo, is now the person trying to safeguard the values threatened by a changing world. Marriage, which so often sorts out Hollywood morality, is used in this instance for a comic inversion of Hammett's paradigm: rather than using it as a strategy for upward mobility as Madvig does, Leo has fallen in love with a triple outcast, Verna. In place of Janet's proposing to go off with Beaumont, Verna, rising above her family and ethnic ties, proposes marriage to Leo, just as Janet escaped her WASP background. In the Coen brothers' allegory, to use The Dane's words, "Up is down, black is white." The ethnic criminals, however—Italian and Jewish—are still purged from the story, as are the three figures who challenge the dominant heterosexual order.

Untangling this allegory, we can see the difficulty of trying to narrowly articulate the meaning of the Coens' film. It is the difficulty of postmodernism, to borrow Linda Hutcheon's phrase, "an ironic dialogue with the past of both art and society."[30] In what sense are we to understand its re-creation of the past when so much about the film deliberately prevents us from accepting it, even as a nostalgia film? There is, for example, the exaggerated acting, which creates a sense of conspiratorial pretending; the obsession with costuming details, especially the men's hats; music that washes the film in sentiment and helps further stylize its narration; and the aestheticism of Barry Sonnenfeld's cinematography with its long lenses, static framing, and luxurious pallet of carefully coordinated colors. *Miller's Crossing* "doesn't look like a gangster movie," Roger Ebert wrote; "it looks like a commercial intended to look like a gangster movie."[31] Then there are the cameo appearances of well-known director Sam Raimi, of actress Frances McDormand after her prominent roles in *Blood Simple* (1984) and *Raising Arizona* (1987), and the name Lars Thorvald, a character from *Rear Window* (Alfred Hitchcock, 1954), on a boxing poster in Drop Johnson's room—all these are a wink to the Coen brothers' knowing audience, not to mention cross-dressing extras in the women's bathroom scene along with one of the film's stars, Albert Finney, in a maid's uniform.

All these aspects contribute to a "depthlessness" and a "waning of affect" that characterize the postmodern, an extension of the film's pastiche of other texts.[32] "The fiction of the creating subject," as Douglass Crimp wrote of Robert Rauschenberg's use of reproduction and parody, "gives way to the frank confiscation, quotation, excerptation, accumulation and repetition of already existing images. Notions of originality, authenticity and presence . . . are undermined."[33] Rather than comment directly either on the earlier work or on society, this film will not "emit propositions," to use Jameson's phrase, or "have the appearance of making primary statements or of having positive (or affirmative) content."[34]

From our perspective, more important than the Coen brothers' success—or failure, for those who do not appreciate *Miller's Crossing*—is the fact that Hammett is the object of "confiscation, quotation, [and] excerptation" by important contemporary filmmakers. The film is evidence of Hammett's transformation during the final quarter of the twentieth century from a flamboyant and controversial author of influential detective fiction to an iconic presence in the landscape of American literary and intellectual history.

Conclusion

Dashiell Hammett and the Movies

Hammett's most recognizable impact on the film industry began with *The Thin Man*'s success, making Myrna Loy a star and reinvigorating William Powell's career. The film spawned not only the series of *Thin Man* films and helped to pair the actors in a half-dozen other pictures, it also contributed, along with *It Happened One Night* (Frank Capra, 1934), to establishing screwball comedy as a popular sub-genre, while creating a precedent for films featuring married couples lovingly at war with one another. *The Maltese Falcon* (1941) had a similar effect, augmenting Humphrey Bogart's success on his way to the triumph of *Casablanca* (1943) and inaugurating John Huston's career as a director. There is no question that the Spade/Bogart embodiment of the hard-boiled detective set off a ripple effect that not only rolled through film noir and the later neo-noir retrospective, but that continues into the present.

Mention of the hard-boiled detective also raises the question of Hammett's wider, if less direct influence on cinema as a whole, especially in but not limited to film noir. The Huston/Bogart film led to Bogart's role as Philip Marlowe in *The Big Sleep* (Howard Hawks, 1946), which doubly reflects Hammett's influence: Raymond Chandler, author of the latter film's source novel and other works important for film noir—as well as the screenplays for *Double Indemnity* (Billy Wilder, 1944), *The Blue Dahlia* (Fritz Lang, 1946), and *Strangers on a Train* (Alfred Hitchcock, 1951)—acknowledged Hammett as his mentor and model. Indeed, during the 1970s and 1980s, as Hammett was lionized as an artist and rebel of the past, his importance as a seminal figure for film noir was simply assumed. Yet during this same period, film scholars found his influence to be less evident: the more closely one looked at the ever-expanding body of films in the genre, the harder it was to make specific associations between them and Hammett's writing.

This represented a change in how Hammett's influence was understood. In the postwar French context of 1946, Nino Frank immediately linked the American films he labeled as "noir" to Hammett. They were, he argued, "to traditional crime drama what the novels of Dashiell Hammett are to those of Van Dine or Ellery Queen."[1] Raymond Borde and Étienne Chaumeton, in their influential *Panorama du film noir américain, 1941–1953*, went further: "The immediate source of film noir is obviously the hard-boiled detective novel of American or English origin. Dashiell Hammett, whose earliest writings go back to around 1925 [actually 1923], is both the creator of this new American literary current and an author whose talent largely transcends the framework of the genre. . . . But then the fact that the first great film noir is precisely *The Maltese Falcon* [1941], adapted from one of his finest tales, underlines Dashiell Hammett's importance."[2] Not all French critics made a direct link between film noir and Hammett as the creator of hard-boiled fiction, however,[3] and even Borde and Chaumeton placed this "immediate source" among broader conditions of the genre's formation. Indeed, British and American critics emphasized such conditions until Hammett was barely cited in a list of circumstances and causes that included everything from the Great Depression to existentialism to Orson Welles's *Citizen Kane* (1941) and the photographs of Weegee.[4] Chandler was more frequently cited, and attention turned to Cornell Woolrich to the point that Tony Williams could write in 1982, "Woolrich (1904–68) is now recognized as an important force in the literary background of film noir, offering a significant alternative to the 'hard-boiled' school of Hammett, [James M.] Cain, and Chandler with their emphasis on phallic pleasures of control and mastery."[5] William Luhr's *Film Noir*, an informed overview of the genre published in 2012, is representative of recent consensus: Luhr mentions Hammett's name exactly twice, allowing only that "substantial foundations for film noir had been laid in 1941 with movies such as *The Maltese Falcon*, with its themes of widespread evil and deviant, as well as manipulative, sexuality."[6]

The underlying links between Hammett and film noir are, in fact, profound, but they are not so unique to Hammett that he can be identified as the principal route through which they arrive in that long and diverse cycle of crime films. Commonalities include the role of the femme fatale and its complement, a sense of threatened masculinity. Many of Hammett's early stories featured a caricature of the femme fatale, very much the figure Ann Kaplan describes as central to film noir. As Kaplan writes, they "symbolize all that is evil and mysterious. Sexuality being the only weapon women have in relation to men, they use it to entrap the investigator and prevent him from accomplishing his task. Dangerous because their sexuality is so openly displayed and so irresistible, women become the element that the male investigator must guard against if he is to succeed in his quest."[7] In Hammett's early stories, this sexuality is indeed "openly displayed," but as we have seen, his women characters evolved, so that Dinah Brand in *Red Harvest* would offer a considerably more complex version, as would Brigid O'Shaughnessy in *The Maltese Falcon*. Particularly as played by Mary Astor, she is noteworthy less for her direct erotic appeal than for her talents of dissimulation, the quality that differentiates the femme fatale of film noir from the vamp of earlier cinema.

The vulnerability of Hammett's male protagonists is less obvious, because they show themselves to be tough, even if their success is tempered by loss. Yet as Frank Krutnik has written, toughness in these 1940s thrillers is a result of a sense of masculine identity that "has to be perpetually protected against various forms of deviance and disruption."[8] The category of film noir to which Hammett contributed, the tough investigative thriller, uniquely portrays the continuing consolidation of masculine identity, emphasizing the challenges to it and the fact that such a consolidation can never be fully secure. Krutnik takes Bogart's Spade in *The Maltese Falcon* as the seminal example for this strain of the genre.

Hammett's narrators, however, are vulnerable far beyond challenges to their masculine identity—their struggle to remain anchored and clear-headed is a result of living in a world cut loose from moorings of objective truth or a definitive basis of morality to guide human behavior. Thus Hammett's detectives become a metaphor for a process of trying to understand a world that can never be fully understood, a truth that cannot be discovered. They live by a provisional code with no more solid foundation than repressed feelings and remembered values. The Op looks to the Old Man and the Continental Detective Agency for a set of rules. Sam Spade looks only to himself—the true meaning of being an independent private eye. Ned Beaumont states frankly that he believes in nothing. Nick Charles is beyond worrying about it, grateful for whatever good cheer and affection survive in a world devoid of broader significance. This is the logic that underlies the evolution of Hammett's protagonists. The Op typically found himself trying to reconstruct, based on a few facts, the best story he could for the Old Man. And this attempt to construct a story that makes sense is the dilemma faced by all Hammett's protagonists, from the first-person narrators in *Red Harvest, The Dain Curse*, and *The Thin Man*, to the carefully restricted third-person perspective, close to Spade and Beaumont's points of view, in *The Maltese Falcon* and *The Glass Key*. It is the impact of the protagonist's situation on his outlook and feelings that take him beyond most genre fiction and give Hammett a kinship with Ernest Hemingway, or even with Franz Kafka and Samuel Beckett. And this also links Hammett with film noir, a world of deceptive surfaces that promise one thing only to snatch it away and leave the protagonist disillusioned. But if Hammett's world is already that of film noir, the angst of both Hammett and film noir are shared widely across early twentieth-century Western experience. Hammett is one of its many vehicles into hard-boiled fiction and, later, into film noir.

James Naremore argues that it was Hammett's "skepticism" that kept him from having a greater influence on film noir. "In the 1940s and for a long time afterward," Naremore concluded, "an accurate rendition of this popular, yet radically skeptical novelist would have been politically controversial, morally challenging, and perhaps excessively artful in the eyes of the major studios."[9] Yet whether or not this explains why Hammett's novels were not revived for films in the late 1940s and 1950s, his unacceptable "skepticism"—sometimes closer to nihilism—is the obvious reason that the studios made no "accurate renditions" of his novels in the 1930s and early 1940s. The movie industry addressed a much wider and more diverse audience than pulp fiction, and film was viewed as having a dangerously powerful influence on its viewers. Thus between aiming for the greatest number of ticket buyers and—under pressure from social reformers and religious moralists—trying to avoid federal regulation, Hollywood films preferred anodyne assumptions about life, enacted within a limited number of narrative patterns. All source material would be shaped accordingly, nonconforming impulses disguised. And so for the films, as we have seen, Hammett's books were all tamed. *Red Harvest* was reimagined as comedy. A shadow of bitter reality was eliminated from *The Thin Man*. Rather than rescue her male counterpart through decisive action as Luise Fischer does in *Woman in the Dark*, Louise Loring in the film version must be saved by the strong arms of John Bradley. The ambiguity and sordid fate of Sam Spade disappear in all versions of *The Maltese Falcon*, although it is only with difficulty that honesty and devotion to the law seem to get the upper hand on self-interest in the 1941 version. And the cruel intelligence of Ned Beaumont in *The Glass Key* is softened in the 1935 film to an appreciation of Madvig's big heart, and in the 1942 version by passion to allow Alan Ladd to be coupled with Veronica Lake. Even Hammett's stories for hire had to be reshaped for Hollywood's more optimistic paradigm: the Kid's pathology was converted to a laudable independence for *City Streets*; Dynamite's dishonesty was trivialized and subordinated to good-humored generosity in *Mister Dynamite*. Only when the times changed—with the anxiety of the approaching war, of men threatened by the massive movement of women into the workforce, of the Cold War and nuclear weapons—would Hollywood reflect a public mood closer to that of Hammett. The Coen brothers' *Miller's Crossing*, of course, an entirely different case from the films of classic Hollywood, embraces Hammett's "radical skepticism" for its own purposes.

Yet divergence from Hammett's work is only part of the story, emphasizing the ways in which he failed to influence film. More to the point is what the industry made of the narratives, characters, imagery, and dialogue repurposed by studios and the army of individuals elaborating the films; in this we see how Hammett's writing nourished the system, integrating the products of one sensibility into the creative process of new and vivid works of collaborative and commercial art, that is, exemplary Hollywood rather than inferior Hammett. Each instance is unique, of course, as when Ben Hecht brushed *Red Harvest* aside in favor of ideas from his own previous screenplay for *Underworld*. Or the outline for *City Streets* that drew on a character in *The Maltese Falcon*. Or the trajectory of Hammett's experiment with a dishonest detective that, under the influence *The Thin Man*'s success, ends up with the wisecracking couple of *Mister Dynamite*.

The adaptation of *The Thin Man* ultimately proved to be a vital extension of Hammett's novel within a much broader cultural sphere. Its success, aesthetically and financially, depended on Hunt Stromberg and W. S. Van Dyke's recognizing the book's values and on their craft in pursuing the project through the screenplay, the casting, the creation of an effective mise-en-scène, and, above all, the actors being enabled to deliver their incomparable performances. But the film's real achievement—deeply rooted in Hammett's novel—was its engagement of a pivotal cultural moment, the triumph over Prohibition in the culture war it represented. Not even Stromberg and Van Dyke fully realized the timeliness of their effort—they were surprised by the magnitude of its success.

Each of the versions of *The Maltese Falcon*, by contrast, embraces aspects of Hammett's novel according to the circumstances of its production. For the first film, a search for box office success emphasized the femme fatale's seductive powers—it was to be a "sex picture," and everything from the screenplay to the casting of Ricardo Cortez and Bebe Daniels to Daniels's wardrobe and performance would articulate this selective reorientation of Hammett's narrative. The film was written, shot, and edited under the influence of fraught negotiations between the studio and the Hays Office, and was ultimately released in defiance of the Motion Picture Producers and Distributors Association. *Satan Met a Lady* provides the appropriate industry sequel: it represents one response to increased enforcement of the Production Code. Offering screwball comedy in place of sex, the film employs Bette Davis to underscore the femme fatale's intelligence and even recasts Hammett's sexually ambiguous arch-villain, Casper Gutman, as a woman. The Huston/Bogart version of *The Maltese Falcon*, in a complete turnabout, promotes the hard-boiled detective, and while all versions drew deeply from the book, this one, in some degree like *The Thin Man*, extended its reach across the culture and into the future.

As a final example, the films from *The Glass Key* similarly develop out of different strands of Hammett's novel, the earlier film expanding the trust between Beaumont and Madvig into a quality of human goodness that, in motivating Beaumont, carries all before it. Yet the film is perhaps most interesting in the way it engages Hammett's theme of a meritocracy entailing assimilation and trumping ethnic and class divisions. Wary of the reactions of both immigrant and foreign audiences, the studio cleansed the film of all signs of ethnicity through its casting and performances, while underneath this surface makeover, the mise-en-scène, particularly its lighting, mines the novel for imagery, leaving the film haunted with social and sexually motivated violence that comes together in Jeff's execution of O'Rory. The later film, though reestablishing Hammett's ethnic allegory and maintaining the violent elimination of the ethnic gangster, develops the repressed love story of the novel between Beaumont and Janet Henry, from her opening slap that turns Paul Madvig's head to the final departure of Beaumont and Janet, ultimately motivated by the studio's desire to promote Ladd and Lake as a screen couple.

Retrospectively, *Miller's Crossing* continues the work of the earlier films' digesting and extending Hammett in new forms, but it does so with a particular self-consciousness and lucidity—it is a film about the relationship of *The Glass Key*, Hammett's entire body of work, and the gangster and film noir genres to our world, with its own ethnic, sexual, gender, and aesthetic politics. *Miller's Crossing* exhibits in itself the reason for the present study, to retain and specify the continuing role of the novelistic texts within the films. Individually, each adaptation—whether or not it was received "as an adaptation"—helps us to understand more precisely the active role of the precursor works, and the active embrace of them in the process of creating something new. Taken together, the films yield a portrait of the dynamic role of an author's oeuvre in the embrace of the industry through which it is diffused in the wider public sphere of cinema. Finally, in observing the set of interrelations around Hammett's work in film, we expose the process of interweaving such source materials with local, even accidental elements of lives and careers under industry imperatives, studio styles, and ideological censorship within the flux of broader, less recognized historical currents.

Without an awareness of their literary precursors, these films are certainly poorer, while the novels themselves are enriched through our understanding of their continued development in the films.

NOTES

INTRODUCTION: INFERIOR HAMMETT OR EXEMPLARY HOLLYWOOD?

1. Dashiell Hammett, *Red Harvest* (New York: Vintage, 1992), 85.
2. Dudley Andrew, *Concepts in Film Theory* (New York: Oxford University Press, 1984). Reprinted in *Film Theory and Criticism*, ed. Leo Braudy and Marshall Cohen (New York: Oxford University Press, 2009), 375.
3. James Naremore, ed., *Film Adaptation* (New Brunswick, N.J.: Rutgers University Press, 2000), 21.
4. Thomas Leitch, *Film Adaptation and Its Discontents: From Gone with the Wind to The Passion of Christ* (Baltimore: Johns Hopkins University Press, 2007), 127.
5. Linda Hutcheon, *A Theory of Adaptation* (New York: Routledge, 2006), xv.
6. Robert Stam and Alessandra Raengo, eds., *Literature and Film: A Guide to the Theory and Practice of Film Adaptation* (Malden, Mass.: Blackwell, 2005), 46 (emphasis added).
7. Hutcheon, *A Theory of Adaptation*, xvii.
8. Stam and Raengo, *Literature and Film*, 27.
9. Hutcheon, *A Theory of Adaptation*, xvii.
10. Ibid., 6.
11. Braudy and Cohen, *Film Theory and Criticism*, 373 (emphasis added).
12. Hutcheon, *A Theory of Adaptation*, xvi.

CHAPTER 1   THREE EARLY FILMS: *ROADHOUSE NIGHTS* (1930), *CITY STREETS* (1931), AND *MISTER DYNAMITE* (1935)

1. Richard Layman, *Shadow Man: The Life of Dashiell Hammett* (New York: Harcourt, Brace, Jovanovich, 1981), 90.
2. Diane Johnson, *Dashiell Hammett: A Life* (New York: Random House, 1983), 74–76.
3. Ibid., 76.
4. Layman, *Shadow Man*, 116.
5. Dashiell Hammett, *Dashiell Hammett: Selected Letters*, ed. Richard Layman with Julie M. Rivett (Washington, D.C.: Counter Point, 2001), 52.
6. Layman, *Shadow Man*, 125.
7. Ibid., 126.
8. Ibid., 130.
9. Carlos Clarens, *Crime Movies: An Illustrated History from D. W. Griffith to Pulp Fiction* (New York: Da Capo Press, 1997), 82.

10. William F. Nolan, *Hammett: A Life at the Edge* (New York: Congdon & Weed, 1983), 112.

11. Layman, *Shadow Man*, 130.

12. Nolan, *Hammett*, 114.

13. Richard Corliss, *The Hollywood Screenwriters* (New York: Avon, 1972), 65.

14. Layman, *Shadow Man*, 125.

15. Nolan, *Hammett*, 112.

16. Ibid., 113.

17. Clarens, *Crime Movies*, 81.

18. Robert Warshow, *The Immediate Experience: Movies, Comics, Theatre, and Other Aspects of Popular Culture* (Cambridge, Mass.: Harvard University Press, 2001), 101–102.

19. Tom Milne, *Rouben Mamoulian* (Bloomington: Indiana University Press, 1970), 29.

20. Dashiell Hammett, *The Maltese Falcon* (New York: Vintage, 1992), 93–94.

21. Dashiell Hammett, film treatment for *City Streets* (also catalogued under the title "The Kiss-off"), 5. Available at the Harry Ransom Center, University of Texas at Austin.

22. As early as June 1929, Hammett had considered writing a story focused on a gunman. He was dissuaded by Herbert Asbury, who told him it had already been done by William R. Burnett in a novel published that year, *Little Caesar*. Hammett, *Selected Letters*, 50.

23. After an affair with Cooper, Carole Lombard is supposed to have said, "In conversation, by the time he opens his mouth it's tomorrow." Jeffrey Meyers, *Gary Cooper: American Hero* (New York: William Morrow, 1998), 69.

24. Ibid., 61.

25. Milne, *Rouben Mamoulian*, 33.

26. Mark Spergel, *Reinventing Reality: The Art and Life of Rouben Mamoulian* (Metuchen, N.J.: Scarecrow Press, 1993), 10–11. Mamoulian revealed very little in interviews later in his life, preferring to stay with a few repeated formulas.

27. Hammett, *Selected Letters*, 72.

28. Ibid., 74.

29. Ethan Mordden, *The Hollywood Studios: House Style in the Golden Age of the Movies* (New York: Simon & Schuster, 1988), 339, 325.

30. Hammett, *The Maltese Falcon*, 215.

31. Layman recounts the story of "On the Make" in detail. Layman, *Shadow Man*, 155–156.

32. See *Shall We Dance* (Mark Sandrich, 1937), for example, where ballet, Petrov, Lady Carrington, and Europe are rejected in favor of Peter P. Peters, Linda Keene, tap dancing, and jazz derived from African American popular culture.

CHAPTER 2   CELEBRITY: *THE THIN MAN* (1934)

1. Diane Johnson, *Dashiell Hammett: A Life* (New York: Random House, 1983), 79.

2. Richard Layman, *Shadow Man: The Life of Dashiell Hammett* (New York: Harcourt, Brace, Jovanovich, 1981), 115.

3. Lillian Hellman, *An Unfinished Woman* (New York: Barnes & Noble, 2001), 183.

4. Dashiell Hammett, *Nightmare Town* (New York: Vintage, 1999), 5.

5. Dashiell Hammett, *The Continental Op* (New York: Vintage, 1989) 56.

6. Ibid., 60.

7. William K. Everson, *The Detective in Film* (Secaucus, N.J.: Citadel Press, 1972), 50, 60.

8. William F. Nolan, *Hammett: A Life at the Edge* (New York: Congdon & Weed, 1983), 139.

9. "Excited" is still found in the most widely read 1992 Vintage edition, 151. Other references to sex in the novel are modest, always indirect, so it was most likely the freedom of the couple in their marriage—which Richard Layman suggests "might have been described as 'open' in the 1960s"—that worried editors. Layman, *Shadow Man*, 145.

10. Scott Eyman, *Lion in Hollywood: The Life and Legend of Louis B. Mayer* (New York: Simon & Schuster, 2005), 185.

11. According to Breen, *The Thin Man* was the "most interesting screen entertainment which we have witnessed in a long time." Motion Picture Association of America, Production Code Administration records; Margaret Herrick Library, Academy of Motion Picture Arts and Sciences (hereafter MHL).

12. Nolan, *Hammett*, 141.

13. *Lux Radio Theatre*, "The Thin Man," June 8, 1936.

14. Nolan, *Hammett*, 141.

15. In a memoir written with James Kotsilibas-Davis, Loy describes how this became her image, beginning with a "small but showy part" in *What Price Beauty* (Buckingham, 1925) in which Natacha Rambova, the writer and star of the film, dubbed her "the intellectual type of vampire without race or creed or country." James Kotsilibas-Davis and Myrna Loy, *Myrna Loy: Being and Becoming* (New York: Alfred A. Knopf, 1987), 42. Bosley Crowther wrote that the success of *The Desert Song* (Del Ruth, 1929) "tagged [Loy] for Oriental roles." Bosley Crowther, *The Lion's Share: The Story of an Entertainment Empire* (New York: Dutton, 1957), 222. One was Nubi the Gypsy in Alexander Korda's *The Squall* (1929). Remembering Loy in the part, Loretta Young emphasized Nubi's sexuality, as a "seductive creature [who] goes through all the men in the house, the husband, the father, the sweethearts, the male servants, the gardeners, everybody, and the women can't wait to get rid of her." Kotsilibas-Davis and Loy, *Myrna Loy*, 59.

16. Kotsilibas-Davis and Loy, *Myrna Loy*, 59.

17. Ibid., 74.

18. Charles Francisco, *Gentleman: The William Powell Story* (New York: St. Martin's Press 1985), 86.

19. Everson, *The Detective in Film*, 87.

20. See, for example, the narrative offered by film historian Rudy Behlmer in the documentary *William Powell: A True Gentleman*, packaged with *The Complete Thin Man Collection* DVD box set.

21. *New York Times*, March 11, 1934. In *Manhattan Melodrama*, childhood friends Blackie (Clark Gable) and Jim Wade (William Powell) become racketeer and district attorney, respectively; Eleanor (Loy), who is drawn to both of them,

ultimately chooses the virtuous Jim over the roguish Blackie. A hint of Nora
Charles's persona is evident in an early scene after Blackie's illegal gambling
establishment is raided. Eleanor knocks at the door and recognizes the policeman who opens it for her. "Good evening, Inspector," she says. "Are you the new
doorman?" Then, as the men on the force begin to parade out, Eleanor stops
one of them: "Just a minute, McGinty. Why, you have caviar all over your badge."
And she quips, as Nora Charles might, "That's just what the police department
needs, a woman's touch." Accounts of Loy's first introduction to Powell during the production suggest that the actors immediately responded well to each
other. She was nervous, and their meeting was held off by Van Dyke until a
scene where Blackie hustles Eleanor into a taxi where his old friend Jim is waiting. Thrown by Gable into the taxi, Loy landed in Powell's lap. "Miss Loy, I presume?" he asked, the beginning of a beautiful screen friendship. Rudy Behlmer,
*W. S. Van Dyke's Journal: White Shadows in the South Seas, 1927–1928: and Other Van
Dyke on Van Dyke* (Lanham, Md.: Scarecrow Press, 1996), 85.

22. Francisco, *Gentleman*, 131.
23. Behlmer, *W. S. Van Dyke's Journal*, 102–103.
24. Dashiell Hammett, *The Thin Man* (New York: Vintage, 1992), 190.
25. Ibid., 21.
26. Ibid., 47.
27. James Naremore is the exception here: "With only a slight turn of the screw, *The
    Thin Man* could have been as disturbing as any of Hammett's previous writings."
    James Naremore, *More Than Night: Film Noir in Its Contexts* (Berkeley: University
    of California Press, 1998), 54–55.
28. Hammett, *The Thin Man*, 95.
29. Ibid., 147.
30. Ibid., 112–113.
31. Kotsilibas-Davis and Loy, *Myrna Loy*, 69.
32. Behlmer, *W. S. Van Dyke's Journal*, 85.
33. Ibid., 92.
34. Ibid.
35. David Bordwell, Kristin Thompson, and Janet Staiger, *The Classical Hollywood
    Cinema: Film Style and Mode of Production to 1960* (New York: Columbia University
    Press, 1985), 62.
36. Martha Nochimson, *Screen Couple Chemistry: The Power of 2* (Austin: University
    of Texas Press, 2002), 89–90.
37. Ibid., 91.
38. Behlmer, *W. S. Van Dyke's Journal*, 93.
39. Ibid.
40. Nick suggests that he and Nora go there after they attend the opening of
    Radio City Music Hall, which occurred on December 27, 1932. This first visit to
    Studsy's speakeasy is brief, but it gives Nora the opportunity to meet the ex-con
    Burke, who again evokes Nick's past by saying, "A wife, think of that." Ham-
    mett, *The Thin Man*, 78. Nora marvels at Studsy's manner of speaking, telling

Nick, "Half his sentences I can't understand at all." Hammett, *The Thin Man*, 81. She is a tourist in foreign territory, an idea repeated after their second visit to the Pigiron Club: "Your wife is drunk, Nicky. Listen, you've got to tell me what happened—everything. . . . I don't understand a thing that was said or a thing that was done. They're marvelous." Hammett, *The Thin Man*, 127. Nora shudders when she first tastes Studsy's liquor, asking Nick, "Do you suppose this could be the 'bitter vetch' they used to put in crossword puzzles?" Wit and irony exist in both high and low speech—contrast her educated language to Morelli's colorful turn of phrase to describe being beaten by the police: "They had me resisting some more arrest just for good measure before they turned me loose." Nora is amused by Morelli, but she is appalled by the conduct of the police. She asks Nick, "Did you do things like that?" Hammett, *The Thin Man*, 118–119. Only the fact that Nick has been part of the corrupt world allows him to serve as Nora's Virgil.

41. Layman, *Shadow Man*, 152.
42. Nolan, *Hammett*, 147.

CHAPTER 3 AFTER *THE THIN MAN*: FROM SEQUEL TO SERIES

1. Carolyn Jess-Cooke, *Film Sequels: Theory and Practice from Hollywood to Bollywood* (Edinburgh: Edinburgh University Press, 2009), 5.
2. Ibid., 3.
3. Ibid., 5.
4. Carolyn Jess-Cooke and Constantine Verevis, *Second Takes: Critical Approaches to the Film Sequel* (Albany: State University of New York Press, 2010), 33.
5. Ibid., 38.
6. *New York Times*, May 21, 1944.
7. Richard Layman, *Shadow Man: The Life of Dashiell Hammett* (New York: Harcourt, Brace, Jovanovich, 1981), 152.
8. Ibid., 157.
9. James Kotsilibas-Davis and Myrna Loy, *Myrna Loy: Being and Becoming* (New York: Alfred A. Knopf, 1987), 115–116.
10. Layman, *Shadow Man*, 159.
11. Ibid.
12. Dashiell Hammett, *Dashiell Hammett, Selected Letters*, ed. Richard Layman with Julie M. Rivett (Washington, D.C.: Counter Point, 2001), 93.
13. Diane Johnson, *Dashiell Hammett: A Life* (New York: Random House, 1983), 117.
14. William F. Nolan, *Hammett: A Life at the Edge* (New York: Congdon & Weed, 1983), 146.
15. Dashiell Hammett, *The Thin Man* (New York: Viking, 1992), 59–60.
16. Layman, *Shadow Man*, 159–160; Nolan, *Hammett*, 153.
17. Jess-Cooke and Verevis, *Second Takes*, 5.
18. The studio recognized Stewart's talent—he appeared in seven other pictures that year.
19. Nolan, *Hammett*, 153.

20. Hammett, *Selected Letters*, 113.

21. Layman, *Shadow Man*, 166.

22. Ibid.

23. Hammett, *Selected Letters*, 119.

24. Layman, *Shadow Man*, 168.

25. Hammett, *Selected Letters*, 128.

26. Ibid., 133.

27. Ibid., 131.

28. Nolan, *Hammett*, 166.

29. Ibid.

30. *New York Times*, November 24, 1939.

31. Layman, *Shadow Man*, 170.

32. Hammett, *Selected Letters*, 128.

33. Johnson, *Dashiell Hammett*, 221.

34. Kostilibas-Davis and Loy, *Myrna Loy*, 162.

35. Claire Porter (Stella Adler), a.k.a. Clara Peters, wears hats that are as attention-getting as Nora's. But Claire, like Mimi Jorgensen in *The Thin Man*, is a fraud. Nick says to her at one point, "Don't look now, your accent is showing." Nora describes her to Nick as a "fur-bearing animal."

36. Ian Scott, *In Capra's Shadow: The Life and Career of Screenwriter Robert Riskin* (Lexington: University Press of Kentucky, 2006), 158.

37. Roy Kinnard, *The Films of Fay Wray* (Jefferson, N.C.: McFarland, 2005), 217.

38. Clayton R. Koppes, "Regulating the Screen: The Office of War Information and the Production Code Administration," in *Boom and Bust: American Cinema in the 1940s*, ed. Thomas Schatz (Berkeley: University of California Press, 1997), 269.

39. The first film version was *The Maltese Falcon* (Roy Del Ruth, 1931), starring Ricardo Cortez and Bebe Daniels.

4 LILLIAN HELLMAN: *WOMAN IN THE DARK* (1934) AND *WATCH ON THE RHINE* (1943)

1. Diane Johnson, *Dashiell Hammett: A Life* (New York: Random House, 1983), 95.

2. Ibid., 105–106.

3. Ibid., 108.

4. Ibid.

5. Ibid.

6. William F. Nolan, *Hammett: A Life at the Edge* (New York: Congdon & Weed, 1983), 116.

7. Johnson, *Dashiell Hammett*, 100.

8. The production was scheduled to begin on June 19; it concluded on July 7. *New York Times*, June 8 and July 7, 1934.

9. *Woman in the Dark* was announced as the first of twelve films that Select planned to make at Biograph studios; *New York Times*, June 8, 1934. Only two of the films were made.

10. The impressive list of directors Ruttenberg worked with includes Fritz Lang, Frank Borzage, Julian Duvivier, King Vidor, William Wyler, Busby Berkeley, and

Anthony Mann, as well as four films each for George Cukor and Vincente Min-
nelli. His later credits include films ranging from the Marx Brothers' *A Day at the
Races* (Sam Wood, 1937), to *The Women* (1939), *The Philadelphia Story* (1940), and
Gaslight (1944) for Cukor, *Mrs. Miniver* (1942) for Wyler, and *The Thin Man Goes
Home* (Richard Thorpe, 1945).

11. Both Bellamy and Melvyn Douglas had only been acting in films for four years in
    1934, but Bellamy had worked in thirty-one films in contrast to Douglas's nine.
12. Johnson, *Dashiell Hammett*, 147.
13. Alice Kessler-Harris. *A Difficult Woman: The Challenging Life and Times of Lillian
    Hellman* (New York: Bloomsbury Press, 2012), 107–108.
14. Johnson, *Dashiell Hammett*, 156.
15. Ibid., 157.
16. Ibid., 164.
17. Bernard F. Dick, *Hal Wallis: Producer to the Stars* (Lexington: University Press of
    Kentucky, 2004), 86.
18. Deborah Martinson. *Lillian Hellman: A Life with Foxes and Scoundrels* (New York:
    Counterpoint, 2005), 173.
19. Ibid., 174.
20. Dick, *Hal Wallis*, 76.
21. Bernard F. Dick, *Hellman in Hollywood* (Rutherford, N.J.: Fairleigh Dickinson Uni-
    versity Press, 1982), 88; Martinson, *Lillian Hellman*, 174.
22. Alan Brinkley, *The Unfinished Nation: A Concise History of the American People*
    (New York: McGraw-Hill, 2010), 663.
23. Lillian Hellman, *Six Plays by Lillian Hellman* (New York: Vintage Books, 1979), 301.
24. Martinson, *Lillian Hellman*, 175.
25. Dick, *Hellman in Hollywood*, 88.
26. Ibid., 91.
27. Martinson, *Lillian Hellman*, 174.
28. Apparently Hellman wrote the dialogue for the scene at the Washington Monu-
    ment. The soft patriotic music particularly evokes Capra's Mr. Smith visiting
    the Lincoln Memorial in *Mr. Smith Goes to Washington* (1939).
29. Dick, *Hellman in Hollywood*, 94; Martinson, *Lillian Hellman*, 176.
30. Dick, *Hellman in Hollywood*, 95.
31. Martinson, *Lillian Hellman*, 175.
32. As a film director, Shumlin was not a success; he directed only one other film,
    Confidential Agent (1945).
33. Dick, *Hellman in Hollywood*, 96.
34. There is a complex relationship between *Watch on the Rhine* and *Casablanca*
    that stems not only from their addressing the same question of American
    involvement in the war, but also because the characters of Kurt Müller and Vic-
    tor Laszlo were most likely based on the same person—a Moscow-trained agent
    named Otto Katz who operated out of pre-Hitler Germany and then France.
    Hellman was friendly with him when he produced *The Spanish Earth* in support
    of the Republicans during the Spanish Civil War and when he raised money for

the antifascist cause in Hollywood in the late 1930s. Hellman's widely known play preceded the screen adaptation of *Casablanca*, while the release of *Casablanca* preceded the release of *Watch on the Rhine*. Without overstating the similarities, it is interesting to consider *Watch on the Rhine* as the story of Victor Laszlo after he leaves Casablanca for the United States. For Katz's story see Jonathan Miles, *The Dangerous Otto Katz: The Many Lives of a Soviet Spy* (New York: Bloomsbury, 2010).

CHAPTER 5   SEXUAL POLITICS: *THE MALTESE FALCON* (1931), *SATAN MET A LADY* (1936), AND *THE MALTESE FALCON* (1941)

1. The price was $8,500. Richard Layman, *Shadow Man: The Life of Dashiell Hammett* (New York: Harcourt Brace Jovanovich, 1981), 125.

2. Dashiell Hammett, *The Maltese Falcon* (New York: Vintage, 1992), 57.

3. Ibid., 89.

4. As Edward Said wrote, "To speak of Orientalism is to speak mainly . . . of a British and French cultural enterprise, a project whose dimensions take in such disparate realms as the imagination itself, the whole of India and the Levant, the Biblical texts and Biblical lands, the spice trade, colonial armies." Edward W. Said, *Orientalism* (New York: Vintage, 1979), 4. Brigid O'Shaughnessy invokes "the Orient" as the site of her initial involvement with the falcon, and Gutman's detailed narration begins with the Crusades and spans the globe from the Middle East to North Africa, from Turkey to China and Russia. Cairo's name additionally evokes Egypt, while the business card of an insurance broker in his wallet connects him to Shanghai. His homosexuality is meant to add yet another dimension of exoticism.

5. The ambiguity is evident in disagreement among scholars. See, for example: Steven Marcus, "Introduction," in Dashiell Hammett, *The Continental Op* (New York: Vintage, 1994), xv–xvii; Ilsa J. Bick, "The Beam That Fell and Other Crises in *The Maltese Falcon*," in *The Maltese Falcon, John Huston, Director*, ed. William Luhr (New Brunswick, N.J.: Rutgers University Press, 1995), 181–199; John J. Irwin, *Unless the Threat of Death Is Behind Them: Hard-Boiled Fiction and Film Noir* (Baltimore: Johns Hopkins University Press, 2006), 7.

6. Sid Wise, an attorney who protects Spade from City Hall by spreading around cash in a way that anticipates *The Glass Key*, is similarly cut for the more compact feature films.

7. Motion Picture Association of America, Production Code Administration records; Margaret Herrick Library, Academy of Motion Picture Arts and Sciences, Beverly Hills (hereafter MHL).

8. James Naremore, *More Than Night: Film Noir in Its Contexts* (Berkeley: University of California Press, 1998), 56.

9. A substantial part of its revenue came from a contract with Western Electric, which supplied much of the equipment for sound in theaters.

10. Eve Golden, *Golden Images: 41 Essays on Silent Film Stars* (Jefferson, N.C.: McFarland, 2001), 19.

11. Daniels and her husband Ben Lyon had a second career in England, with the enormously successful *Life with the Lyons* radio and television series from 1950 to 1961.

12. Bick sees Spade as failing to match Wonderly's image with the card, helping her make the argument of a "lack of certainty" in defining the "domain of the female." "The Beam That Fell," 185.

13. Hammett, *The Maltese Falcon,* 209.

14. Richard Maltby, "The Production Code and the Hays Office," in *Grand Design: Hollywood as a Modern Business Enterprise, 1930–1939,* ed. Tino Balio (New York: Charles Scribner's Sons, 1993), 48.

15. Hammett, *The Maltese Falcon,* 40.

16. Ibid., 196.

17. Ibid.

18. Note to Jason Joy from Darryl Zanuck, January 6, 1931, Motion Picture Association of America, Production Code Administration records, MHL.

19. Letter to Zanuck from Joy, January 16, 1931, Motion Picture Association of America, Production Code Administration records, MHL.

20. Memo to Mr. Hays, April 14, 1931, Motion Picture Association of America, Production Code Administration records, MHL. A more accurate description would have emphasized that Spade found women irresistible. After the release of the film, Lamar Trotti, then an MPPDA executive assistant in New York, would push the logic of "deniability" further, writing to Hays, "It did not seem to me that the scene indicated anything more than that Cortez . . . has had a petting party in the office. Certainly there is no indication that the woman was being paid." "Col. Joy's Resume," April 21, 1931, Motion Picture Association of America, Production Code Administration records, MHL. It is a long stretch from a petting party to paying a prostitute, which someone must have suggested to Trotti as a possible interpretation of the action.

21. Hammett, *The Maltese Falcon,* 92.

22. Motion Picture Association of America, Production Code Administration records, MHL.

23. Ibid. By April 21, a jury including "Mr. Schnitzer of R.K.O., Mr. Wurtzel of Fox, and Mr. Christie of the Christie Studio" had been convened and delivered its opinion: "It was the unanimous opinion of the jury that Warner Bros. should delete from their production the scenes in question." Motion Picture Association of America, Production Code Administration records, MHL.

24. Motion Picture Association of America, Production Code Administration records, MHL.

25. Hammett, *The Maltese Falcon,* 12.

26. Bick, "The Beam That Fell," 184.

27. The "Saracens" are nearly all that remains of Orientalism here, a further reduction of this strand of the plot.

28. James Wingate, the New York censor, commented on how to adapt the Mae West play *Diamond Lil:* "Develop the comedy elements, so that the treatment will

invest the picture with such exaggerated qualities as automatically to take care of possible offensiveness." Quoted in Maltby, *Grand Design*, 55.

29. Andrew Sarris, *"You Ain't Heard Nothin' Yet": The American Talking Film, History and Memory, 1927–1949* (New York: Oxford University Press, 1998), 95.

30. Joseph Breen still found cause for complaint. In a letter to Jack Warner dated January 31, 1935, he declared an early draft to be in violation of the Code because Shane was "a criminal operating as a private detective," a criticism repeated in a letter of June 4, which also requested eliminating the unflattering view of the police and "sexual suggestions, touching, Murgatroyd on Shane's lap, etc." The screenwriters must have been deliberately baiting him: specifically cited as offensive is a line of Spade to Murgatroyd, "You play wet nurse." Motion Picture Association of America, Production Code Administration records, MHL.

31. Lawrence Quirk, *Fasten Your Seat Belts: The Passionate Life of Bette Davis* (New York: William Morrow, 1990), 47.

32. Charlotte Chandler writes that *Satan Met a Lady* was "the film that precipitated Bette's decision to break her Warner Bros. contract." Charlotte Chandler, *The Girl Who Walked Home Alone: Bette Davis, A Personal Biography* (New York: Simon & Schuster, 2006), 111. In fact, *Satan* was just one of a series of films, beginning with *The Golden Arrow* (1936), that brought her to rebel. Following completion of *Satan*, she was assigned *God's Country and the Woman* (1937), eventually made with Beverly Roberts instead of Davis, which was the final straw—she fled to England. Only with *Jezebel* (Wyler, 1938) would Warner Bros. recognize her value.

33. Quirk, *Fasten Your Seat Belts*, 56–57.

34. Ibid., 58.

35. Although Breen had pronounced the script "basically acceptable" by the time it was shot in December 1935, as late as January 16, 1936, he was insisting on a recutting of the morning scene with the bootblack to remove any suggestion that Shane had remained "out all night in Valerie's apartment." Letters to Jack Warner, December 27, 1935, and January 16, 1936, Motion Picture Association of America, Production Code Administration records, MHL. Again, the principle of deniability: there is no other explanation, but nothing proves that he has come directly from her apartment. During its development, the film had undergone a number of title changes from *Money Man* to *Filthy Lucre* and finally to *Men on Her Mind* and *Satan Met a Lady*; the changes register a gradual shift in emphasis from the detective to the money to the woman and finally to the duel between Shane and Purvis—the film's final title and theme reverse the formula of Josef von Sternberg's *The Devil Is a Woman* (1935), released one year before.

36. William Luhr, "John Huston: A Biographical Sketch," in Luhr, *The Maltese Falcon, John Huston, Director*, 18–20.

37. James Agee, "Undirectable Director," in *Reflections in a Male Eye: John Huston and the American Experience*, ed. Gaylyn Studlar and David Dresser (Washington, D.C.: Smithsonian Institution Press, 1993), 265.

38. In John Engell's words, "a close inspection of his many screenplay adaptations of novels . . . proves that he habitually lifted much of his dialogue from the fiction

being adapted. More importantly, . . . he always strove to 'capture the spirit' as well as the letter of his literary source." John Engell, "Traven, Huston, and the Textual Pleasures of the Sierra Madre," in *Reflections in a Male Eye,* 82.

39. William F. Nolan, *John Huston: King Rebel* (Los Angeles: Sherbourne Press, 1965), 40.

40. Robert Emmet Long, ed., *John Huston: Interviews* (Jackson: University Press of Mississippi, 2001), 75.

41. Ibid., 34.

42. Ibid., 28.

43. *New York Times,* October 4, 1941.

44. James Naremore, "John Huston and *The Maltese Falcon,*" in Luhr, *The Maltese Falcon, John Huston, Director,* 149–160.

45. Lucile Watson as Maggie's aunt Ada anticipates her role as Fanny Farrelly, mother of Sara Müller, played by Davis in *Watch on the Rhine.*

46. *New York Times,* October 4, 1941.

47. Stefan Kanfer, *Tough without a Gun: The Life and Extraordinary Afterlife of Humphrey Bogart* (New York: Alfred A. Knopf, 2011), 45.

48. Robert Sklar, *City Boys: Cagney, Bogart, Garfield* (Princeton, N.J.: Princeton University Press, 1992), 134–135.

49. Kanfer, *Tough without a Gun,* 65.

50. Letter to Darryl Zanuck, January 16, 1931, Motion Picture Association of America, Production Code Administration records, MHL.

51. Letter to Jack Warner, May 23, 1941, Motion Picture Association of America, Production Code Administration records, MHL.

52. Letter to Jack Warner, June 6, 1941, Motion Picture Association of America, Production Code Administration records, MHL.

53. Certificate of Approval, Motion Picture Association of America, Production Code Administration records, MHL.

54. Mary Ann Doane, *Femmes Fatales: Feminism, Film Theory, Psychoanalysis* (New York: Routledge, 1991), 2.

55. See, for example, Kanfer, *Tough without a Gun,* 68.

56. Letter to Jack Warner, May 27, 1941, Motion Picture Association of America, Production Code Administration records, MHL.

57. Hammett, *The Maltese Falcon,* 105.

58. Ibid., 126.

59. Ibid., 108–109.

60. Ibid., 109.

61. Ibid., 126.

62. Thomas Leitch, *Crime Films* (Cambridge: Cambridge University Press, 2002), 198.

63. For the passage in the novel see Hammett, *The Maltese Falcon,* 213–214.

64. See Hammett, *The Maltese Falcon,* 215.

65. Gaylyn Studlar, "Shadowboxing: *Fat City* and the Malaise of Masculinity," in *Reflections in a Male Eye: John Huston and the American Experience,* ed. Gaylyn Studlar and David Dresser (Washington, D.C.: Smithsonian Institution Press, 1993), 183. For Agee, see note 37 above.

66. William Luhr, "*The Maltese Falcon*, the Detective Genre, and *Film Noir*," in Luhr, *The Maltese Falcon, John Huston, Director*, 5.

CHAPTER 6   ETHNIC POLITICS: *THE GLASS KEY* (1935 AND 1942)

1. Letter from B. P. Schulberg to Jason Joy, March 24, 1931, Motion Picture Association of America, Production Code Administration records, Margaret Herrick Library, Academy of Motion Picture Arts and Sciences, Beverly Hills (hereafter MHL).

2. "Col. Joy's Resume" of the meeting with Lloyd Sheldon and Bartlett Cormack, March 25, 1931, Motion Picture Association of America, Production Code Administration records, MHL.

3. Memorandum from Stewart to Dr. Wingate, December 20, 1934, Motion Picture Association of America, Production Code Administration records, MHL. The title "Colonel" refers to the rank Joy attained in the army.

4. Richard Layman, *Shadow Man: The Life of Dashiell Hammett* (New York: Harcourt Brace Jovanovich, 1981), 81–82.

5. Dashiell Hammett, *The Glass Key* (New York: Vintage, 1989), 160.

6. Ibid., 83.

7. Ibid., 61.

8. Ibid., 69.

9. Ibid., 63, 66, 73, 99.

10. Alan Brinkley, *The Unfinished Nation: A Concise History of the American People* (New York: McGraw-Hill, 2010), 480.

11. Vivian Sobchack, "Postmodern Modes of Ethnicity," in *Unspeakable Images: Ethnicity and the American Cinema*, ed. Lester Friedman (Urbana: University of Illinois Press, 1991), 329.

12. Ella Shohat, "Ethnicities in Relation: Toward a Multicultural Reading of American Cinema," in Friedman, *Unspeakable Images*, 234.

13. Hammett, *The Glass Key*, 9.

14. Given Hammett's wide and eclectic reading of history, it is not impossible that he even had in mind the Vikings who invaded England between the eighth and eleventh centuries.

15. Hammett, *The Glass Key*, 68.

16. Ibid., 171.

17. For a very different reading of Beaumont's liaison with Janet, see Sean McCann, *Gumshoe America: Hard-Boiled Crime Fiction and the Rise and Fall of New Deal Liberalism* (Durham, N.C.: Duke University Press, 2000), 122.

18. The PCA insisted that Madvig's club not be presented as a site of professional gambling, which accounts for their betting on which blade of an old fan will stop in a certain position. Memorandum from Mr. Steward to Dr. Wingate, December 20, 1934, and letter from Joseph Breen to John Hammell at Paramount Studios, December 22, 1934, Motion Picture Association of America, Production Code Administration records, MHL.

19. Shohat, "Ethnicities in Relation," 218.

20. Jonathan Munby, "*Manhattan Melodrama*'s 'Art of the Weak': Telling History from the Other Side in the 1930's Gangster Film," *Journal of American Studies* 30, no. 1 (1996): 101–103.

21. Catholics, wary of the program of assimilation to a normative Protestant Americanism, were equally distressed that "the only way ethnic concerns could get a voice within a culture traditionally steeped in nativist symbols and definitions of Americanness, was under the stigma of criminality." Jonathan Munby, *Public Enemies, Public Heroes: Screening the Gangster from Little Caesar to Touch of Evil* (Chicago: University of Chicago Press, 1999), 105. Ruth Vasey has documented the response of international audiences and distributors. In one extreme instance the Italian government told an intermediary of the MPPDA that "no films featuring Italians or bearing Italian names could be distributed in Italy unless those characters were completely sympathetic." Ruth Vasey, *The World according to Hollywood, 1918–1939* (Madison: University of Wisconsin Press, 1997), 143.

22. Vasey, *The World according to Hollywood*, 137.

23. Ibid., 101, 108.

24. *The Glass Key* production file, MHL.

25. According to William Nolan, "It is generally agreed among film critics that he gave the best performance of his career as Ned Beaumont." William Nolan, *Hammett: A Life at the Edge* (New York: Congdon & Weed, 1983), 151.

26. *Diamond Jim* (A. Edward Sutherland, 1935), released three months after *The Glass Key*, made Arnold a star, and he would continue with these roles in films like *Come and Get It* (Howard Hawks, Robert Rossen, William Wyler, 1936) as Barney Glasgow, an empire-building lumberman, or as J. B. Ball, who throws his wife's mink coat out the window in *Easy Living* (Mitchell Leisen, 1937).

27. The Production Code Administration was concerned with the level of violence. See the letter from Joseph Breen to John Hammell of Paramount Studios, May 9, 1935, Motion Picture Association of America, Production Code Administration records, MHL.

28. Hammett, *The Glass Key*, 164.

29. Mark Winokur, *American Laughter: Immigrants, Ethnicity and 1930s Hollywood Film Comedy* (New York: St. Martin's Press, 1996), 4.

30. Winokur reads *Manhattan Melodrama* (1934) in a similar way: the assimilated Jim Wade (William Powell) seeks the execution of his childhood friend Blackie (Clark Gable), who had taken the alternative path of remaining unassimilated and a gangster. Winokur, "Improbable Ethnic Hero: William Powell and the Transformation of Ethnic Hollywood," *Cinema Journal* 27, no. 1 (Fall 1987): 12–13.

31. Letter from Joseph Breen to John Hammell of Paramount Studios, May 9, 1935, Motion Picture Association of America, Production Code Administration records, MHL.

32. Hammett, *The Glass Key*, 91.

33. Ibid., 185. Joseph Breen's letter to Hammell on December 22, 1934, recommended cutting the word "massacrist" because of its "obvious connotations." Motion Picture Association of America, Production Code Administration records, MHL.

34. Hammett, *The Glass Key*, 186.

35. Vasey, *The World according to Hollywood*, 128.

36. Richard Maltby, "The Production Code and the Hays Office," in *Grand Design: Hollywood as a Modern Business Enterprise 1930–1939*, ed. Tino Balio (New York: Charles Scribner's Sons, 1993), 70.

37. Unsigned letter from the Production Code Administration, February 6, 1942, Motion Picture Association of America, Production Code Administration records, MHL.

38. Lake later wrote that she had not learned to pull punches and Donlevy was stunned after she hit him. Veronica Lake and Donald Bain, *Veronica* (New York: Bantam, 1972), 90.

39. Ibid., 51. Hornblow gave her the name Veronica Lake, and in her autobiography she claims that during the screen test for him her hair blew across her left eye in the way that inspired her signature "peek-a-boo" look.

40. Ibid., 92.

41. Hammett, *The Glass Key*, 214.

42. Class and ethnicity meet in vernacular speech, with or without a particular accent. Munby's analysis of Blackie (Clark Gable) in *Manhattan Melodrama* illuminates an example of this: "Blackie's world is rooted in the vernacular, in the popular realm." Munby, "*Manhattan Melodrama*," 106.

43. Ibid., 102.

44. *New York Times*, May 14, 1936.

45. The PCA made a point of telling Paramount not to present her surrounded by white men. Letter to Luigi Luraschi, February 6, 1942, Motion Picture Association of America, Production Code Administration records, MHL.

46. This repeats the pattern of *Manhattan Melodrama* in which Blackie refuses to accept help from Jim Wade because it will compromise Wade's integrity.

CHAPTER 7   HAMMETT IN RETROSPECT: *MILLER'S CROSSING*

1. Richard Layman, *Shadow Man: The Life of Dashiell Hammett* (New York: Harcourt, Brace, Jovanovich, 1981), 221.

2. *New York Times,* July 10, 1951.

3. *New York Times,* January 11, 1961.

4. Layman, *Shadow Man*, 224.

5. Alice Kessler-Harris, *A Difficult Woman: The Challenging Life and Times of Lillian Hellman* (New York: Bloomsbury Press, 2012), 211. When Hammett died, the government seized his estate for back taxes. Hellman made the IRS an offer of $5,000, which was refused, but her friend Arthur Cowan acquired it at auction for $5,000 and gave it to Hellman. "Under [Hellman's] guiding hand," in the words of Kessler-Harris, and "helped no doubt by the revival of the hard-boiled-detective-and-tough-dame style that Hammett had originated, the estate flourished. Hellman controlled Hammett's legacy tightly, asking not only for generous fees but also for the right of approval."

6. See Kessler-Harris, *A Difficult Woman*, especially 244–249. Hellman received wide publicity and condemnation as an organizer of a pro-Soviet conference

of leftist intellectuals at New York's Waldorf Astoria—the Cultural and Scientific Conference for World Peace—in March 1949, though in fact her role in that conference was minor. With her testimony before McCarthy and the House Un-American Activities Committee (HUAC) in May 1952, however, four months after Hammett was released from prison, her reputation—as a defender of civil rights—rebounded. She refused to name names, and a letter to the committee, released to the press when committee chair John Wood requested that it be entered into the record, contained what became a tagline of her testimony: "I cannot and will not cut my conscience to fit this year's fashions." Kessler-Harris, *A Difficult Woman,* 262. Hellman remained at odds with many New York intellectuals, both conservatives and liberal former leftists who during the Cold War became outspoken anticommunists.

7. Ibid., 114.

8. Hellman quickly lost her renewed popularity, particularly during an extended dispute with and lawsuit against Mary McCarthy, who branded her a liar on *The Dick Cavett Show* in October 1979, and when some stories in her memoirs, especially "Julia," were discovered to have been invented.

9. Joe Gores, *Hammett* (London: Orion, 1975), 235.

10. See Fredric Jameson's use of "pastness" in relation to the "nostalgia film." Fredric Jameson, "Postmodernism and Consumer Society," in *Critical Visions in Film Theory: Classic and Contemporary Readings,* ed. Timothy Corrigan and Patricia White (New York: Bedford/St. Martin's, 2011), 1032.

11. Ibid.

12. Nielsen ratings placed the first episode, with a 22.6 percent share of households with television sets, third among all programs for the week; with an 18.2 percent share the third episode ranked eleventh; with a 17.9 percent share the second episode ranked thirteenth. *New York Times,* June 1, 1978.

13. Bob Rafelson, the film's director, was involved in numerous significant projects in the 1960s and 1970s. He produced *Easy Rider* (1969) and *The Last Picture Show* (1971), and he both produced and directed *Five Easy Pieces* (1970), *The King of Marvin Gardens* (1972), and *The Postman Always Rings Twice* (1981), all staring Jack Nicholson.

14. Fredric Jameson, *Postmodernism, or, The Cultural Logic of Late Capitalism* (Durham, N.C.: Duke University Press, 1991), 20.

15. Eddie Robson, *Coen Brothers* (London: Virgin, 2003), 72.

16. Ibid., 81.

17. *New York Times,* September 21, 1990.

18. *Chicago Sun-Times,* October 5, 1990.

19. *Village Voice,* September 25, 1990.

20. One reviewer wrote that the Coen brothers were lucky not to have been sued by Hammett's estate. John Harkness, *Sight and Sound* (Winter 1990–91), cited by Sabine Horst, *"Miller's Crossing,"* in *Joel & Ethan Coen,* ed. Peter Körte and Georg Seesslen (New York: Limelight Editions, 2001), 96. In a 1998 interview, Ethan Coen answered a question about the film's debt to Dashiell Hammett by saying

that the film is "an *homage* [pause] or a rip-off, depending on how you look at it." *The Big Lebowski*, DVD (Universal Home Entertainment, 1998). But "rip-off" suggests trying to get away with something, while "homage" throws attention on the object of veneration—*Miller's Crossing* goes well beyond worshipful celebration.

21. Robson, *Coen Brothers*, 68.

22. Some are used as they were in the novel, such as Beaumont's line, "How far has this dizzy blond daughter of his got her hooks into you," which becomes Reagan's "How far has she got her hooks into you." And Beaumont's "As far as I'm concerned we're quits" becomes Reagan's "We're quits, as far as I'm concerned." But many phrases are inserted in significantly different contexts. When Leo says, "Call me a big-hearted slob," he is echoing Jeff's phrase in the novel, "I'm just a good-natured slob," uttered after strangling O'Rory and memorably delivered by both Guinn Williams in the 1935 film and William Bendix in the 1942 version. Delivered by Leo, the similar line focuses our attention on characteristics Leo shares with Jeff in the earlier versions: physical power and limited intelligence. O'Doole, the anxious police chief modeled on District Attorney Farr—especially as performed by Donald MacBride in the 1942 film—becomes the target of a line initially thrown by Madvig at Beaumont in the novel: "Don't anything ever suit you?" In the revenge scene in the films and the novel, which occurs in Hammett's chapter "The Heels," Jeff refers to Beaumont and O'Rory/Varna as "a couple of heels." In *Miller's Crossing*, Verna says to Reagan, "We're a couple of heels," when she is apparently contrite at her betrayal of Leo with Reagan, or at least chagrinned at losing Leo. The line given Caspar, "Just me, Mink, and my friend Roscoe," mixes Jeff's reference to a gun as a "Roscoe" with his comment to Beaumont—in the films only—that his secret concerning who killed Sloss is between "me and Shad [in the 1935 film] and the lamppost." The Dane's reference to Reagan as "Little Miss Punching Bag" is similar to Jeff's comments to Beaumont, but The Dane's contemptuous feminizing of Reagan also contrasts with Jeff's sadomasochistic feminizing of Beaumont as his "sweetheart." As Sabine Horst notes, Reagan's "'Lo, Shad" on the telephone with the police is a Beaumont mannerism. *"Miller's Crossing,"* 98. Yet by applying "Shad," the first name of the Irish gangster in the novel and 1935 film, to a cop, the Coens encourage us to notice and reflect on the change. Of course this conversation, in which Reagan has taken the receiver from Verna who has called the police, also recalls *The Big Sleep* (Howard Hawks, 1946), in which Vivian Sternwood (Lauren Bacall) calls the police and then gives the phone to Marlowe (Humphrey Bogart).

23. Ronald Bergan, *The Coen Brothers* (New York: Thunder's Mouth Press, 2000), 120.

24. There are various accounts of how the Irish characters acquired accents, but all agree that Gabriel Byrne—born in Dublin with a mother from Galway and who claimed that he took his cue from the rhythm of the writing—suggested reading Reagan's part with his Irish accent. "'We were skeptical,' says Joel, 'but we said, fine, go ahead. He did it and we liked the way it sounded.'" Robson, *Coen Brothers*, 70.

25. An irony that would not be lost on the Coen brothers is that John Turturro's family roots are in Sicily and Puglia. Audiences for *Miller's Crossing* when it was released in October 1990 would have associated him with the loudly bigoted Italian American Pino in Spike Lee's *Do the Right Thing*, which had appeared to great acclaim in June 1989. *Miller's Crossing* was filmed the following winter.

26. Robson, *Coen Brothers*, 78.

27. Ibid., 70.

28. Ibid., 88.

29. As Eddie Robson writes, "It is worth considering that there is a possible gay subtext in the dynamic between Tom and Leo, a reading that has become popular with many Coen commentators." *Coen Brothers,* 94. This reading centers on the idea that Reagan expresses little passion for Verna and that it is jealousy of Verna's closeness to Leo that drives Reagan to sleep with her. And interestingly, the decisive moment echoes that of *The Maltese Falcon* (1941) when Spade looks away from Brigid past the blowing curtain to Wilmer on the street corner. Rowell looks for evidence of Reagan's passion for Leo in a dissolve from the blowing curtains at Verna's place to those in Leo's bedroom, where he is about to be attacked. Erica Rowell, *The Brothers Grim: The Films of Joel and Ethan Coen* (Lanham, Md.: Scarecrow Press, 2007), 84. By pushing a "queer" reading of the film to its limits, Rowell does us the service of testing conclusions that run the full gamut from the obviously valid to the highly speculative.

30. Linda Hutcheon, *A Poetics of Postmodernism: History, Theory, Fiction* (New York: Routledge, 1988), 4.

31. *Chicago Sun-Times,* October 5, 1990.

32. Jameson, *Postmodernism,* 6, 10.

33. Hutcheon, *A Poetics of Postmodernism,* 11.

34. Jameson, *Postmodernism,* 392.

CONCLUSION: DASHIELL HAMMETT AND THE MOVIES

1. Nino Frank, "A New Kind of Police Drama: The Crime Adventure," in *Film Noir Reader 2*, ed. Alain Silver and James Ursini (New York: Limelight Editions, 2003), 16.

2. Raymond Borde and Etienne Chaumeton, *A Panorama of American Film Noir, 1941–1953* (San Francisco: City Lights Books, 2002), 15.

3. See articles by Jean-Pierre Chartier, Henri-Francois Rey, Pierre Duvilars, Roger Taileur, Pierre Kast, and Madeleine Vives, in *Perspectives on Film Noir*, ed. R. Barton Palmer (New York: G. K. Hall, 1996), which variously highlight film noir's pessimism, the return of the vamp, the struggle between good and evil, and a humanist perspective.

4. The pool of films grew as attention shifted to broader historical and cultural explanations. Mentioned along with crime have been disillusionment following the stock market crash, World War II, the Cold War, and fear of war with Korea; intellectual and artistic movements from naturalism and modernism, to expressionism, surrealism, existentialism, the Ashcan School of American

painting, and Edward Hopper; French poetic-realism; the gangster and horror genres; the German influence in cinematography, Italian neorealism, documentary film, and melodrama. Specific émigré industry personnel were identified, from the cinematographers, lighting technicians, and set designers to directors—particularly Fritz Lang, Robert Siodmak, Billy Wilder, Anthony Mann, and Otto Preminger—and production realities at B-picture and poverty-row studios. See Paul Kerr, "Out of What Past? Notes on the B Film Noir," in Alain Silver and James Ursini, eds., *Film Noir Reader* (New York: Limelight Editions, 1996), 107–128. Sources in visual culture beyond cinema include photojournalism, a postwar iconography of diners, bars, drugstores, bus stops, and train stations, and urban spaces representing a "nightmare of special regimentation, consumer manipulation and corporate control." Edward Dimendberg, *Film Noir and the Spaces of Modernity* (Cambridge, Mass.: Harvard University Press, 2004), 14.

5. Tony Williams, "Phantom Lady, Cornell Woolrich, and the Masochistic Aesthetic," in Silver and Ursini, *Film Noir Reader*, 130.

6. William Luhr, *Film Noir* (Malden, Mass.: Wiley-Blackwell, 2012), 25.

7. E. Ann Kaplan, "The Place of Women in Fritz Lang's *The Blue Gardenia*," in *Women in Film Noir*, ed. E. Ann Kaplan (London: BFI, 1998), 81.

8. Frank Krutnik, *In a Lonely Street: Film Noir, Genre, Masculinity* (New York: Routledge, 1991), 88.

9. James Naremore, *More Than Night: Film Noir in Its Contexts* (Berkeley: University of California Press, 1998), 63.

BIBLIOGRAPHY

Agee, James. "Undirectable Director." In *Reflections in a Male Eye: John Huston and the American Experience,* ed. Gaylyn Studlar and David Dresser. Washington, D.C.: Smithsonian Institution Press, 1993.

Andrew, Dudley. *Concepts in Film Theory.* New York: Oxford University Press, 1984.

Astor, Mary. *Mary Astor: A Life on Film.* New York: Bantam, Doubleday, Dell, 1972.

Balio, Tino, ed. *Grand Design: Hollywood as a Modern Business Enterprise, 1930–1939.* New York: Simon & Schuster, 1993.

Behlmer, Rudy. *W. S. Van Dyke's Journal: White Shadows in the South Seas, 1927–1928: and Other Van Dyke on Van Dyke.* Lanham, Md.: Scarecrow Press, 1996.

Bergan, Ronald. *The Coen Brothers.* New York: Thunder's Mouth Press, 2000.

Bick, Ilsa J. "The Beam That Fell and Other Crises in *The Maltese Falcon.*" In *The Maltese Falcon, John Huston, Director,* ed. William Luhr. New Brunswick, N.J.: Rutgers University Press, 1995.

Borde, Raymond, and Étienne Chaumeton. *A Panorama of American Film Noir, 1941–1953.* San Francisco: City Lights Books, 2002.

Bordwell, David, Kristin Thompson, and Janet Staiger. *The Classical Hollywood Cinema: Film Style and Mode of Production to 1960.* New York: Columbia University Press, 1985.

Braudy, Leo, and Marshall Cohen. *Film Theory and Criticism.* New York: Oxford University Press, 2009.

Brinkley, Alan. *The Unfinished Nation: A Concise History of the American People.* New York: McGraw-Hill, 2010.

Chandler, Charlotte. *The Girl Who Walked Home Alone: Bette Davis, a Personal Biography.* New York: Simon & Schuster, 2006.

Chudacoff, Howard P., and Judith E. Smith. *The Evolution of American Urban Society.* Englewood Cliffs, N.J.: Prentice-Hall, 1988.

Clarens, Carlos. *Crime Movies: An Illustrated History from D. W. Griffith to Pulp Fiction.* Updated by Foster Hirsch. New York: Da Capo Press, 1997.

Corliss, Richard. *The Hollywood Screenwriters.* New York: Avon, 1972.

Crowther, Bosley. *The Lion's Share: The Story of an Entertainment Empire.* New York: Dutton, 1957.

Dick, Bernard F. *Hal Wallis: Producer to the Stars.* Lexington: University Press of Kentucky, 2004.

————. *Hellman in Hollywood.* Rutherford, N.J.: Fairleigh Dickinson University Press, 1982.

Dimendberg, Edward. *Film Noir and the Spaces of Modernity.* Cambridge, Mass.: Harvard University Press, 2004.

Doane, Mary Ann. *Femmes Fatales: Feminism, Film Theory, Psychoanalysis.* New York: Routledge, 1991.

Engell, John. "Traven, Huston, and the Textual Pleasures of the Sierra Madre." In *Reflections in the Male Eye: John Huston and the American Experience,* ed. Gaylyn Studlar and David Dresser. Washington, D.C.: Smithsonian Institution Press, 1993.

Everson, William K. *The Detective in Film.* Secaucus, N.J.: Citadel Press, 1972.

Eyman, Scott. *Lion of Hollywood: The Life and Legend of Louis B. Mayer.* Simon & Schuster, 2005.

Francisco, Charles. *Gentleman: The William Powell Story.* New York: St. Martin's Press, 1985.

Friedman, Lester D. *Unspeakable Images: Ethnicity in American Cinema.* Urbana: University of Illinois Press, 1991.

Golden, Eve. *Golden Images: 41 Essays on Silent Film Stars.* Jefferson, N.C.: McFarland, 2001.

Gores, Joe. *Hammett.* London: Orion Books, 2002.

Hammett, Dashiell. *The Continental Op.* New York: Vintage, 1989.

————. *The Dain Curse.* New York: Vintage, 1989.

————. *Dashiell Hammett: Selected Letters.* Ed. Richard Layman with Julie M. Rivett. Washington, D.C.: Counterpoint, 2001.

————. *The Glass Key.* New York: Vintage, 1989.

————. *The Maltese Falcon.* New York: Vintage, 1992.

————. *Nightmare Town.* New York: Vintage, 1999.

————. *Red Harvest.* New York: Vintage, 1992.

————. *The Thin Man.* New York: Vintage, 1992.

Haycraft, Howard. *Murder for Pleasure: The Life and Times of the Detective Story.* New York: Carroll & Graf, 1941.

Hellman, Lillian. *Pentimento.* Boston: Little, Brown, 1973.

————. *Scoundrel Time.* Boston: Little, Brown, 1976.

————. *Six Plays by Lillian Hellman.* New York: Vintage Books, 1979.

————. *An Unfinished Woman.* New York: Barnes & Noble, 2001.

Horst, Sabine. "*Miller's Crossing.*" In *Joel & Ethan Coen,* ed. Peter Körte and Georg Seesslen. New York: Limelight Editions, 2001.

Hutcheon, Linda. *A Poetics of Postmodernism: History, Theory, Fiction.* New York: Routledge, 1988.

————. *A Theory of Adaptation.* New York: Routledge, 2006.

Irwin, John J. *Unless the Threat of Death Is Behind Them: Hard-Boiled Fiction and Film Noir.* Baltimore: Johns Hopkins University Press, 2006.

Jameson, Fredric. "Postmodernism and Consumer Society." In *Critical Visions in Film Theory: Classic and Contemporary Readings,* ed. Timothy Corrigan and Patricia White. New York: Bedford/St. Martin's, 2011.

————. *Postmodernism, or, The Cultural Logic of Late Capitalism.* Durham, N.C.: Duke University Press, 1991.

Jess-Cooke, Carolyn. *Film Sequels: Theory and Practice from Hollywood to Bollywood.* Edinburgh: Edinburgh University Press, 2009.

Jess-Cooke, Carolyn, and Constantine Verevis. *Second Takes: Critical Approaches to the Film Sequel.* Albany: State University of New York Press, 2010.

Johnson, Diane. *Dashiell Hammett: A Life.* New York: Random House, 1983.

Kanfer, Stefan. *Tough without a Gun: The Life and Extraordinary Afterlife of Humphrey Bogart.* New York: Alfred A. Knopf, 2011.

Kaplan, E. Ann, ed. *Women in Film Noir.* London: BFI Publishing, 1998.

Kerr, Paul. "Out of What Past? Notes on the B Film Noir." In *Film Noir Reader,* ed. Alain Silver and James Ursini. New York: Limelight Editions, 1996.

Kessler-Harris, Alice. *A Difficult Woman: The Challenging Life and Times of Lillian Hellman.* New York: Bloomsbury Press, 2012.

Kinnard, Roy. *The Films of Fay Wray.* Jefferson, N.C.: McFarland, 2005.

Koppes, Clayton R. "Regulating the Screen: The Office of War Information and the Production Code Administration." In *Boom and Bust: American Cinema in the 1940s,* ed. Thomas Schatz. Berkeley: University of California Press, 1997.

Körte, Peter, and Georg Seesslen, eds. *Joel & Ethan Coen.* New York: Limelight Editions, 2001.

Kotsilibas-Davis, James, and Myrna Loy. *Myrna Loy: Being and Becoming.* New York: Alfred A. Knopf, 1987.

Krutnik, Frank. *In a Lonely Street: Film Noir, Genre, Masculinity.* New York: Routledge, 1991.

Lake, Veronica, and Donald Bain. *Veronica.* New York: Bantam, 1972.

Layman, Richard. *Shadow Man: The Life of Dashiell Hammett.* New York: Harcourt Brace Jovanovich, 1981.

Leitch, Thomas. *Crime Films.* Cambridge: Cambridge University Press, 2002.

———. *Film Adaptation and Its Discontents: From Gone with the Wind to The Passion of Christ.* Baltimore: Johns Hopkins University Press, 2007.

Long, Robert Emmet, ed. *John Huston Interviews.* Jackson: University Press of Mississippi, 2001.

Luhr, William. *Film Noir.* Malden, Mass.: Wiley-Blackwell, 2012.

———. "John Huston: A Biographical Sketch." In *The Maltese Falcon, John Huston, Director,* ed. William Luhr. New Brunswick, N.J.: Rutgers University Press, 1995.

———. "*The Maltese Falcon,* the Detective Genre, and *Film Noir.*" In *The Maltese Falcon, John Huston, Director,* ed. William Luhr. New Brunswick, N.J.: Rutgers University Press, 1995.

MacAdams, William. *Ben Hecht.* New York: Barricade Books, 1995.

Maltby, Richard. "The Production Code and the Hays Office." In *Grand Design: Hollywood as a Modern Business Enterprise, 1930–1939,* ed. Tino Balio. New York: Charles Scribner's Sons, 1993.

Marcus, Steven. "Introduction." In *The Continental Op,* by Dashiell Hammett. New York: Vintage, 1994.

Martinson, Deborah. *Lillian Hellman: A Life with Foxes and Scoundrels.* New York: Counterpoint, 2005.

McCann, Sean. *Gumshoe America: Hard-Boiled Crime Fiction and the Rise and Fall of New Deal Liberalism*. Durham, N.C.: Duke University Press, 2000.

Meyers, Jeffrey. *Gary Cooper: American Hero*. New York: William Morrow, 1998.

Miles, Jonathan. *The Dangerous Otto Katz: The Many Lives of a Soviet Spy*. New York: Bloomsbury, 2010.

Milne, Tom. *Rouben Mamoulian*. Bloomington: Indiana University Press, 1970.

Mordden, Ethan. *The Hollywood Studios: House Style during the Golden Age of Movies*. New York: Simon & Schuster, 1988.

Munby, Jonathan. "*Manhattan Melodrama's* 'Art of the Weak': Telling History from the Other Side in the 1930's Gangster Film." *Journal of American Studies* 30, no. 1 (1996).

——. *Public Enemies, Public Heroes: Screening the Gangster from Little Caesar to Touch of Evil*. Chicago: University of Chicago Press, 1999.

Naremore, James, ed. *Film Adaptation*. New Brunswick, N.J.: Rutgers University Press, 2000.

——. "John Huston and *The Maltese Falcon*." In *The Maltese Falcon, John Huston, Director*, ed. William Luhr. New Brunswick, N.J.: Rutgers University Press, 1995.

——. *More Than Night: Film Noir in Its Contexts*. Berkeley: University of California Press, 1998.

Nochimson, Martha. *Screen Couple Chemistry: The Power of 2*. Austin: University of Texas Press, 2002.

Nolan, William F. *Hammett: A Life at the Edge*. New York: Congdon & Weed, 1983.

——. *John Huston: King Rebel*. Los Angeles: Sherbourne Press, 1965.

Palmer, R. Barton, ed. *Perspectives on Film Noir*. New York: G. K. Hall, 1996.

Porter, Dennis. *The Pursuit of Crime: Art and Ideology in Detective Fiction*. New Haven, Conn.: Yale University Press, 1984.

Quirk, Lawrence. *Fasten Your Seat Belts: The Passionate Life of Bette Davis*. New York: William Morrow, 1990.

Riese, Randall. *All about Bette: Her Life from A to Z*. Chicago: Contemporary Books, 1993.

Robson, Eddie. *Coen Brothers*. London: Virgin, 2003.

Rowell, Erica. *The Brothers Grim: The Films of Joel and Ethan Coen*. Lanham, Md.: Scarecrow Press, 2007.

Said, Edward W. *Orientalism*. New York: Vintage, 1979.

Sarris, Andrew. *"You Ain't Heard Nothin' Yet": The American Talking Film, History and Memory, 1927–1949*. New York: Oxford University Press, 1998.

Schatz, Thomas, ed. *Boom and Bust: The American Cinema in the 1940s*. Berkeley: University of California Press, 1997.

Scott, Ian. *In Capra's Shadow: The Life and Career of Screenwriter Robert Riskin*. Lexington: University Press of Kentucky, 2006.

Shohat, Ella. "Ethnicities in Relation: Toward a Multicultural Reading of American Cinema." In *Unspeakable Images: Ethnicity in American Cinema*, ed. Lester D. Friedman. Urbana: University of Illinois Press, 1991.

Silver, Alain, and James Ursini, eds. *Film Noir Reader*. New York: Limelight Editions, 1996.

——. *Film Noir Reader 2*. New York: Limelight Editions, 2003.

Sklar, Robert. *City Boys: Cagney, Bogart, Garfield.* Princeton, N.J.: Princeton University Press, 1992.

Sobchack, Vivian. "Postmodern Modes of Ethnicity." In *Unspeakable Images: Ethnicity and the American Cinema,* ed. Lester D. Friedman. Urbana: University of Illinois Press, 1991.

Spergel, Mark. *Reinventing Reality: The Art and Life of Rouben Mamoulian.* Metuchen, N.J.: Scarecrow Press, 1993.

Stam, Robert, and Alessandra Raengo, eds. *Literature and Film: A Guide to the Theory and Practice of Film Adaptation.* Malden, Mass.: Blackwell, 2005.

Studlar, Gaylyn, and David Dresser, eds. *Reflections in a Male Eye: John Huston and the American Experience.* Washington, D.C.: Smithsonian Institution Press, 1993.

Vasey, Ruth. *The World according to Hollywood, 1918–1939.* Madison: University of Wisconsin Press, 1997.

Warshow, Robert. *The Immediate Experience: Movies, Comics, Theatre, and Other Aspects of Popular Culture.* Cambridge, Mass.: Harvard University Press, 2001.

Williams, Tony. "Phantom Lady, Cornell Woolrich, and the Masochistic Aesthetic." In *Film Noir Reader,* ed. Alain Silver and James Ursini. New York: Limelight Editions, 1996.

Winokur, Mark. *American Laughter: Immigrants, Ethnicity and 1930s Hollywood Film Comedy.* New York: St. Martin's Press, 1996.

———. "Improbable Ethnic Hero: William Powell and the Transformation of Ethnic Hollywood." *Cinema Journal* 27, no. 1 (Fall 1987).

INDEX

Page numbers in *italics* refer to illustrations.

Cowan, Arthur, 192n.5
Cowling, Bruce, 78
CPUSA (Communist Party of the USA), 89; Hammett defends leaders of, 90; linked to Civil Rights Congress, 155
Crimp, Douglas, 170
Cromwell, John, 32
Crosland, Alan, 21, 49
Crowther, Bosley, 117, 181n.15
Cukor, George, 40, 185n.10
Cultural and Scientific Conference for World Peace, 193n.6
Curtiz, Michael, 32, 80, 109, 118, 136

The Dain Curse (Hammett), 9, 21, 28, 96, 175
The Dain Curse (TV miniseries, 1978), 157–158, *159*, 193n.12
Daly, Carroll John, 1
Dangerous Female (1931 *Maltese Falcon* adaptation), 2, 5, 96, 97, 99–108; uncertain domain of the female in, 187n.12. See also *The Maltese Falcon* (1931); Ruth Wonderly
Daniels, Bebe, 7, 32, 96, 99, 100–104, *103, 104*, 107, 117, 121, 177, 187n.11
"Danny Boy" (song), 167
The Dark Horse (1932), 110
Dark Victory (1939), 91
Davies, Marion, 64
Davis, Bette, 7, 91–92, 109–110, *112*, 117, 121, 177, 188n.32
Davis, Elmer, 76
A Day at the Races (1937), 185n.10
Days to Come (Hellman), 80
deathbed scene, in *Woman in the Dark*, 86, *87*
Del Ruth, Roy, 100, 101, 105, 181n.15
DeMille, Cecil B., 29, 100, 150
Denning, Richard, 145
The Desert Song (1929), 181n.15
desire, Gary Cooper as object of, 17, 19
The Devil Is a Woman (1935), 188n.35
Diamond Jim (1935), 191n.26
Diamond Lil (West), 187–188n.28. See also *She Done Him Wrong*
Dick, Bernard, 90, 92, 94
Dieterle, William, 80
Dietrich, Marlene, 16, 17, 83
Dishonored (1931), 83
disillusionment, post-1929 crash, 195n.4
Dixon, Jean, 10, 23
Dmytryk, Edward, 79
Doane, Mary Ann, 121
documentary films, 196n.25
Dodd, Claire, 133
Donlevy, Brian, 145, 146, 147, 150, 192n.38
Do the Right Thing (1989), 195n.25
Double Indemnity (1944), 79, 158, 160, 172
Douglas, Melvyn, 84, 185n.11

Dreier, Hans, 145
drinking, 28, 30, 48; in *Another Thin Man*, 66; as contest, 28; end-of-Prohibition celebration of, 43; in 1935 *Glass Key*, 135; Hammett's and Hellman's, 81; in Hammett's *Thin Man*, 182–183n.40; in 1941 *Maltese Falcon*, 119, 122–124; as mark of gender equality, 44–45; in script for *Dangerous Female*, 105. See also alcohol
Duck Soup (1933), 24
Dunn, Emma, 134
Durante, Jimmy, 12, 14
Duvivier, Julian, 184n.10
Dvorak, Ann, 138

Eastman, George, 18
Easy Living (1937), 191n.26
Easy Rider (1969), 193n.13
Ebert, Roger, 161, 170
Ed Beaumont (1935 *Glass Key*), *134*, 138, *143*, 144, 176. See also Ned Beaumont
Eddy, Nelson, 62
Edeson, Arthur, 119
Eighteenth Amendment, repeal of, 26, 48. See also Prohibition
Engel, John, 188–189n.38
Equality magazine, 89
Escapade (1935), 54
ethnicity: and class, intersection of, in *Manhattan Melodrama*, 192n.42; easy mixing, at nightclub, 59; erasure of, in 1935 *Glass Key*, 137, 144, 177; and gangsters, 15, 132, 191n.21, 191n.30; in 1942 *Glass Key*, 150–153; in *Miller's Crossing*, 160, 165–168, 169; and politics, Hammett's treatment of, 8 (see also *The Glass Key*); voter, and 1920s immigration laws, 131
Evans, Herbert, 139
Evelyn Prentice (1934), 54
Everson, William, 28
existentialism, 195n.4
exoticism, and homosexuality, 186n.4
expressionism, 195n.4

family: in *After the Thin Man*, 56; and childcare, scenes of, in *Another Thin Man*, 69, 70, *70*; as imperiled by alcohol, 43; in later *Thin Man* films, 52; lead couple defined by other couples, in *The Thin Man*, 35–40; and wealth, in *Another Thin Man*, 67–68
"The Farewell Murder" (Hammett), 66
fascism, resistance to, 89
The Fat Man (1951), 154
The Fat Man (radio series), 154
femmes fatales, 27, 31, 80, 97, 99, 108, 121, 174, 181n.15; eradication of, 126; stripped of sexuality, 124
Fields, W. C., 24

ABOUT THE AUTHOR

WILLIAM H. MOONEY is a professor of English and the coordinator of film and media at the Fashion Institute of Technology, State University of New York. He has published a range of both short fiction and criticism. His writing credits for film include *Effects* (1980) and *Donor Unknown* (1995). *Dashiell Hammett and the Movies* is his first book.